PIANO INFORMATION GUIDE

MUSIC RESEARCH
AND INFORMATION GUIDES
(VOL. 10)
GARLAND REFERENCE LIBRARY
OF THE HUMANITIES
(VOL. 806)

MUSIC RESEARCH AND INFORMATION GUIDES

PIANO INFORMATION GUIDE
An Aid to Research

Robert Palmieri

GARLAND PUBLISHING, INC. • NEW YORK & LONDON
1989

Library of Congress Cataloging-in-Publication Data

Palmieri, Robert, 1930–
    Piano information guide : an aid to research / Robert Palmieri.
    p. cm. — (Music research and information guides; vol. 10)
(Garland reference library of the humanities; vol. 806)
    Bibliography: p.
    Includes indexes.
    ISBN 0-8240-7778-4 (alk. paper)
    1. Piano—Bibliography. 2. Piano music—Bibliography. I. Title.
II. Series. III. Series: Garland reference library of the
humanities ; vol. 806.
ML128.P3P34 1989
016.7862'1—dc19   88-38631
                                       CIP
                                       MN

Printed on acid-free, 250-year-life paper
Manufactured in the United States of America

Contents

Preface

Numerous bibliographic lists as well as many annual and periodic lists dealing with the piano's history, construction, and other pertinent topics have been scrutinized. Listings in *The Music Index* and *Repertoire international de littérature musicale* (RILM Abstracts) have been utilized when appropriate. The majority of items present in the bibliography are available in this country, including the Russian books and periodicals. I have supplied full bibliographic data with each entry; when available, the International Standard Book Number (ISBN) has been incorporated and the On-line Computer Library Center, Inc. (OCLC) number has also been included. OCLC is an on-line bibliographic data base constituting one of the largest cataloging records in the world. There are well over 10 million records, representing books and other publications in over 6,000 library collections available to its members across the United States and around the globe. OCLC's Interlibrary Loan subsystem enables scholars and librarians to borrow materials from distant institutions. This formidable link of library holdings and speed of retrieving data greatly facilitates the search process.

The photographs have been reproduced with the kind permission of *Da Capo Press, Vestal Press,* and the Piano Technicians Guild, Inc..

I would like to thank the library staff members of the many libraries that I visited in my quest for literature on the piano; their assistance was always welcomed. Special thanks goes to my wife, Margaret Walsh Palmieri, whose gift for languages and skill in editing helped expedite the completion of the volume. I thank also the Research Council of Kent State University for its support of this project, as well as Michael R. Cole, Kerry Kean, Michael A. Rogers, Jack W. Scott, and Richard W. Schindle, all of Kent State University. My gratitude also to master bibliographer Guy A. Marco, Nora M. Palmieri, and David and Sigrid Anderson. The expertise, interest, and support of all concerned is greatly appreciated.

Introduction

Early records on the history of the piano reveal an uncertainty concerning its originator. In France it was believed that Jean Marius was the inventor; in Germany (Dresden) the contender was Christoph Gottlieb Schröter; and in Italy it was the Paduan instrument builder Bartolomeo Cristofori, *cembalaro* for the Medici, who was believed to have invented the first keyboard instrument with a hammer action. This uncertainty about who was the first to invent the pianoforte prevailed for years but was eventually put to rest when Edward Francis Rimbault, in *The Pianoforte, Its Origin, Progress, and Construction* (1860), wrote in a chapter titled "Claimants to the Invention of the Pianoforte," that findings regarding Cristofori's work satisfactorily cleared up the origin of the pianoforte. Rimbault's conviction was reinforced by Curt Sachs, who in 1920 wrote (*Handbuch der Musikinstrumentenkunde*), "Der Streit um die Krone ist heute verstummt. CRISTOFORI blieb Sieger." [The battle for the crown is silenced today. CRISTOFORI remained the victor.]

A great number of early builders made pianos that were magnificent in design and structure: the sleek lines of the Walter Hammerflügel, the strength of the Broadwood grand, the beauty of the decorated case work of the Erard and Pleyel, and the elegant flowing pyramids and giraffes of Frederici and Van der Hoef all reflect the builders' ingenuity. These are but a few of the remarkable pianos of the past. It is obvious, upon viewing instruments such as these, that many relatively early artisans had an inspired commitment towards building a musical instrument with distinctive line, design, and esthetic balance. It is evident from tracing the evolution of the piano that the prime motivating factor in construction considerations, throughout its development, has been to produce a piano with greater tone, both in volume and sustainability.

Interestingly, a turnabout has occurred; today there is a trend toward performing on the smaller-toned period instruments. It appears that the instruments of the past are being re-evaluated and appreciated for what they were rather than being compared with our present day instrument.

As for the future, we are now at a crossroad where the electronic piano may possibly surpass the "acoustic" piano. But is the electronic piano really a piano? In a sense, the tone sounds similar to a piano; however, the electronic piano lacks the soul of the acoustic piano: the integral hammer striking the string, the resonance of its total mass with its varieties of woods, and the complex vibration of the strings, including its characteristic inharmonicity.

I believe this overview of literature about the piano and its music clearly demonstrates that the true essence of pianism is the collaboration of builder, composer, and performer. The integration of all of these elements is essential.

The subject of the piano and its music is vast and complex, therefore limitations in scope were necessary for this volume. I have attempted to restrict coverage to the instrument, and to literature that describes music for the piano. Obviously, it would be impossible to include all the literature on these topics; works selected seem to best represent the developmental evolution of the piano as well as the historical unfolding of piano literature. Topics not considered are biographies, performance, pedagogy, pianists in general, and jazz, as these topics are not directly germane to the volume's thrust; besides, any one of these topics could easily fill a bibliographic survey of its own.

It is hoped that *Piano Information Guide* will make evident the varied accomplishments of the diverse piano builders and companies, the colorful evolution and history of the instrument, the great variety of music for the piano, and of utmost importance as we approach its three hundredth birthday, the significance of the instrument in the lives of so many. May the piano's future be steadfast and may it continue to enrich humanity for many more years.

PIANO INFORMATION GUIDE

THE INSTRUMENT

I. Encyclopedias and Dictionaries

1. *Britannica Book of Music.* Edited by
    Benjamin Hadley; consulting editors,
    Michael Steinberg, George Gelles.
    Garden City, N.Y.: Doubleday/Britan-
    nica Books, 1980. ISBN 0-3851-4191-2
    OCLC 5102051   ML 100 B848

    Good coverage of the piano; includes
    important dates and pertinent informa-
    tion. Handles the history of the first
    upright (a controversial subject) in an
    understanding manner. Observes modern
    innovations. Entry on "Mechanical Instru-
    ments" offers a concise survey of several
    automatic keyboard instruments e.g., Pi-
    anola, Welte, etc.. Bibliography.

2. *Concise Encyclopedia of Music and Musi-
    cians.* Edited by Martin Cooper. Con-
    tributors: John Barbirolli, *et al.*
    New York: Hawthorn Books, 1958. 516 p.
    OCLC 598312   ML 100 C78

    Great deal of attention to construction
    of the piano, from the time of Cristofori
    on. "Piano Music" entry traces selected
    compositions for the piano, from Lodovico
    Giustini's early work (1732) through Mozart,
    Beethoven, Liszt, Chopin, and a few twen-
    tieth-century works. No coverage of auto-
    matic pianos.

3. *Concise Oxford Dictionary of Music.* Third
    edition by Michael Kennedy. Based on the
    original publication by Percy Scholes.
    Oxford; New York: Oxford University Press,
    1980. 724 p. ISBN 1-9311-1315-5   OCLC
    8347070   ML 100 K35 1980

4. *New Oxford Companion to Music.* General
    editor, Denis Arnold. Oxford; New York:
    Oxford University Press, 1983. 2 v. (xii,
    2017 p.) ISBN 0-1931-1316-3   OCLC 1009-
    6883   ML 100 N5 1983.

5. *Oxford Dictionary of Music.* Michael
    Kennedy. [Rev. and enl. ed. of: *The Con-
    cise Oxford Dictionary of Music.* 3rd ed.
    1980] Oxford; New York: Oxford University
    Press, 1985. 810 p. ISBN 0-1931-1333-3
    OCLC 11289135   ML 100 K35 1985.

All three Oxford reference works are based
on Percy Scholes' work. The *Companion* first
appeared in 1938 and the *Dictionary* in 1952,
both compiled by Scholes. All have undergone
revision in subsequent editions. The *New
Oxford Companion* (1983) offers the best coverage of the piano, primarily because of the
length of the work itself. It allows more
breadth of subject examination. It also contains data on early public performances and
repertoire. Unfortunately, *New Companion*
still retains some of Scholes' statements that
today, because of new findings, are incorrect
e.g., "two, and only two, of Cristofori's
instruments still remain..." and the date of
Cristofori's first instrument as 1709. This
same misinformation was also present in the
Concise Dictionary (1980) under headings of
"piano," and "Cristofori." The information
is brought up to date (i.e., three extant
Cristofori instruments and 1700 for the first
piano) in *Oxford Dictionary* (1985). Illustrations and bibliography in *New Oxford Companion.*

6. *Dizionario Ricordi della musica e dei musicisti.* Direttore: Claudio Sartori; Redattori: Fausto Broussard, *et al.* Milano: Ricordi, 1959. xii, 1155 p. OCLC 850782   ML 100 D65

   Strong on the structure of the piano; sketchy on the history of the instrument. Bibliography (good selection).

7. *Encyclopedia Americana.* International Edition. Danbury, Conn.: Grolier, 1984. 30 v.   ISBN 0-7172-0115-5   OCLC 1018-3134   AE 5 E333 1984

   Description of the operation of the piano in lay terms. Concisely reviews actions, strings, soundboard, dampers, pedals, etc.. Repertoire is briefly surveyed, from Giustini to Crumb and Cage. Does not reflect changes of historic dates resulting from recent research findings. A very short entry for player pianos. Illustrations, bibliography (7 items); set is indexed. Piano coverage in the 1971 edition (by Curt Sachs) of the *Americana* has much more detailed explanation of the instrument, plus pertinent historical data as to innovations and builders.

8. *Encyclopedia of Music in Canada.* Edited by Helmut Kallmann, Gilles Potvin, Kenneth Winters. Toronto; Buffalo: University of Toronto Press, 1981. xxix, 1076 p. ISBN 0-8020-5509-5   OCLC 7995924   ML 106 C3 E5

   A survey of piano-building in Canada from 1820. First builders in Canada were skilled British and German craftsmen. Contains a tabulation of builders in Canada and a summary of the growth of the Canadian piano industry. The "Player Piano" entry traces the history of Canadian manufacturers of that genre from 1906 (Higel Co.). Illustrations, bibliography.

9. *Enciclopedia Salvat de la música.* Esta
   obra ha sido dirigida por Françoise
   Michel con la colaboracion de Françoise
   Lesure y Vladimir Fedorov, Revisión y
   adaptción española por Manuel Valls Gorina.
   Barcelona: Salvat, 1967. 4 v. OCLC 27-
   6929   ML 100 E48 1967

10. *Encyclopédie de la musique.* Publié sous
    la direction de Françoise Michel en col-
    laboration avec Françoise Lesure et
    Vladimir Féderov ... Paris: Fasquelle.
    1958-61. 3 v. OCLC 860571   ML 100 E48

    Strong on examination of piano construction
    and innovations. Only brief coverage of the
    history of the piano. Deals with acoustics,
    composers for the piano, actions (with illus-
    trations), early builders, etc.. Does not
    always attach dates to important structural
    innovations. Highlights selected piano com-
    posers and a few of their works according to
    region i.e., Germany and Central Europe,
    France, Russia and Scandinavia, Italy, and
    Spain. The text is the same in both edi-
    tions. Illustrations are superior in the
    Spanish edition. Bibliography.

11. Heinitz, Wihelm. *Instrumentenkunde.*
    Wildpark-Potsdam: Akademische Verlags-
    gesellschaft Athenaion, 1929. 159 p.
    OCLC 6793997   ML 160 B9 S3. In *Hand-
    buch der Musikwissenschaft.* [13 v.]
    Herausgegeben von [edited by] Ernst Bücken
    in Verbindung mit [in collaboration with]:
    Heinrich Bessler, Friedrich Blume, [et
    al]. Potsdam: Akamademische Verlagsgesell-
    schaft Athenaion, 1929-31. OCLC 13278777
    ML 160 B9; Reprint of *Instrumentenkunde*
    by Wilhelm Heinitz (edition of 1928-31,
    which was issued as v. [11-12, 1, 13] of
    Handbuch der Musikwissenschaft, hrsg.
    von Ernst Bücken). New York: Johnson Re-
    print Corp., 1973   ISBN 0-3842-2093-2
    OCLC 572760   ML 160 H44

History of keyboard instruments, from early precursors to the the hammerklavier. Historical aspects of the piano start with the
"Pantaléon" and continue through to the
Emanuel Moòr double keyboard instrument and
quartertone-tuned instruments. Action mechanisms and other construction features are
examined. Contains schematic diagrams of
Tastenanordnungen für Vierteltonklaviere
[keyboard layouts of quartertone pianos] including the *Vierteltonflügel* of August
Förster (c.1924). Illustrations, musical
examples.

12. *International Cyclopedia of Music and Musi-
      cians*. Editor in Chief, Oscar Thompson.
      10th ed. Editor, Bruce Bohle. New York:
      Dodd, Mead & Co.; London: J.M. Dent & Sons
      LTD, 1975. 2511 p. ISBN 0-3960-7005-1
      OCLC 1301271   ML 100 T47 1975

     General historical survey of the piano.
     Does not reflect new information derived from
     recent research. Data on pedals, while being
     correct, obscures the fact that damper rais-
     ing stops/levers and *una corda* shifts were
     in use years prior to the pedal device. Con-
     cisely surveys keyboard literature from Bach
     and Scarlatti to Prokofiev and Rachmaninoff.
     A mechanical instrument entry examines the
     piano mécanique, piano-organs, and player
     pianos (Pianola).

13. *Macmillan Encyclopedia of Music and Musi-
      cians*. Compiled and edited by Albert
      E. Wier. New York: Macmillan Co., 1938.
      2089 p. OCLC 861908   ML 100 W64 M3

     Good coverage, though concise, of the
     piano, from Cristofori on. Mentions a
     few composers in relation to the piano.
     Very little information on player pianos.

14. Marcuse, Sibyl. *Musical Instruments: A Com-
     prehensive Dictionary.* Garden City, N.Y.:
     Doubleday, 1964.   xiv, 608 p.   OCLC 765359
     ML 102 I5 M37

     Inspired by Curt Sachs' *Real-Lexikon der
     Musikinstrumente* (1913), Marcuse offers a
     comparable reference work to Sachs' early
     volume and presents some post-1913 research
     on the subject. Sources are documented.
     The piano entry covers the history of the
     instrument, its structure and innovations,
     and also describes the many variant in-
     struments allied to the piano i.e., piano-
     organ, pianola, pianoctave, etc.. Illus-
     trations, sources.

15. Meer, John Henry van der. *Musikinstrumente:
     von der Antike bis zur Gegenwart.* [Musical
     instruments: from antiquity to the present]
     München: Prestel, 1983.   302 p.   ISBN 3-
     7913-0656-1   OCLC 11186437   ML 460 M4

     Beautifully illustrated history of musical
     instruments. Presents a useful survey of pi-
     ano builders, as well as a concise overview
     of historical instruments. It exhibits repre-
     sentative historical pianos by: Stein (Hammer-
     flügel), Graf (Hammerflügel), Broadwood,
     Nannette Streicher & Sohn, Erard, Clementi &
     Co., Johann Christian Schleip (Lyraflügel),
     Mathias Müller (pianino), etc.. There is an
     interesting illustration and description of a
     Johann Andreas Stein Pianoforte *"vis-à-vis
     Flügel"* (1777), which is housed in the *Museo
     di Castelvecchio* in Verona. It is a rectan-
     gular instrument with four keyboards: three
     keyboards on one side and one keyboard on the
     opposite side. Two manuals are used for the
     harpsichord and two are used for the piano-
     forte. It is a "combination instrument" i.e.,
     can be played as a piano and/or a harpsichord.
     Illustrations, bibliography (extensive), list
     of museums, instrument index, name index.
     The Stein *"vis-à-vis Flügel"* is also il-

lustrated in Franz Josef Hirt's *Stringed Key-board Instruments* (1955; 1981).

16. *Musical Instruments of the World: An Illus-trated Encyclopedia by the Diagram Group.*
New York: Paddington Press, 1976. 320 p.
ISBN 0-8467-0134-0   OCLC 2332111   ML 102
I5 D5

More illustrations than text. Contains correct data as to the first Cristofori piano (1700). There are illustrations of histori-cal pianos e.g., Cristofori's 1720 instru-ment, giraffes, Jankó's keyboard, as well as an exploded view of the interior of a modern piano and other detailed pictures. Automatic pianos are viewed briefly, as are electric pianos and an example of the innovation of our period: a Moog Sonic-Six. Unusual layout of the volume presents instruments in an at-tractive pictorial chronology.

17. *New Grove Dictionary of Music and Musicians.*
Edited by Stanley Sadie. London: Macmillan Publishers; Washington, D.C.: Grove's Dic-tionaries, 1980. 20 v. ISBN 0-3332-3111-2
OCLC 5676891   ML 100 N48

18. *New Grove Dictionary of Musical Instruments.*
Edited by Stanley Sadie. London: Macmillan Press; Washington, D.C.: Grove's Diction-aries, 1984. 3 v.   ISBN 0-9438-1805-2
OCLC 10754317   ML 102 I5 N48 1984

The *New Grove Dictionary of Music and Musi-cians* offers major coverage of the piano divided into 8 sections: "Origins to 1750"; "Germany and Austria 1750-1800"; "England and France to 1800"; "Viennese piano from 1800"; "England and France 1800-60"; "North America to 1860"; "1860-1915"; "From 1915". Histori-cal and mechanical descriptions, with atten-tion to innovations, of piano(forte)s by Cristofori, Silbermann, Stein, Walter, Zumpe,

Broadwood, Stodart, and others. There is a
great deal of detail, especially on the English
piano and on the various actions that developed
in the early years of the piano. There are
good action schematics and many illustrations
of historical instruments. The *New Grove Dictionary of Music and Musicians* concludes
its coverage of the piano c.1970 with an account of the Asian export piano market. The
New Grove Dictionary of Musical Instruments
contains the identical articles on instruments
that appear in the *New Grove Dictionary of
Music and Musicians*, with a few minor cor-
rections and additions. A well-done survey
of the history of the piano. Illustrations,
bibliography.

19.   *New Grove Dictionary of American Music.*
      Edited by H. Wiley Hitchcock and Stanley
      Sadie. New York: Grove's Dictionaries
      of Music, 1986. 4 v. ISBN 0-9438-1836-2
      OCLC 13184437   ML 101 U6 N48 1986

      A broad historic overview of the piano
      in the USA from the 1770s to the second half
      of the twentieth century. Traces the early
      builders who settled in the eastern states.
      Special attention is given: Alpheus Babcock,
      Jonas Chickering, and Steinway & Sons.
      There is very little attention given to the
      many other fine American piano manufactur-
      ers. One wishes the entry were twice as
      long as it is. Illustrations, bibliography
      (8 items).

20.   *New Harvard Dictionary of Music.* Edited by
      Don Michael Randel. [Rev. ed. of: Harvard
      Dictionary of Music/ Willi Apel. 2nd ed.
      1969] Cambridge, Mass.: Belknap Press of
      Harvard University Press, 1986. xxi, 942
      p. ISBN 0-6746-1525-5   OCLC 13333674
      ML 100 N485 1986

      A completely new *Harvard Dictionary of Mu-*

sic, with very little material carried over
from previous editions. The piano entry is
written in non-technical language and briefly surveys its history and construction.
There are a few points that make the entry
disconcerting. Is the date of the invention
of the pianoforte purposely avoided because
of controversy or is it an oversight? (The
research done by Mario Fabbri recorded in
L'alba del pianoforte [c.1968] establishes
the date of Cristofori's first instrument.)
Also, Cristofori's dates are set at 1655-
1731, not 1655-1730. True, the *una corda*
pedal came later, but it should also be mentioned that Cristofori's instrument of 1720
already had an *una corda* shift that was
operated by levers. The "Player Piano" entry offers minimum information, although more
can be found under the entry of "Automatic
Instrument." The *Harvard Dictionary* does
offer excellent action schematics in both
rest and strike positions and a concise summary of the instrument. Illustrations, bibliography (arranged by subject: history, literature, technique, tuning and maintenance).

21.   *New Oxford Companion to Music.* Oxford;
       New York: Oxford University Press, 1983.
       See under *Concise Oxford Dictionary of
       Music.*

22.   *Oxford Dictionary of Music.* Oxford; New
       York: Oxford University Press, 1985. See
       under *Concise Oxford Dictionary of Music.*

23.   Ripin, Edwin M.   "A Scottish Encyclopedist
       and the Piano Forte." *Musical Quarterly*
       55 (October 1969): 487-99.

       A critical examination of John Robison's
       (1739-1805) article on the piano, which ap-
       peared in the *Supplement* volume (1801) of
       the *Encyclopaedia Britannica* 3d ed. (1797).
       Author Ripin draws a thorough description of

John Robison. He comments on Robison's contribution to the *Britannica*, which is fully
quoted in this article. Encyclopedist Robison's writing is of interest to those seeking
information about the harpsichord-piano transition period, the early English piano, work
of William Mason, as well as the overview of
keyboard instruments in England at that time.
Illustration.

24.   Sachs, Curt. *Real-Lexikon der Musikinstru-*
      mente Berlin: J. Bard, 1913.   xvii,
      442 p. OCLC 1749022   ML 102 I5 S2; Re-
      print. [Rev. and enl. ed.] New York: Dover,
      1964. OCLC 171598   ML 102 I5 S2 1964;
      Reprint. Hildesheim/New York: Olms, 1979.
      ISBN 3-4870-0205-1   OCLC 12297762   ML
      102 I5 S2 1979

      Sachs' concise Hammerklavier entry covers
      the history of the piano. He makes note of
      Scipione Maffei's article of 1711 in *Giornale*
      dei Letterati d'Italia, which described
      Cristofori's invention of the "*gravecembalo*
      col piano e forte (term used by Maffei).
      Sachs mentions the early contributions of
      Marius, Schröter, Silbermann, and Stein.
      A chronology chart of keyboard ranges of 44
      pianos built from 1720 (Cristofori) to 1876
      (Ibach) concludes the Hammerklavier entry.
      There are many minor entries on keyboard in-
      struments that readers can examine, such as:
      Pianino, Piano chanteur, Aliquotflügel,
      Giraffenklavier, etc.. Bibliography (arranged
      chronologically; earliest written in 1817 and
      latest in 1911).

25.   Viotta, Henri Anastase. *Lexicon der Toon-*
      kunst. door Henri Viotta, met medewerking
      van de heeren: Peter Benoit, Frans Coenen..
      ..enz. enz... Amsterdam: Bührmann & Rooth-
      laan, 1881-85. 3 v. OCLC 861735   ML 100
      V46

Of historic value only. A concise survey of
the history of the piano. Does not delve into
great detail but does point out important highlights such as innovations (e.g., Erard's action) and principal builders. Bibliography
(5 entries).

THE INSTRUMENT

II. Historical Studies

General Histories

26. Badura-Skoda, Paul. "Pianist's View: Paul
     Badura-Skoda Looks at the History of the
     Piano." *Music and Musicians* 17 (Feb-
     ruary 1969): 42-43,70; "Pianist's View-
     2." 17 (March 1969): 44-45,78; "Pianist's
     View-3." 17 (April 1969): 32-33.

     A three-part article on the history of the
     piano. Pianist Badura-Skoda became inter-
     ested in old instruments when he first pre-
     sented a lecture "Beethoven on Old and New
     Pianofortes" to the Royal Music Association.
     First installment of the article deals with
     similarities of the early piano to the clavi-
     chord and harpsichord, J.S. Bach's reaction
     to the pianoforte, C.P.E. Bach's essay of
     1753, and early German and English piano
     builders. Part Two of Badura-Skoda's his-
     torical survey includes material on:
     Mozart's comments on the superiority of
     Stein's instruments, the Walter piano,
     Beethoven's music, and the pianos he pre-
     ferred, etc.. Part Three concludes with:
     Beethoven's music and his pianos, the Erard
     piano, the upright piano, and a quick look
     at construction innovations. Illustrations.

27. Barthold, Kenneth van, and David Buckton.
     The Story of the Piano. London: British
     Broadcasting Corporation, 1975. ISBN 0-

14

5631-2580-2   OCLC 2202910   ML 650 V36

Historical overview of the evolution of the
piano in concise form and in non-technical
language. Barthold and Buckton's book is an
outgrowth of a movie that the two authors
collaborated on, titled "How Did It Sound to
Beethoven - The Story of Piano Sound Through
250 Years." Their research for the movie
project inspired this volume. Various actions are described and illustrated, and the
evolution and progress of the instrument are
examined. Recommended for the layperson and
amateur musician. Illustrations, action
schematics, musical examples, appendixes;
lacks an index.

28. Bie, Oscar. *History of the Pianoforte and
     Pianoforte Players.* Translated (from Bie's
     Das Klavier und seine Meister. München:
     Bruckmann, 1898. OCLC 3225879 ML 650 B475)
     and revised by E.E. Kellett and E.W. Naylor.
     London: Dent; New York: Dutton, 1899. xi,
     336 p. OCLC 408793   ML 700 B586; Reprint.
     New York: Da Capo Press, 1966. OCLC 681882
     ML 700 B586 1899a

     A colorfully written illustrated survey of
     music for the piano, beginning with pre-piano
     composers such as those represented in *Par-
     thenia* (Byrd, Bull, Gibbons), and the *cla-
     vecinistes* i.e., Rameau, François Couperin,
     Domenico Scarlatti, etc., and continuing to
     Liszt and his contemporaries. The handsome
     volume, though now out of date, contains basic
     material on the instrument, technique, form,
     the virtuoso pianists of the time, and other
     aspects of the development of keyboard litera-
     ture. Beethoven, Chopin and Liszt receive
     greatest coverage. For its time (written
     scarcely a year after Brahms' death) the vol-
     ume represented a good overview of the his-
     tory of keyboard literature. Illustrations,
     music, musical examples, name and subject
     index, directory of illustrations.

29. Blom, Eric. *The Romance of the Piano.* Lon-
     don: Foulis, 1928. xiii, 241 p. OCLC 20-
     85518 ML 650 B6; Reprint. New York: Da
     Capo Press, 1969. OCLC 5395

     A history of the piano, beginning with con-
     cise descriptions of very early, remote pre-
     cursors of the piano such as the dulcimer
     and the psaltery. Blom quickly moves on to
     the organ and the clavichord. Short chap-
     ter on early keyboard music (from *Fitzwil-
     liam Virginal Book* and *Parthenia* to Bach)
     is followed by a chapter "First Real Piano
     Music," where he picks up with Haydn and
     Mozart. Blom traces the early manufactur-
     ers through to the modern builders, always
     giving special attention to the British
     contribution to the history of the instru-
     ment. Illustrations, bibliography (32 en-
     tries), index.

30. Bonaventura, Arnaldo. *Storia e letteratura
     de pianoforte.* Terza edizione riveduta,
     ampliata e coordinata ai nuovi programmi
     d'esame. [History and literature of the
     pianoforte. Third edition, revised, en-
     larged and coordinated to the new examina-
     tion programs] Livorno: Raffaello Giusti,
     1934. 183 p. ML 650 B6

     Designed as a review in preparation for
     conservatory exams in history and literature
     of the piano. The volume virtually covers
     all aspects of piano study in concise terms.
     A quick survey of forms (sonata, fugue, etc.)
     is followed by the history of the piano,
     starting with the monochord, and further ex-
     amining English, Italian, French, and Ger-
     man harpsichord composers. The invention of
     the piano is noted as occuring before Marius
     and Schröter (i.e., before 1711). The au-
     thor delves into descriptions of various
     early pianofortes. Muzio Clementi is given
     extended coverage. Composers of works for
     piano from different nations are surveyed.

The unit on French composers notes many minor
composers and does not focus on the important
ones. Attention is given throughout to composers of piano methods (i.e., exercises,
studies, etc.). Coverage of Italian composers starts with Giovanni Sgambati, as a connecting link with the past, and concludes
with Mario Castelnuovo-Tedesco. Bibliography
(extensive), name index.

31. Brancour, René. *Histoire des instruments
de musique.* Préface de Ch.-M. Widor.
Paris: Henri Laurens, 1921. iv, 280 p.
OCLC 3946167   ML 460 B8

The author was *conservateur du Musée du
Conservatoire National de Musique* (Paris)
at time of publication. The chapter covering
keyboard instruments starts with the clavichord. There are descriptions of various
keyboard instruments and brief comment on
some of the composers who wrote for the instrument. Cristofori is given credit for in-
venting the piano (often a controversial subject in early works about the piano). Piano
builders are duly noted and their contributions to the craft described. Jean Marius,
Sébastien Erard, and Ignace Pleyel are giv-
en special attention. Six keyboard instruments housed in the Conservatory of Paris
Museum are illustrated; three are pianos: an
Erard square (1813), Empire style vertical
(n.d.), and a small Empire square (n.d.).
Illustrations, bibliography (by instrument
classification), instrument index, proper
name index.

32. Brinsmead, Edgar. *The History of the Piano:
With an Account of the Theory of Sound and
Also of the Music and Musical Instruments
of the Ancients.* London: Novello, Ewer and
Co., 1879. Reissue. Detroit, Mich.: Singing
Tree Press, 1969. xii, 201 p.   OCLC 54982
ML 652 B85 1969

A history of the piano that commences with
the science of acoustics and the history of
plucked stringed instruments. Brinsmead often
refers to the piano as the "orchestra of the
drawing-room." He comments on the "crowd of
claimants and appropriators" of the first piano and holds out for Cristofali [sic] as the
first inventor because of evidence of authenticity. As to the name change for Cristofori
(Cristofali), Mario Fabbri in his work *L'alba
del pianoforte* (c.1968) remarks on the numerous spellings of the name encountered in literature, and lists several examples: Christof-
fori, Cristofari, Cristofoli, Cristofolli,
Cristofali, Cristofalli, Cristofani, and Cris-
toffani. Brinsmead traces the progress of
the piano, noting innovations and refinements.
Contributions made by John Brinsmead to the
industry are noted. Illustrations, appendixes
(inventions patented [1693-1879] and acoustics); lacks an index.

33. Casella, Alfredo. *Il Pianoforte.* Roma-
     Milano: Tumminelli, 1937. 242 p. OCLC 4-
     952320   ML 650 C33 P5; 4th ed., rev. and
     enl. Milano: Ricordi, 1954, 1967. viii,
     252 p.   OCLC 1308524   ML 650 C33 P5 1967

A useful compilation of material for the
pianist, pegagogue, and historian. Casella
effectively covers the history of the piano,
with particular information on Cristofori,
and generally highlights the Italian contribution to the evolution of the instrument;
surveys the construction of the piano (includes schematic drawings); gives an overview
of the history of piano literature from Haydn
to Schönberg and Hindemith; comments on pianists from Clementi to Busoni; includes a major chapter on how to play the piano, covering
style, technique, memorization, fingering, etc.;
includes a pedagogical chapter observing diverse teaching methods, noting methods of Clementi, Chopin, Liszt, Leschetizky, and Busoni;
looks at transcriptions for piano and includes

observations on arrangements by J.S. Bach (of works by Vivaldi), Liszt, Busoni, von Bülow, Godowsky, Stravinsky, and Casella. The author concludes with concise surveys of piano concerti and piano chamber music. Illustrations, musical examples, name index.

34. ------. "L'esthétique du piano." *La Revue internationale de musique* 1 (Numéro spécial Avril 1939): 785-88.

An exuberant tribute to the magnificence of the piano. Quotes an extract of an article in *Gazette musicale* (1837) written by Liszt, in which the pianist-composer reveals his love for the instrument. Casella evaluates the powers of the piano in superlative terms.

35. Closson, Ernest. "Histoire du piano." *La Revue internationale de musique* 1 (Numéro spécial Avril 1939): 789-800.

A brief descriptive survey of keyboard instruments, including historical data, beginning with the clavichord and continuing to the upright piano and diverse unique innovative instruments. Closson attributes the inspiration for the invention of the piano to Pantaléon Hebenstreit.

36. ------. *History of the Piano.* Translated by Delano Ames. London: Paul Elek, 1947. 168 p. OCLC 897125 ML 650 C582 (1st ed. *Histoire du piano.* Bruxelles: Editions Universitaires, c.1944. 172 p. OCLC 644-1491); 2d ed., rev. and ed. by Robert Golding. London: Paul Elek, 1974. OCLC 99-7126; Also, 2d ed., rev. and ed. by Robert Golding. New York: St. Martin's Press, 1974. OCLC 1149067; Reprint of English ed. [1947] St. Clair Shores, Mich.: Scholarly Press, 1977. OCLC 3345850

Since the first edition in 1944, Closson's
volume on the history of the piano has undergone several printings. A very informative
work that begins with the clavichord, describing its function and its composers, and continues through the evolution of the piano.
Closson gives a detailed view of the development of the piano and also sheds some light on
the early piano in Belgium. There are some
excellent schematics of early actions, i.e.,
Cristofori (1712), Zumpe (1766), Stein (1786),
Taskin (1787), and Erard (1795, 1822). The
science of acoustics is not overlooked in Closson's account of the development of the instrument. Illustrations, schematics (by Jaques
Closson), musical examples, bibliography (100
entries, many pre-twentieth-century works),
index.

37.   Clutton, Cecil. "The Pianoforte." In *Musical
      Instruments Through the Ages*, edited by
      Anthony Baines. Baltimore, Md.: Penguin
      Books, 1961. 383 p. OCLC 604159   ML460
      B14; Reprint. New York: Walker, 1966.
      344 p.   OCLC 3000440   ML 460 B14 1966a;
      Reprint. Baltimore, Md.: Penguin Books,
      1969, 1971. OCLC 593882   ML 460 B14
      1969

      A concise account of a portion of the his-
      tory of the piano from Cristofori to Erard.
      The author briefly touches on the early build-
      ers. Of particular interest is Clutton's
      experience playing the Cristofori instrument
      in the Metropolitan Museum of Art in New York
      and his comparison of this piano to a 1770
      Stein. Illustrations, musical examples, glos-
      sary, bibliogaphy (only three entries for
      pianoforte), index.

38.   Colt, C.F. "Early Pianos: Their History and
      Character." *Early Music* 1 (January 1973):
      27-33.

Concise history of the piano, with attention to restoration of old instruments, early actions and their regional popularity, uprights, development of the iron frame, and construction techniques. Colt illustrates and describes ten early pianos: Broadwood grands (1794 and 1819), Thomas Haxby square (1789), Broadwood square (1812), unsigned square (c.1825-35), Heilmann fortepiano (1825), unsigned (attributed to George Haschka) forte-piano (c.1825), Schmidt-Pressburg grand forte-piano (1830), Broadwood cottage upright (1825), and a Pape console [upright] (1843).

39. Dallapiccola, Laura. "Histoire et bibliographie du piano en italie." *Revue Internationale de musique* 1 (Numéro spécial Avril 1939): 965-68.

A brief review of Cristofori's invention, describing the instrument's action as well as presenting a rationale for why the piano was not further developed in Italy after Cristofori's initial construction of the instrument. Cristofori's dates are incorrect, evidently an error in typesetting, as the date of birth is stated as 1565 rather than 1655. The bibliography appended to this article is annotated (13 works).

40. Debaar, Mathieu. *Le piano, son historique, ses maitres et sa littérature.* [The piano, its history, its masters and its literature] Pepinster: H. Thoumsin, 1945. 96 p. OCLC 15362710 ML 650 D4

A history of the piano, designed primarily for the piano student and the amateur musician. Offers a general overview of the history of the instrument, its literature and its great composers and performers. Debaar delves quite a bit into the *clavecinistes* and their literature. Of special interest is

the list of contemporary pianists of various
nations. Illustrations, name index.

41.   Dolge, Alfred. *Pianos and Their Makers.*
      Covina, Cal.: Covina Publishing Co., 1911.
      478 p.   OCLC 1268025   ML 652 D6

      A history of the development of the piano
      from the monochord to the player piano. Ma-
      jor portion of Dolge's work centers around
      the construction of the instrument and the
      men who were involved in its evolution.
      There are many action schematics of early
      instruments (Schröter, Marius, Cristofori,
      Silbermann, Stein, Zumpe) as well as views
      of more modern actions (Steinway, Erard,
      Langer, Broadwood, etc.). Dolge traces the
      development of the piano industry in Italy,
      Germany, France, England, and the USA.
      There are photos of the "art piano" (highly
      decorated), pedal piano, and player piano.
      He also points out the influence of piano
      virtuosi on the industry. Useful for its
      many schematic drawings and the view of the
      piano industry at the turn of the century.
      The volume boasts 300 illustrations. Appen-
      dix (list of piano firms), indexes.

42.   Ehrlich, Cyril. *The Piano: A History.*
      London: Dent, 1976. 254 p. ISBN 0-4600-
      4246-7   OCLC 2615827   ML 652 E4

      The author aims to depict the rise and
      eventual fall of the piano. Technology and
      production of the piano is traced from its
      infancy to the emergence of Japanese instru-
      ments on the international market. Ehrlich's
      introduction briefly views the predecessors
      of the piano, then quickly moves on to de-
      scribe early pianos (1770-1830). The volume
      primarily covers the growth and development
      of the piano industry, while also noting in-
      novations and refinements made to the instru-
      ment during this development. Growth in pi-

ano production of major nations, i.e., England,
USA, Germany, and France, is documented. The
English piano industry is given the greatest
depth of study. Illustrations, production
charts, appendixes, bibliography (extensive),
index.

43. Epstein, Abraham. "The Stick, the Log, and
the String." *American Music Teacher* 12
(July-August 1963): 18,35.

The evolution of the piano from the very
primitive beginning of a stick and a hollow
log to the monochord, psaltery, dulcimer,
clavichord, and through to Babcock's development of the iron frame. A compressed view
of the history of the instrument.

44. Fabbro, Beniamino dal. *Crepuscolo del
Pianoforte.* Milan: Giulio Einaudi
editore, 1951. 234 p. ML 700 F3 C7

Very interesting musings by Fabbro on various musical aspects associated with the piano. Though the work is chronologically or-
dered in its historical overview, it casually
reverts to the past at various intervals;
this is its charm. Fabbro interweaves his
musings on the instrument and its music in
a very readable fashion. He disusses the
history of the piano, the major composers of
piano music, social aspects of the piano,
contemporary pianists, and other topics, never in a pedantic style, but rather in a con-
versational manner. There are many literary
references. Lacks documentation. Illustrations, appendix (advice for young pianists),
name index.

45. Gaines, James R., ed. *The Lives of the Piano.*
New York: Holt, Rinehart and Winston, 1981.
viii, 215 p. ISBN 0-0305-7974-0 OCLC 759-
7536 ML 650 L58

Collection of essays on various aspects of
the piano. Anthony Burgess writes: "The
Well Tempered Revolution: A Consideration of
the Piano's Social and Intellectual History";
Annalyn Swan: "Enlightenment's Gift to the
Age of Romance: How the Piano Came to Be";
Anthony Liversidge: "Of Wood and Iron Wrought:
The Making of a Bösendorfer"; Dominique
Browning: "Finding the Sound: Portrait of a
Master Technician" [Steinway's Franz Mohr];
Ned Rorem: "Beyond Playing: A Composer's Life
With the Piano"; William Bolcom: "Song and
Dance: The American Way of Pianism"; Samuel
Lipman: "The Ordeal of Growth: Confessions
of a Former Prodigy"; and Richard Sennett:
"Pianists in Their Time: A Memoir." A fas-
cinating collection, informative as well as
interesting, covering the history of the
instrument, its construction, artists (e.g.,
Lhévinne, Hofmann, Curzon, etc.), many
composers and teachers, etc.. Well illustrated, name index.

46. Galpin, Francis William. *Old English Instru-*
     ments of Music. Their History and Character.
     London: Methuen and Co., 1910. xxv, 327 p.
     OCLC 89663   ML 501 G2; Also, 4th ed. rev.
     with supplementary notes by Thurston Dart.
     London: Methuen and Co., 1965. xxviii, 254 p.
     OCLC 896676   ML 501 G2 1965a; Also, 4th ed.
     rev. with supplementary notes by Thurston
     Dart. New York: Barnes and Noble, 1965.
     OCLC 744403   ML 501 G2 1965; Reprint of
     the 1910 edition. Clair Shores, Mich.:
     Scholarly Press, 1978.   ISBN 0-4030-1562-6
     OCLC 4365-87   ML 501 G2 1978

     Galpin just touches on the piano, referring
     often to Alfred James Hipkins' work of 1896,
     Description and History of the Pianoforte and
     the Older Keyboard Stringed Instruments.
     Galpin notes Cristofori's instrument, and Zumpe's
     work (square piano). The scope of the vol-
     ume is limited to early instruments. Musical
     examples, illustrations, appendix, name index.

47. ------. *A Textbook of European Musical
Instruments, Their Origin, History, and
Character.* London: Williams & Norgate,
1937. 256 p. OCLC 892362   ML 460 G14;
New York: J. de Graff, 1937.   OCLC 4748-
566   ML 460 G14 1937; Reprint. London:
E. Benn, 1956.   OCLC 2338107   ML 460 G14
T35 1956; Reprint. Westport, Conn.: Green-
wood Press, 1976.   ISBN 0-8371-8648-X
OCLC 2270746   ML 460 G14 T35 1976

A short description of the history of
the piano. In the foreword, Galpin states
that he directs this book towards young
people and tries to refrain from overly
technical descriptions. The reader will
note that Galpin is personally familiar
with the older pianoforte. His observations are brief but thorough. He touches
on actions of Cristofori and the Viennese
style and also discusses the early uprights,
the sostenente piano, and various early
automatic instruments. Illustrations,
bibliography (arranged by instrument classification), index.

48. Geiringer, Karl. *Musical Instruments, Their
History in Western Culture From the Stone
Age to the Present.* Translated by Bernard
Miall. New York: Oxford University Press,
1945. xviii, 3-278 p. OCLC 2571292   ML 460
G4 1945; Also, London: Allen and Unwin, 1943.
OCLC 2828659   ML 460 G4

Geiringer began work on his book on musical
instruments in Vienna in 1936, continuing in
London through 1938-39 and finishing in New
York in 1940. The volume was first published
in London in 1943. Concise descriptions of
various early instruments and their characteristics i.e., Cristofori's pianoforte, English
action, Viennese action, square piano, upright piano, Jankó and Moòr keyboards, and
other instruments. This is not the work to
refer to for in-depth investigation of the

piano; the encompassing scope of the volume
necessarily limits the information on any one
instrument. Illustrations, bibliography, index. There is better coverage of the piano
in Geiringer's revised and enlarged subsequent third edition of this work titled *Instruments in the History of Western Music*
(1978).

49. ------. *Instruments in the History of
     Western Music.* 3d ed. New York: Oxford
     University Press, 1978. 318 p. ISBN 0-
     1952-0057-7   OCLC 4135384   ML 460 G4
     1978

     Piano is discussed in regard to its role
     in particular periods of music. The piano
     is first presented in the Classical Period
     (because this is the period when the instru-
     ment actually came into use, informs Gei-
     ringer), where coverage traces its beginnings
     and notes later innovations through to the
     upright piano (c.1800). The piano in the
     Romantic and Avant-Garde Period is repre-
     sented by various innovations and builders,
     with a look at the Neo-Bechstein (electri-
     cally amplified tone), and other experimen-
     tal pianos (Jankó and Moòr). There is some
     mention of mechanical keyboard instruments
     and the Moog Synthesizer. A well-laid-out
     presentation of the history of musical in-
     struments. This is better coverage of the
     piano than that exhibited in Geiringer's pre-
     vious second edition of this work titled
     *Musical Instruments, Their History from the
     Stone Age to the Present Day* (1945). Il-
     lustrations, bibliography (extensive), name
     index, instrument index.

50. Gill, Dominic, ed. *The Book of the Piano.*
     Ithaca, N.Y.: Cornell University Press,
     1981. 288 p. ISBN 0-8014-1399-0   OCLC 7-
     57952   ML 650 B64

A lavishly illustrated volume depicting
the history of the piano and its literature.
There are photographic reproductions of line
engravings, paintings, autograph manuscripts,
portraits, scores, instruments, etc.. Chap-
ters dealing with the instrument are by:
Dominic Gill "Prologue," Derek Adlam "Anatomy
of the Piano," William Brooks "American Piano,"
Andrew Clements "Piano Makers" and "Eccentric
Pianos." Other chapters deal with piano lit-
erature, styles, and pianists: Nicholas Kenyon
"Classical Piano," Misha Donat "Cross Currents:
Schubert, Schumann, Mendelssohn, Brahms,"
David Murray "Romantic Piano: Chopin to Ravel,"
Charles Rosen "Romantic Pedal," Bryce Morrison
"Notes on the Grand Romantic Virtuosos and
After" and a "Chronology of Pianists," Martin
Cooper "Chamber Piano," Susan Bradshaw "Piano
in the Twentieth Century," Wilfred Mellers
"Jazz Piano" and "Popular Piano." The volume
concludes with reminiscences by the late
Clifford Curzon. An interesting survey of
the literature of the piano, beautifully il-
lustrated. Glossary, discography, bibliogra-
phy (57 entries), illustrations, index.

51. Gil-Marchex, Henri. "Some Remarks on the Beginnings of the Piano in France." Trans.
by Rita Benton. *American Music Teacher* 12
(July-August 1963): 24-25.

Evolutionary growth of the piano in France
(1789-1831) and reflections on the Erard
brothers, the harpsichord, Chopin, Liszt,
and other composers. Translator Benton gives
no information as to date and origin of Gil-
Marchex's text.

52. Good, Edwin Marshall. *Giraffes, Black Drag-
ons, and Other Pianos: A Technological
History from Cristofori to the Modern Concert Grand.* Stanford, Cal.: Stanford University Press, 1982. xvii, 305 p. ISBN 0-
8047-1120-8   OCLC 8856758   ML 652 G6 1982

It is Good's purpose to demonstrate technological differences in the piano throughout
its evolution, reveal the delay between innovation and adoption, and to carry on, im-
prove and extend work done by his predecessors
e.g., Harding (*The Piano-Forte*), Loesser (*Men,
Women and Pianos*), and Ehrlich (*The Piano*).
A technological survey of the development of
the piano approached chronologically, using
particular period instruments as models and
including short chapters on the player piano
and the modern electronic piano. A choice
contemporary technological survey to use in
conjunction with Harding. Good's work is
principally a study of the instrument itself;
it is not concerned with music for the piano.
Illustrations, bibliography (extensive), index.

53. Greenfield, Jack. "Piano Actions - From
     Cristofori to Erard." *Piano Technicians
     Journal* 22 (December 1979): 18-20.

     Greenfield has written several series of
     articles for the *Piano Technicians Journal*
     on the history of the piano. This article
     deals largely with the history of the instru-
     ment from Cristofori to Erard, with attention
     to the work of Silbermann, Schröter, Zumpe,
     Stein, and Backers. Greenfield incorporates
     the results of recent investigation on the
     date for Cristofori's first pianoforte (1700).

54. ------. "The Piano's Century of Progress:
     1770's - 1870's." *Piano Technicians
     Journal* 23 (January 1980): 19-23.

     A chronological survey of piano builders
     from Cristofori to Steinway. Family units
     that constructed pianos are examined e.g.,
     Stein-Streicher, Shudi-Broadwood, Sébastisn
     and Jean Baptiste Erard, Chickerings, Stein-
     ways, etc.. Beethoven's influence on the
     development of the instrument is noted. The

author cites innovations by various builders,
such as Chickering's use of the Babcock one-
piece cast-iron plate, Erard's repetition
action, Steinway's duplex scale, as well as
innovations by others. He also presents an
interesting comparison of the English and
Viennese piano. A concise but well-struc-
tured history of piano development in its
early years.

55. Grover, David S. *The Piano: Its Story from
    Zither to Grand.* London: Hale, 1976.
    223 p. ISBN 0-7091-5673-1 OCLC 2836926
    ML 650 G75; Also, New York: Scribner, 1978.
    ISBN 0-6841-5781-0 OCLC 4343565 ML 650
    G75 1978

    As the title states, this is a study of the
    piano from primitive zithers to the refine-
    ments of the piano of the 1970s. Grover ef-
    fectively links the technical development
    of the piano with parallel social and musi-
    cal growth. He includes units on perform-
    ers and piano virtuosi of the period c.1830-
    1914, e.g., Gottschalk, Leschetizky, Pade-
    rewski, to mention a few. Grover's work is
    somewhat similar to Loesser's *Men, Women and
    Pianos* in that it is socially oriented.
    The interplay of musical development and pi-
    ano evolution is done well. Illustrations,
    musical examples, schematics, index.

56. Harding, Rosamond Evelyn Mary. *The Piano-
    forte: Its History Traced to the Great
    Exhibition of 1851.* Cambridge: Cambridge
    University Press, 1933. xviii, 432 p.
    OCLC 3356964 ML 652 H26; Reprint. New
    York: Da Capo Press, 1973. ISBN 0-306-710-
    84-6 OCLC 415237 ML 652 H26 1973; Re-
    print. St. Clair Shores, Mich.: Scholarly
    Press, 1976. OCLC 2597854 ML 652 H26
    1976; Reprint. Old Woking, Surrey: Gresham
    Books, 1978. ISBN 0-9054-1831-X OCLC 49-
    67531 ML 652 H26 1978

A significant survey of the state of piano
construction to 1851. Contains detailed descriptions of the inventions by Cristofori,
Schröter, and Marius. Presents Scipione Maffei's
report of Cristofori's invention (from *Giornale
dei Letterati d'Italia*, 1711) in Italian and
in English translation (by E. F. Rimbault).
Observes tone-sustaining and octave coupler
devices of the early nineteenth century, influence of Turkish and program music on the
instrument, innovations, and experimental
instruments. Good coverage of the upright
piano. Contains many action schematics, including several down strike models. Of particular interest is patent data, present in
the text and in the bibliography. Concludes
with a chapter on the care of the instrument.
An important source for research. Illustrations, appendixes (8) including: list of patents, bibliography (96 entries), prices of
pianos 1815-1851 (in sterling), list of piano
builders (London & environs 1760-1851), and
pedal indications; name-instrument index,
patentees and pianoforte makers index.

57.   Harrison, Sidney. *Grand Piano.* London:
      Faber, 1976. 272 p. ISBN 0-5711-0386-3
      OCLC 3070087   ML 650 H33

Harrison's work examines the history of
the piano and the major composers of piano
music. The volume's units are captioned in
a manner similar to the way Arthur Loesser
titled his chapters in *Men, Women and Pianos*
(New York: Simon and Schuster, 1954). That
is to say, like Loesser, Harrison has a sense
of humor in his approach to the subject.
The history of the piano is woven throughout
the book, with the author returning to the
subject in different eras. The text reads
in a reflective and musing fashion, making
it easy even for the non-musician to compre-
hend. Harrison discusses the piano, composers, some of their compositions, and pianists. The inclusion of a bibliography would

have assisted the reader in finding the works
that Harrison often quotes.   References are
not always fully documented.   Illustrations,
musical examples, name index.

58.   Hipkins, Alfred James. *A Description and His-
       tory of the Pianoforte and of the Older Key-
       board Stringed Instruments.* London: Novello,
       1896. Reprint. AMS Press, 1977. 130 p. ISBN
       0-4041-2971-4   OCLC 3255647   ML 652 H66 1977

       Hipkins does not follow a chronological for-
       mat in his work but instead opens with a de-
       scription of the piano of 1820-95.   This is
       followed by historical material on various
       keyboard instruments dating from the early
       organ to the year 1820. Hipkins then surveys
       the piano of 1709-1820. A fully documented
       work that includes a great deal of informa-
       tion.   Engraved action schematics were done
       by the author. A useful volume. Illustra-
       tions, glossary, name index.

59.   James, Philip. *Early Keyboard Instruments
       From Their Beginnings to the Year 1820.*
       London: Holland Press, 1930 (reprint 1960)
       xvii,   153 p. OCLC 918613   ML 549 J2
       1930a; New York: Stokes, 1930.   OCLC 36-
       41288; Reprint. New York: Broude Bros.,
       1960   OCLC 5580149   ML 549 J2 1960;
       Reprint. New York: Barnes & Noble, 1970.
       ISBN 0-3890-4082-7   OCLC 143928   ML 549
       J2 1970; Reprint. London: Tabard Press,
       1970.   ISBN 0-9019-5103-X   OCLC 298945
       ML 549 J2 1970

       A well-documented keyboard history, from
       the psaltery to William Stodart's applica-
       tion of a metal frame to the piano (1820).
       Pianofortes illustrated and described:
       Cristofori's 1720 instrument; an English
       Zumpe Square Pianoforte (1767); an English
       Beck Square Pianoforte (1775); an English
       W. Southwell Pianoforte (in the shape of a

semicircular side-table c.1785); an English
Longman & Broderip Square Pianoforte (c.1790);
a Viennese Grand Pianoforte (c.1795); an
English William Stodart Upright Pianoforte
(1801); an English R. Jones Upright Pianoforte (1808); and the Dutch Van der Hoef Cabinet
Giraffe Pianoforte (c.1810). A well-laid-
out illustrated history of the piano. Illustrations, name index.

60. Juramie, Ghislaine. *Histoire du piano.* Pre-
     face by Alfred Cortot. Paris: Editions Pri-
     sma, c.1947. 167 p. OCLC 918617 ML 650
     J87

     A historical survey of the development of
     the piano, beginning with descriptive essays
     on the psaltry and the clavichord and con-
     cluding with a chapter on the modern piano.
     Juramie interjects historical data in regard
     to France's contribution to the development of
     the piano. Of interest is the emphasis placed
     on the evolution of the upright piano. Refer-
     ences to composers and concert artists in
     France (e.g., Fauré, Saint-Saëns, Cortot,
     Gieseking) are also of interest to the casual
     reader or the researcher. Errata, illustra-
     tions.

61. Kelley, Edgar Stillman. *Musical Instru-
     ments.* Boston: Oliver Ditson, 1925.
     243 p. OCLC 343125 MT 6 K29

     Designed as text book (third-year course
     in understanding music). The portion deal-
     ing with the piano discusses its evolution,
     briefly regarding the piano's predecessors.
     Kelley views square pianos, English and Ger-
     man actions, and American improvements (some
     of which are not American in origin) e.g.,
     overstringing, agraffe, and other innovations.
     A very concise overview of the piano. Illus-
     trations, musical examples, name-instrument
     index.

62. Krehbiel, Henry Edward. *The Pianoforte and
    Its Music.* New York: Scribner, 1911. ix,
    314 p.   OCLC 1264303   ML 700 K73

    Opens with a relatively short chapter on
    the history of the piano, in which Krehbiel
    gives equal credit to three craftsmen for
    inventing the piano: Cristofori in Italy,
    Schröter in Germany, and Marius in France.
    This is followed by the major portion of the
    work, which deals with piano music and com-
    posers of piano music. Works by Pistoia to
    Bach and Handel are described; Classicism and
    the sonata are noted; chapters on Beethoven,
    Romantic school, National schools, and per-
    formers (style and technique) complete the
    volume. The work is dated by its flowery
    and poetic narrative. Illustrations, musi-
    cal examples, index.

63. Locard, Paul, and Rémey Stricker. *Le piano.*
    4th ed., rev. Paris: Presses Universitaires
    de France, 1966. 128 p.   OCLC 6647989
    ML 650 L6 1966.

    Brief mention of the origin of the instru-
    ment (Marius and Cristofori) is followed by
    a description of the modern piano and its
    builders. A concise chapter on the early
    virtuosi (e.g., Clementi, Czerny, Heller)
    precedes descriptions of Chopin's and Liszt's
    styles. Units on teaching techniques, great
    pianists, repertoire (Haydn to Barber), and
    piano chamber music are offered. Bibliogra-
    phy (lacking data), no index.

64. Loesser, Arthur. *Men, Women and Pianos: A So-
    cial History.* Preface by Jacques Barzun.
    New York: Simon and Schuster, 1954. xvi,
    654 p.   OCLC 269089   ML 650 L64

    This distinctive survey of the life of the
    piano is interwoven with highly descriptive
    views of its environment, from its inception

through c.1953. Loesser begins his socially
guided piano tour with the Reformation and
concludes with twentieth century democracy
and totalitarianism. He traces the history
of the piano in Italy, Germany, Austria,
England, France, and the USA. Loesser does
note functional aspects of the instrument as
well as innovations and refinements. He
weaves a colorful historical survey of the
instrument. The clever sense of humor that
marks his style is apparent in the banner-
headline-style chapter titles and in his keen
appreciation for the ridiculous. A very useful volume. Unfortunately, sources are not
documented, but it is apparent that the extensive bibliography served as source references. Name-subject index.

65.   Montagu, Jeremy. *The World of Baroque and*
      Classical Musical Instruments. Woodstock,
      N.Y.: Overlook Press, 1979. 136 p. ISBN
      0-8795-1089-7   OCLC 4493095   ML 465 M65;
      Newton Abbot (Eng.): David & Charles, 1979.
      ISBN 0-7153-7593-8   OCLC 5222412   ML 465
      M65

      A concise history of the pianoforte through
      the Classical period. Beautifully illustrated.
      There are only a few illustrations of pianos:
      the Cristofori 1722 pianoforte, a Zumpe Square
      Piano (1767), a Broadwood Grand Pianoforte
      (1794), and a Mathaeus Heilmann Fortepiano
      (1775). Data on the illustrated instruments
      is minimal. Illustrations, bibliography,
      name index.

66.   ------. *The World of Romantic and Modern*
      Musical Instruments. Woodstock, N.Y.:
      Overlook Press, 1981. 136 p. ISBN 0-
      8795-1126-5   OCLC 6916620   ML 471 M66

      A continuation of Montagu's series on mu-
      sical instruments. Begins with the piano
      of the nineteenth century, noting construc-

tional innovations and a few prominent
craftsmen. Pianos illustrated are: square
pianos by Steinway (1877) and William Swift
(1835); uprights by Broadwood (1815) and
Hawkins (1801). Illustrations, bibliography,
index.

67. Nalder, Lawrence Marcuse. *The Modern Piano.*
    London: Musical Opinion, 1927. 192 p.
    OCLC 5356837 ML 652 N3 M7; Reprint. Old
    Woking: Unwin Brothers, 1977.   ISBN 0-
    9054-1810-7 (hbk.), 0-9054-1811-5 (pbk.)
    OCLC 4229006   ML 652 N3 M7 1977

    An excellent piano handbook. The vol-
    ume warrants reprinting. Nalder's text is
    written in narrative fashion, transporting
    the reader through a varied historical over-
    view of the piano. Construction is thorough-
    ly examined; a study of tone is presented;
    action schematics are well done and accom-
    panied by explanations of how the actions
    operate. Discusses the history of the pi-
    ano; includes material on the innovative
    Jankó keyboard and the Wood two-manual piano.
    A unit on the history of the keyboard is of
    special value, as this portion of the instru-
    ment is often slighted. As Nalder's book
    was published in 1927, a few dates do not
    reflect the changes documented by recent re-
    search e.g., Cristofori's dates, first pi-
    anoforte. Illustrations; unfortunately,
    lacks an index.

68. Neupert, Hanns. *Vom Musikstab zum Modernen
    Klavier.* [from the monochord to the modern
    piano] 3 Auflage. Berlin: Erweiterte. Son-
    derdruck aus Herbert Junghanns, *Der Piano
    und Flügelbau.* Berlin; Fachverlag Otto
    Krause, 1952. 55 p. ML 650 N4 V6 1952;
    4th ed. Berlin: Krause, 1960. OCLC 11979845
    ML 650 N48 V6

    An expanded excerpt from *Der Piano und*

Flügelbau by Herbert Junghanns. Neupert
offers a survey of the history of the piano
and covers forerunners of the piano e.g.,
cordophones, monochords, the psaltery, zither,
clavichord, and harpsichord. Chapters dealing with the piano discuss the Cristofori
action as well as others', and various modern pianos. Includes diagrams, charts (piano's family tree, etc.), illustrations, bibliography (concerning the history of the piano), no index.

69. Newman, William S. "A Capsule History of the
    Piano." *American Music Teacher* 12 (July-
    August 1963): 14-15.

    A concise history of the piano, noting re-
    search sources, evolution of the instrument,
    structural details, Ludovico Giustini's early
    piano composition (*12 Sonate da cimbalo di
    piano e forte detto volgarmente di martelli*),
    composers for the piano, and the piano's pop-
    ularity.

70. Palmieri, Robert. "Artist and Artisan."
    American Music Teacher 12 (July-August
    1963): 26-27.

    The indirect influence of particular pian-
    ist-composers on the innovative process of
    piano construction. A look at several com-
    posers' favored instruments, i.e., Mozart's
    Späth, Stein; Beethoven's Streicher, Broad-
    wood, Graf; Chopin's Pleyel, Erard.

71. Paul, Oskar. *Geschichte des Claviers vom
    Ursprunge bis zu den modernsten Formen
    dieses Instruments nebst einer Uebersicht
    über die musikalische Abtheilung der
    Pariser Weltausstellung im Jahr 1867.*
    [History of the piano from its origin up
    to the most modern forms of this instru-
    ment, also an overview (survey) of the mu-

sic section of the Paris World's Fair (*Exposition universelle*) of 1867] Leipzig: A.H. Payne, 1868. 256 p. OCLC 2097012 ML 652 P32

Study of: acoustics, temperament, history of the piano, various piano craftsmen and their innovations, construction techniques, and piano-building, as viewed at exhibitions. As in other early German studies of the piano, the author ascribes the invention of the pianoforte to Christoph Gottlieb Schröter. Lists prize winners (with appropriate medals) in the classification of piano manufacturers at the Paris World's Fair of 1867. Illustrations (woodcuts), action schematics; lacks an index.

72. Pizzi, Mario. *Histoire du Piano: de 1700 à 1950.* Chambéry: M. Pizzi, 1983. 314 p. ISBN 2-9046-6000-3 OCLC 11289818 ML 652 P6 1983

History of the piano, stressing the evolution of piano manufacturing. Pizzi tracks down many manufacturers, including minor builders, noting regional factories, style of product, quantity manufactured, historical importance, influences, and other pertinent data. Also included are acoustic facts, many action schematics, Stein family lineage, and production charts. Important for the coverage of piano manufacturing in France, especially the progress of the firms of Pleyel and Erard. Illustrations, charts, bibliography (20 entries); lacks an index.

73. Rapin, Eugène. *Histoire du piano et des pianistes.* Paris: Bertout, 1904. 508 p. OCLC 4371136 ML 650 R21

The clavichord marks the beginning of Rapin's history of the piano. It continues
with a survey of the Italian, French, German
and English *clavecinistes*, with major focus
on Rameau, Handel, and J.S. Bach. Early piano construction is traced, from Cristofori
through to Erard and Steinway. Biographical
sketches (with musical examples) of Haydn,
Mozart, Beethoven, Schubert, Weber, Mendelssohn, Schumann, Chopin, Liszt, and their contemporaries comprise the major portion of the
volume. A chapter on music in France and in
other parts of the world at the end of the
nineteenth century concludes the volume.
Good view of the musical world of 1850-1900.
Musical examples, name index.

74.   Rattalino, Piero. *Storia del pianoforte: Lo
       strumento, la musica, gli interpreti.* 364 p.
       Milano: Il Saggiatore, 1982. OCLC 9828075
       ML 700 R37 1982

       Descriptive survey of the history of the pi-
       ano, piano literature, and artists and their
       interpretation. Rattalino, who is artistic
       director of the *Teatro Regio di Torino* and in-
       structs at the *Conservatorio di Milano*, effec-
       tively correlates diverse data regarding piano
       construction, literature, teaching, concert
       activity, interpretation, biographical material,
       and stylistic analysis. Illustrations (of var-
       ious pianos), musical examples, bibliographies
       (the piano, and works cited), name index.

75.   Remnant, Mary. *Musical Instruments of the
       West.* New York: St. Martin's Press, 1978.
       240 p. ISBN 3125-5583-0   OCLC 3361887
       ML 460 R36; London: Batsford, 1978. ISBN
       0-7134-0569-4   OCLC 4307090   ML 460 R36

       Contains a concise history of stringed
       instruments with keyboards, from the organ-
       istrum to the concert grand. The author
       includes current information as to Cristofori's

first piano. Chapter on mechanical instruments includes comment on barrel organs, orchestrions, and the pianola. Illustrations,
glossary, bibliography (arranged by instrument classification), name index.

76. Rimbault, Edward Francis. *The Pianoforte,*
     Its Origin, Progress, and Construction.
     London: Robert Cocks and Co., 1860. xvi,
     420 p. OCLC 1891711   ML 652 R57

     Rimbault's large volume is divided into
     three parts: "History of the Piano"; "Con-
     struction of the Piano"; and "Early Compo-
     sers for the Pianoforte." He traces the
     evolution of the instrument; offers a gener-
     al survey of the construction of the piano,
     noting improvements in the instrument to
     1851 (year of the Great Industrial Exhibi-
     tion); includes commentary on early keyboard
     music (works by William Blitheman [1555] to
     C.P.E. Bach [1760]); action schematics and
     wood-cut illustrations; and statistical data
     on piano manufacturing. The chapter "Claim-
     ants to the Invention of the Pianoforte" is
     important, for Rimbault reports the findings
     in Scipione Maffei's account of Cristofori
     in the *Giornale de' Litterati d'Italia*
     [1711] as evidence to "satisfactorily clear
     up the origin of the Pianoforte." Rimbault
     includes the complete Maffei text in the
     original Italian alongside the first Eng-
     lish translation by W. Chappell, Esq. F.S.A..
     A valuable work for both its informative and
     its historical function. Illustrations, mu-
     sic, schematics, appendixes, name index.
     Compare Mario Fabbri's more recent findings
     concerning Cristofori's invention in his
     work *L'alba del pianoforte: Verità storica*
     sulla nascita del primo cembalo a martel-
     letti.

77. Sachs, Curt. *Handbuch der Musikinstrumenten-*
     kunde. Leipzig: Breitkopf & Hartel, 1920.

xi, 419 p. OCLC 3351708   ML 460 S13; Reprint of 2d ed. [1930]. Wiesbaden: Georg Olms
Hildesheim, 1967.

Sachs' first edition of his musical instrument handbook was published in 1920 and covers
musical instruments of Europe from the Middle
Ages to modern times. In the foreword to the
second edition (1930) Sachs thanks Karl Geiringer for improvements made to the new edition. In describing the Hammerklavier, Sachs
puts to rest the argument of who invented the
hammered instrument- Schröter, Marius, or
Cristofori: "Der Streit um die Krone ist
heute verstummt. CRISTOFORI blieb Sieger."
[The battle for the crown is silenced today.
CRISTOFORI remained the victor.] Sachs offers
a historical account of the pianoforte, describing the mechanical properties of the instrument as well as noting innovations primarily made by German craftsmen. A unit on
Tafelklavier [table clavier] describes Christian Ernst Friederici's square pianoforte and
similar instruments constructed in other countries. The upright piano also receives attention. Illustrations, name index, subject index.

78.   ------. *Das Klavier; Mit 16 Tafeln und 10*
       Textabbildungen. (Handbücher des Instru-
       mentenmuseums der Staatlichen Hochschule
       für Musik. Erster Band.) [The keyboard
       instrument; with 16 tables and 10 text il-
       lustrations. Handbooks [manuals] of the
       Museum of Instruments of the State Conser-
       vatory of Music. Vol.1.] Berlin: Julius
       Bard, 1923. 54 p., 16 p. (appended illus-
       trations). OCLC 2059290   ML 650 S12 K4

Sachs concisely covers the development of
the piano from early stages (monochord) to
innovative concepts (Jankó). He recommends
using the illustrated manual as a guide to
viewing the actual instruments housed (at
the time of this publication) in the *Berlin*
Hochschule der Musik. Sachs' intense in-

volvement with the history of musical instruments is evident in this work of 1923. Besides describing precursors of the piano,
Sachs depicts pianos by various builders e.g.,
Silbermann, Cristofori, Stein, Erard, Friederici, Beck, and others. Details of construction are noted. Musical examples, illustrations, action schematics; lacks an
index.

79. ------. *The History of Musical Instru-
      ments.* New York: Norton, 1940. 505 p.
      OCLC 547845   ML 460 S24 H5

Sachs concisely wraps up the history of
the piano in eight pages. Despite the substantial size of the volume, the vast subject allows only a minimum of historical
coverage on any one instrument; thus, eight
pages for the history of the piano suffices;
but do not expect a great deal of elaboration
on any one aspect of the instrument. Sachs
does offer a fairly good representation (with
illustrations) of the German *prellmechanik*
and *stossmechanik* actions. Illustrations,
index.

80. Santos, Ivone. "História do Piano."
      Boletim do Conservatório Nacional 1 (De-
      zembro 1947): 46-51.

Historical overview, dwelling mainly on
early piano precursors such as monochord,
organistrum, *echiquier*, clavichord, harpsichord, etc.. Material on the pianoforte is
sketchy, with some data that is not accurate
e.g., Erard's *mécanique à double échappement*
[double escapement] was patented in 1821, not
1823.

81. Stierlin, Leonhard. *Das Fortepiano und
      seine Vorgänger.* Zürich: Druck von
      Drell, Füssli und Comp., 1861. 23 p.

OCLC 6692025   ML 5 N48 No.49

Evolution of the piano is traced. Included
are descriptions of the clavichord and harpsichord. The author claims Gottlieb Schröter
as the inventor of the "fortepiano" (1717),
although he mentions Cristofori and Marius as
close rivals for the title. The article surveys the work of many German builders e.g.,
Schröter, Silbermann, Stein, Streicher, and
builders of other nations: Erard, Clementi,
Broadwood, and others. Stierlin quotes the
familiar Mozart letter (1777) to his father
regarding the Stein piano. He describes innovations made for the instrument by various
builders, and also compares actions, case and
frame construction, etc. of various types of
pianos. There are sections dealing with the
Broadwood firm and the musical life of Clementi. An informative work.

82. Sumner, William Leslie. *The Pianoforte.* Lon-
     don: Macdonald, 1966. 201 p. OCLC 1474800
     ML 650 S84; 3d ed., rev. and enl. London:
     Macdonald, 1971. 223 p. ISBN 0-3560-3516-6
     OCLC 163074   ML 650 S84 1971

     Perhaps the best modern English-language
     historical survey of the piano. Unfortunately,
     it is currently unavailable. The fact that
     there is greater material on the piano than
     on its precursors is one facet that differen-
     tiates this volume from others, and there is
     material on acoustics, composers' instruments
     and their styles, variations in technique, as
     well as historical data. The volume deserves
     to be republished. Most sources are documented.
     Illustrations, charts, appendixes, bibliography
     (extensive; entries grouped according to sub-
     ject), name index.

83. Wolters, Klaus. *Das Klavier: Eine Einführung
     in Geschichte und Bau des Instruments und
     in die Geschichte des Klavierspiels.* [The

piano: an introduction into the history and
construction of the instrument and into the
history of piano playing] Bern: Hallwag,
1969. 91 p. OCLC 3124265 ML 650 W64;
Also, Mainz; London: Schott, 1984. ISBN 3-
7957-2351-5 OCLC 12839213 ML 652

Wolters attempts to familiarize the pianist with his/her instrument. He admits that
pianists are poorly acquainted with their
instrument. This beautifully illustrated
volume covers in concise form the history
of the instrument, basics of piano construction, and the development of piano technique.
Wolters is hopeful that the pianist will better appreciate the instrument upon reading
this book. The history of the piano begins
with the clavichord, and the construction
material views the vibrating string, soundboard, mechanism, tuning, care and repair,
among other practical aspects of the instrument. Kullak, Clementi, Liszt, *et al* are
observed in the unit on piano technique.
Illustrations, bibliography, no index.

THE INSTRUMENT

II. Historical Studies

Specialized Historical Subjects

84. Azizbekova, Miriam Akimovna. *Fortepíannoe
     Isskustvo v Muzykal'noĭ zhizni Vil'nuisa
     (1-íà polovina XIX veka).* [Fortepiano
     Art in the Musical Life of Vilnius (first
     part of the 19th century)] Vilnĩus: "Mok-
     slas," 1976. 184 p. ML 734 A97

     The importance of the piano in the history
     of the development of musical arts in Vilnius
     (capital of Lithuania). Details as to the
     distribution of keyboard instruments, piano
     literature, music education, pedagogical prac-
     tices, concert activities, etc. in Vilnius
     during the first half of the nineteenth cen-
     tury are observed. A separate unit investi-
     gates the activities of composer, conductor,
     and pedagogue Stanislav Moniũshko (1819-72),
     who was the first in Lithuania to put forward
     the principle of democratic development of mu-
     sical arts. Musical examples, illustrations,
     bibliography (many Polish-language items),
     name index.

85. Badura-Skoda, Eva. "Prolegomena to a History
     of the Viennese Fortepiano." *Israel Studies
     in Musicology* 2 (1980): 77-99.

     The author dispels the prevailing belief
     that the first public piano solo performance
     was given in 1768 by Johann Christian Bach
     in London. New evidence, states Badura-Skoda,

44

"proves that a concert on a fortepiano was
played in Vienna as early as 1763 in the Burg-
theater." Badura-Skoda investigates the
Viennese fortepiano, the origin of its name
(fortepiano), its builders, and its history.
Conflicting terminology concerning the name
of the instrument is one reason for the dif-
ficulties in research on the subject. Her
article is important for her research on pianofortes belonging to Haydn, Mozart, and
Beethoven, and the composers' reasons for
their instrument preference. Pianos built
by Anton Walter, Johann Andreas Stein,
Johann Schantz, Conrad Graf, etc. and the in-
strument-building climate of the time are observed. Unfortunately, she does not include
the more recent research on Cristofori done
by Mario Fabbri. Note: Badura-Skoda does
acknowledge Fabbri's research on Cristofori's
first pianoforte in her article "Domenico
Scarlatti und das Hammerklavier." *Österreichische Musik Zeitschrift* 40 (October
1985) 524-29.

86. Buchner, Alexander. "Das Sostenente-Piano."
Revue Belge de Musicologie 24-25 (1980-
81): 130-46.

The author describes the development of
the *sostenente* piano: the attempt to produce a piano that could continuously sustain
a tone. Buchner surveys the various *sostenente* instruments and their builders
e.g., *Geigenwerk* by Hans Haiden, *Clavecin-
vielle* by Cuisinié, *Animocorde* by J. Schnell,
and many more. A good descriptive survey of
this type of instrument. Buchner includes
illustrations and schematics of several *sostenente* instruments.

87. Bunger, Richard. *The Well-Prepared Piano.*
Foreword by John Cage. 2d American ed.
San Pedro, Calif.: Literal Arts Press, 1981.
94 p. ISBN 0-9406-1201-1 (lib. bdg.); 0-

9406-1200-3 (pbk.)   OCLC 929106   ML 697
B86 1981

In 1940 John Cage devised the first prepared piano. Bunger instructs performers
and composers in planning and choosing prep-
arations that will not damage the instrument. The volume lists prepared piano literature and describes various materials that
can be utilized in the preparation of the
instrument i.e., bolts, screws, washers,
nuts, coins, wood, bamboo, cloth, rubber,
plastics, etc.. Includes directions for
placing the objects in the piano without
damaging the instrument. An appendix includes three articles by Bunger on the subject for *Contemporary Keyboard*: "Prepared
Piano: Its History, Development, and Practice," "Prepared Piano: Explorations in
Sound," "Prepared Piano: Its First 40 Years."
Useful information on the art of the prepared
piano. Illustrations, musical examples,
appendixes (four); lacks an index.

88.   Carmi, Avner, and Hannah Carmi. *The Immortal
        Piano*. New York: Crown Publishers, 1960.
        286 p.   OCLC 891134   ML 429 C18 A3

The dramatic story of the elaborate "Siena
piano." Piano technician Avner Carmi and his
wife relate the history of this instrument, a
very ornate upright piano which was built by
Sebastiano Marchisio and family (of Torino)
at the end of the eighteenth century and was
owned by Nicodemo Ferri (of Siena), who em-
bellished the case with carvings. In turn,
the city of Siena gave the instrument to King
Umberto I as a wedding gift in 1868. In 1961
the story was seen on television (*"The Immortal Piano"* by David Shaw, Armstrong Cir-
cle Theater, December 21), and there were
recordings of the piano issued on the Esoteric
and Counterpoint labels. Illustrations, no
index.

89. Dent, Edward J. "The Pianoforte and Its In-
     fluence on Modern Music." *Musical Quar-
     terly* 2 (April 1916): 271-94.

     Dent explores the harpsichord's influence
     on music written during the time of that
     instrument's prime. The pianoforte's consid-
     erable influence on music of its time is
     also observed. Dent's theme continues with
     Beethoven's compositional ideas in relation
     to his instrument. Other composers regarded
     in this light are: Mozart, Schumann, Wagner,
     Weber, Liszt, and several others. He con-
     cludes with a look at modern composers' per-
     cussive use of the piano in their works.
     Dent has no kind words for the mechanical
     piano (pianola) of his time.

90. Doerschuk, Bob. "The Piano: Can It Survive
     in the Electronic Age?" *Keyboard Maga-
     zine* 11 (December 1985): 76-94.

     A valuable comparative analysis of the fu-
     ture of the acoustic piano. "Will the piano
     become economically and culturally obsolete?"
     is one of the questions pondered by a group
     of musicians. The participants are: Frederic
     Rzewski, Terry Fryer, John Steinway, David
     Burge, John Chowning, Ray Kurzweil, and Rus-
     sell Sherman, whose occupations in music
     range from session player, FM synthesis pi-
     oneer, piano manufacturing executive, to
     concert pianist and pedagogue. A very per-
     tinent subject, reviewed in a fair manner.
     Some of the statements made: consensus is
     that the acoustic piano will fade from the
     picture; not all of the electronic keyboards
     are as reliable as the acoustic piano in re-
     gard to repeated notes; pianos will be con-
     sidered historic instruments eventually,
     just as harpsichords are today; films still
     employ the acoustic piano with large orches-
     tras because film music is basically classi-
     cally oriented. The subject should be widely
     explored. Illustration.

91. Ernst, Friedrich. *Der Flügel Johann Sebastian
     Bachs; Ein Beitrag zur Geschichte des In-
     strumentenbaues im 18. Jahrhundert.* [The
     grand piano of Johann Sebastian Bach; a
     contribution to the history of instrument
     building in the 18th century] 2d ed. Frank-
     furt: C.F. Peters, 1966. 86 p. OCLC 115-
     5466 ML 651 E7 1966

     Ernst's work first appeared in the Bach
     bicentenary year of 1950, after the complete
     restoration of the Kielflügel Nr. 316 of the
     Staatlichen Sammlung für Musikinstrumente
     in Berlin, an instrument purported to be the
     "Bach Flügel." Ernst questions the authen-
     ticity of this claim. The volume is largely
     concerned with harpsichords of Johann Sebas-
     tian Bach's period, specifically instruments
     of the type owned by Bach. There are many
     references to the pianoforte and to builders
     of the time who constructed harpsichords as
     well as pianofortes. An interesting work in
     understanding the craftsmen of the time, the
     instruments they constructed, and the evolu-
     tion of the piano. Illustrations, name in-
     dex.

92. ------. *Bach und das Pianoforte.* Frankfurt:
     Das Musikinstrumen, [1961]. 23 p. OCLC 1-
     545298   ML 410 B1183 E712; 2d ed. [un-
     changed] 1980. OCLC 12751933 ML 410 B1
     E75 1980

     A study of the keyboard instruments of
     Frederick the Great; the piano in Potsdam
     at the middle of the eighteenth century;
     events in the life of Gottfried Silbermann,
     Johann Sebastian Bach, and Frederick the
     Great. Ernst examines Johann Friedrich
     Agricola's account, published in Adlung's
     Musica Mechanica Organoedi (1768), of the
     meeting between Bach and Silbermann, where
     the composer sampled Silbermann's piano.
     He traces Bach's travels in Germany and
     Bach's associations with Silbermann, Fred-

erick the Great, and others. At the same
time, he attempts to structure into a chronological time-frame the events concerning
Bach and the pianoforte. There is a good
description of Silbermann's pianoforte, as
well as insights into his career and piano
construction practices. A useful study of
the early piano in Germany and Bach's limited association with the instrument. Illustrations, no index.

93. Fabbri, Mario. "Il primo 'pianoforte' di
     Bartolomeo Cristofori." *Chigiana Rassegna
     Annuale di Studi Musicologici* 21 (1964):
     162-72.

     Fabbri's account of his investigative work
     in researching the date of Cristofori's ini-
     tial construction of the pianoforte and the
     date of the first instrument's completion.
     Fabbri's findings in this monograph are
     printed in more complete form in his book
     L'alba del pianoforte, published c.1968.
     There is a useful *sintesi cronologica*
     [chronological synthesis] included with this
     article, which highlights important events
     in the life of Cristofori.

94. ------. *L'alba del pianoforte: Verità
     storica sulla nascita del primo cembalo a
     martelletti*. [Dawn of the pianoforte: The
     true history of the birth of the first ham-
     mered harpsichord] Brescia: V Festival Pi-
     anistico Internazionale "Arturo Benedetti
     Michelangeli", [c.1968]. 26 p. OCLC 374-
     0157   ML 655 F3

     Fabbri discovered documents which indicate
     that Cristofori began working on his innova-
     tive instrument in 1698 and completed it in
     1700. The instrument described in Fabbri's
     findings is referred to as "*Un Arpicimbalo di
     Bartolomeo Cristofori, di nuova inventione,
     che fà il piano e il forte.*" Fabbri further

documents that it is a hammered instrument.
This information supersedes the usual report
of the date 1709 for Cristofori's invention
of the pianoforte. The 1709 date was ascer-
tained from Scipione Maffei's published description of the instrument, noted after his
visit to Prince Ferdinand. Fabbri includes
documentation of his findings. An important
monograph. Illustrations. Material presented
in this article first appeared in Fabbri's
"Il primo 'pianoforte' di Bartolomeo Cristofori." *Chigiana Rassegna Annuale di Studi
Musicologici* 21 (1964): 162-72.

95. Ford, Karrin E. "The Pedal Piano: A Forgot-
     ten Instrument." *American Music Teacher*
     35 (November-December 1985): 43-45.

     A useful article on the pedal piano, which
     had a fleeting success in the nineteenth cen-
     tury. First appearing c.1780, the instrument's
     popularity reached its peak by 1850. The au-
     thor traces its history and describes its
     structure. Composers who wrote for the pedal
     piano are discussed. Two pedal pianos are il-
     lustrated: a grand by Johann Schmidt (c.1778-
     1790) and an upright ("lyre") by Johann Chris-
     tian Schleip (c.1820-44). Well documented.
     Musical examples, illustrations.

96. Grame, Theodore. "The Piano in Mozart's Time."
     American Music Teacher 12 (July-August 1963):
     19,34.

     Description of the eighteenth century forte-
     piano and a comparison with the clavichord.
     The Schantz, Stein and Broadwood fortepianos
     are viewed in regard to their owners.

97. Greenfield, Jack. "Home Pianos - Squares,
     Uprights, and Other Verticals." *Piano
     Technicians Journal* 23 (February 1980):
     33-36.

Greenfield examines the origin, design,
and development of the square and various
vertical pianos. He acknowledges that the
origin of the vertical is in dispute and
examines early examples of a Jean Marius
design (instrument in the Leipzig museum
dated 1735), a Domenico del Mela (1739),
and a Christian Ernst Friederici (1745).
He discusses the John Isaac Hawkins and
Matthias Müller uprights (case to the
floor) and actions designed for the upright
by Robert Wornum, as well as innovations by
Jean-Henri Pape (over-stringing, tempered
steel strings, felt hammers). A useful documented study, especially for the history
and development of the upright piano.

98. Hess, Albert G. "The Transition from Harp-
     sichord to Piano." *Galpin Society Journal*
     6 (July 1953): 75-94.

     Hess examines a representative number of
     titles of printed English keyboard music be-
     tween c.1750-1800 and classifies the wording
     of these titles into three groups: for the
     harpsichord, for the harpsichord or piano-
     forte, and for the pianoforte. A comparison
     is made between the transition of harpsichord
     to pianoforte that took place in England and
     that which developed in Paris during the
     same time period. English keyboard composi-
     tions of that time were compiled by Hess from
     various catalogues and checked against Barclay
     Squire's *Catalogue of Printed Music in the
     British Museum* (1912). The French statis-
     tics were compiled from inventories made of
     instruments that were confiscated during the
     French Revolution and catalogued at that time
     by Antonio Bartolomeo Bruni and Bernard
     Sarette. An interesting statistical survey.

99. Jankó, Paul von. *Eine neue Claviatur:
     Theorie und Beispiele zur Einführung in
     die Praxis.* [A new keyboard: Theory and

examples as introduction to its use]
Wien: Verlag von Em. Wetzler (Julius
Engelmann), 1886. x, 68 p.; 11 p. (music)
OCLC 12405195   ML 697 J24Z

Jankó's explanatory treatise on his innovative six-tier keyboard. The novel keyboard
allowed playing tenths and twelfths with
ease, as well as making the execution of ar-
peggi simple. The aforementioned feats are
but a few examples of the improvements in
technique made possible by the Jankó keyboard.
In his treatise, Jankó describes his keyboard
in detail, both scientifically and practically.
He also discusses the technique involved in
performing on the keyboard i.e., hand placement, crossing, narrow spans, certainty of
attack, evenness of tone, fingering, etc..
Ideas are well presented. The volume includes
musical examples of various fragments of piano
compositions by Chopin, Schumann, Beethoven,
et al., and scales, chords, octaves, tenths,
etc., all with appropriate fingerings for the
Jankó keyboard. All of this demonstrates the
ease of performance on the Jankó keyboard-a-
dapted instrument. Illustrations, musical examples, schematics; lacks an index. Arthur
Loesser gives a concise explanation of the
keyboard, and a plausible rationale for why
the innovative keyboard never replaced the
traditional keyboard layout, in his *Men,
Women and Pianos: A Social History* New York:
Fireside Book (Simon and Schuster), 1954.

100.   Jepson, Barbara. "Fortepiano: The Born-Again
       Instrument." *Wall Street Journal* (12 Septem-
       ber 1985): 30.

       An interview with Malcolm Bilson on the sub-
       ject of the renewed interest in the fortepiano.
       Bilson comments on: historically appropriate
       music for the instrument, the fortepiano's
       tonal peculiarities, and pertinent Mozart
       concerti.

101. Kiraly, William, and Phillippa. "Erard ver-
      sus Steinway: A Symposium on the Sounds of
      Various Pianos." *Piano Quarterly* 30
      (Spring 1982): 44-45.

      An interesting report of a two-day sym-
      posium held at Kenyon College. The pur-
      pose of the symposium was to compare the
      relative values of a modern grand piano
      (Steinway) and one from the mid-nineteenth
      century (an 1856 Erard). The symposium
      panel consisted of a music critic, a collec-
      tor and restorer, several pianists, a piano
      technician, and a university professor.
      Compositions were performed on the modern
      instrument and on the Erard, and the results
      were compared and discussed by panel mem-
      bers. Consensus from the article was that
      the composers' intentions were better
      brought out on the nineteenth-century in-
      strument.

102. Kirk, Elise K[uhl]. *Music at the White
      House: A History of the American Spirit.*
      Urbana: University of Illinois Press, 1986.
      xviii, 457 p. ISBN 0-2520-1233-X   OCLC
      11815671   ML 200.8 W3 K57 1986

      An excellent overview of musical events
      held in the White House. The piano is very
      much present in Kirk's documentary. Arranged
      chronologically by administration, the work
      first traces the presence of the piano (a
      Thomas Dodd) in the George Washington adminis-
      tration (1789) and continues through the Car-
      ter and Reagan administrations (1983). There
      have been many types of pianos installed and
      used in the White House; the list is long,
      and only a representative group is mentioned
      here: Chickering grand (1857), Astor and Co.,
      Baldwin, William Bradbury, Knabe grand, Scho-
      macker and Co., Alpheus Babcock (1825), Wil-
      liam Hall & Son (1852), Freeborn Garrettson
      Smith (1871), Steinway & Sons grand (1903),
      Hallet & Davis, Erard. A few of the instru-

ments are illustrated: Erard grand (1818), Babcock square (1825-1829), Schomacker grand (1861), Steinway grand (1903), Astor & Co. square (1799-1815), and a Steinway grand (1938). Illustrations, bibliographical essay, name-subject index.

103. Lange, Helmut K.H. "Der Moderator-Zug am Hammerklavier." *Österreichische Musikzeitschrift* 28 (February 1973): 68-75.

The history of the "soft-pedal," "piano-stop," "Jeu de buffle," etc., traced from beginnings. Lange credits Friederici with the first "Pianozuge" [piano-stop], an insertion of a leather strip between hammer and string, as used in his pyramid piano of 1745. A description and photo of this instrument may be seen in Franz Josef Hirt's *Stringed Keyboard Instruments 1440-1880* Boston: Boston Book & Art Shop, 1968. Lange goes on to identify other pianos with piano-stop devices. He also cites pedagogical sources that mention the use of the piano-stop. He discusses positive and negative characteristics of the sound when used in piano compositions of various composers. Illustration (action schematic).

104. Mactaggart, Peter, and Ann Mactaggart, ed. *Musical Instruments in the 1851 Exhibition: A Transcription of the Entries of Musical Interest from the Official Illustrated Catalogue of the Great Exhibition of the Art and Industry of all Nations, with Additional Material from Contemporary Sources.* Welwyn: Mac & Me Ltd, 1986. 109 p., 16 p. of plates. ISBN 0-9507-7826-5   OCLC 15221139   ML 462 L6 G73 1986

The pianoforte section of the Mactaggarts' volume represents instruments built by 45 different builders, some well known and many that are now forgotten. A few of the pianos are described in detail (taken from the *Exhibition Official Catalogue* and the *Exhibition Official Descriptive and Illustrated Catalogue*), though most are not. The text includes material from William Pole's *Musical Instruments in the Great Exhibition*, W. Newton's edition of *London Journal of the Arts* (vol.39, 1851), *The Crystal Palace and Its Contents: An Illustrated Cyclopedia of the Great Exhibition, 1851*, and other works of that time. A *Report on the Pianoforte* by Sigismund Thalberg reveals an unusual account of the history of the piano. He claims Marius as the originator of the piano (1716). The principal builders of the time had their finest instruments in the exhibit: Pape, Nunns & Clark, Collard & Collard, Brinsmead, Broadwood, Chickering, Erard, Kirkman, Stodart, to name a few. An interesting array of instruments (many unique) that impresses one with the state of the art at that time and the importance of the pianoforte in the exhibition by its proportional representation. Fascinating and informative reading. Illustrations, appendix (price list), bibliography, no index.

105.   Mason, Merle H.   "The Jankó Keyboard."
       Piano Quarterly 87 (Fall 1974): 7-10.

An explanation of the Jankó keyboard and how it can facilitate piano performance. In his study, Mason also refers to other keyboard innovators such as: William A.B. Lunn, Paul Perizina, O.T. Wood, H.A. Howe, and Hofrat Hanfling. Another novel keyboard, the *Clavier Hans*, is also mentioned. Mason notes the whereabouts of two instruments with the Jankó keyboard: a Decker Bros. 1885 upright, housed in the Smithsonian Institution, and a Steinway concert grand, located in the Steven Foster Memorial Center (White Springs, Florida). The author wonders if there will be a comeback for redesigned keyboards. Useful, concise, descriptive account of the Jankó keyboard.

106. Meier, Elisabeth Charlotte. "Das Terpo-
      dion." *Das Musikinstrument* 7 (July
      1986): 9-10.

      The "Terpodion," a sostenente-type instru-
      ment, was invented by Johann David Buschmann
      (1775-1852). A pedal-operated cylinder, with
      wooden levers that touched the surface, pro-
      duced the sound of the "Terpodion." In 1817
      Carl Maria von Weber commented on the "new"
      instrument. The Buschmann "Terpodian" is
      housed in the Leipzig Museum. The first model
      had a keyboard of five and a half octaves; a
      subsequent model increased the keyboard to
      six octaves. Illustrations.

107. Mobbs, Kenneth. "Stops and Other Special
      Effects On the Early Piano." *Early Mu-
      sic* 12 (November 1984): 471-76.

      Examines controlling features of stops and
      pedals as: una corda, dampers, moderator
      (celeste, Pianozug), bassoon, percussion (e.g.,
      Turkish triangle, bells, cymbal, drum), piz-
      zicato, harmonic swell, and Venetian swell.
      Mobbs concludes his investigation of these
      sometimes complicated devices with an astute
      observation: "Products of misplaced ingenuity
      perhaps they may be; but it is interesting
      that one does not have to look far today to
      see their modern equivalents in some of the
      effusions of the electronic keyboard indus-
      try." A good historical study of the early
      pedal. Illustrations.

108. Molsen, Uli. comp, *Die Geschichte des Klavier-
      spiels in historischen Zitaten: von den An-
      fängen des Hammerklaviers bis Brahms.* [The
      history of piano playing in historical quota-
      tions: from the beginnings of the hammer-pi-
      ano up to Brahms] Balingen-Endingen: Musik-

Verlag Uli Molsen, 1982. 192 p. ISBN 3-980-06850-1 OCLC 9557987 ML 700 G46 1982

It is the author's contention that study of pertinent historical references in literature (including letters) concerning music performances, criticism, etc. will greatly aid in the understanding and execution of stylistic interpretations. The subject certainly is a valid premise and worth inspecting. Molsen gathers 479 references, from diverse literary sources, to music, the instrument, criticism, performances etc., in an effort to shed some light on how composers' works or performances were perceived and described in their time. Unfortunately, sources are not always identified, so that further investigation is difficult. Entries begin with dates of 1753-89 and progress to dates toward the end of the nineteenth century. Musical examples, bibliography, name index.

109. Parrish, Carl George. "The Early Piano and Its Influence on Keyboard Technique and Composition in the Eighteenth Century." Ph.D. diss., Harvard University, 1939. ix, 438 p. Cambridge, Mass.: Harvard University Library Photographic Dept., 1962. OCLC 7842033 ML 650 P249 1962

Parrish's excellent work is important for its concentration on the transitional period of the newly invented piano and its immediate predecessors. He views the differences and similarities of technique in performing on various instruments, noting scale fingerings, touch, style, etc.. Parrish presents a varied picture of the circumstances surrounding the emergence and acceptance of the piano, contemporary criticism, new problems for the performer, and the influence which the instrument had on the style of keyboard music. The history of the piano is presented in the opening chapter; succeeding units explore the role of the piano in modifying traditional

keyboard technique and present a survey of
pianistic style and technique in keyboard
works up to 1800. Recommended. Musical examples and an extensive bibliography (con-
sulted works).

110.   ------. "Criticisms of the Piano When It
       Was New." *Musical Quarterly* 30 (Octo-
       ber 1944): 428-40.

       An offshoot of Parrish's earlier work,
       The Early Piano and Its Influence on Key-
       board Technique and Composition in the
       Eighteenth Century (Cambridge, Mass.:
       Harvard University, 1939), which partly
       dealt with the subject of the new keyboard
       instrument on the scene. In this article
       for the *Musical Quarterly* Parrish depicts
       the struggle for acceptance that the piano
       underwent at the time the clavichord was
       still considered the finest keyboard instru-
       ment around. Various sources are quoted in
       this survey of instrumental tastes of differ-
       ent European centers. The author points out
       that the clavichord was generally preferred
       by many composers during the last half of
       the eighteenth century. A useful article.
       See also "From Harpsichord to Pianoforte,"
       by Howard Schott in *Early Music* 13 (Febru-
       ary 1985): 28-38.

111.   Pistone, Danièle. *Le piano dans la littéra-*
       ture française, des origines jusqu'en 1900.
       Lille: Atelier reproduction des thèses, Uni-
       versité Lille III; Paris: diffusion, H.
       Champion, 1975. 594 p.   OCLC 2479661
       ML 650 P58 P5 1975

       An unusual study. Pistone examines how
       the piano was introduced into nineteenth
       century French literature. Some 2,000 liter-
       ary items of well-known and lesser-known
       writers were examined for mention of the pi-
       ano, technique, concerts, pianists, amateurs,

etc.. The work points out the social role of
the piano at that time and notes the comparative use of expressions about music (not to
be confused with musical expressions). Antique French musical dictionaries were scrutinized to find out the early terms (names)
for the piano. Major French authors who referred to the piano and its associated terms
in their works are represented by: Stendhal,
Balzac, G. Sand, Flaubert, les Goncourt, and
Zola. A unique and interesting social, historical, and literary study of the piano.
Charts/graphs, bibliography (literary and musical, including dictionaries), indexes (key
words used, authors and musicians).

112.   Rothstein, Edward. "For the Piano, Chords
       of Change." *New York Times*, 27 September
       1987, p.1, sec.2.

       Predictions on the future of the piano.
       Rothstein notes the decline of piano manu-
       facturing in the USA and the increase of
       Asian production, observes the popularity of
       electronic pianos (synthesized sound), and
       reflects on the social history of the "acous-
       tic" piano. Illustrations.

113.   Scholz, Martin. Translated from the German
       by James Engelhardt. "The Early Piano-
       forte and Its Appraisal." *Piano Tech-
       nicians Journal* 12 (August-September
       1969): 15-19.

       Based on a lecture presented at the Second
       International Vacation Course for Piano Build-
       ers, held in Remscheid, Germany in 1960. At
       the time, the author was manager of Hug & Co.
       (Basel, Switzerland), a firm which restores
       antique keyboard instruments and serves as
       sales representative for Neupert, Schueler,
       and Sperrhake. The author stresses that the
       old instruments must be appreciated for what
       they are and not be compared to modern-day

instruments; the old instruments are not
poorer than the new. Scholz formally ap-
praises a pianoforte built between 1810-
1815 (a Johann Schantz grand) and subsequently explains the determining factors in
his appraisal. Scholz also describes the
rebuilding of a "Patent-Flügel" (1825) by
Nanette Streicher & Sohn, which is now housed
in the *Musikhistoriska Museet* (Stockholm).
The rebuilding operation is related in detail. Those interested in instrument appraisal and reconstruction will benefit from
this lecture-based article. Illustrations.

114. Schott, Howard. "From Harpsichord to Pian-
      oforte: A Chronology and Commentary."
      Early Music 13 (February 1985): 28-38.

      A chronological listing of principal events
      in the development of the piano, from 1698 to
      1809, and general commentary on pertinent top-
      ics concerning the transition period from
      harpsichord to pianoforte e.g., expressive
      devices for harpsichords, early music for the
      piano, etc.. Contains documented data about
      the early piano that reflects recent findings.
      An aid to understanding the harpsichord/piano
      transition period. Illustrations. See also
      "Criticisms of the Piano When It Was New," by
      Carl Parrish in *Musical Quarterly* 30 (Octo-
      ber 1944): 428-40.

115. Shead, Herbert A. *The History of the
      Emanuel Moòr Double Keyboard Piano.*
      Old Woking, Surrey: Emanuel Moòr Double
      Keyboard Piano Trust (distributed by
      Unwin), 1978. 310 p. ISBN 0-9506-
      0230-2   OCLC 4833878   ML 697 S53

      Shead divides his history of Moòr's double
      keyboard instrument into five units: Techni-
      cal and Mechanical (construction and manufac-
      turing data); Historical (year by year devel-
      opments); Bibliographical (annotated; includes

a reprint of Donald Tovey's article, "The Pianoforte of Emmanuel Moòr," *Music & Letters* 3
[Jan. 1922]: 29-48); Musical (musical considerations and conclusions); Statistical (repertoire, patents, how many instruments were made,
etc.). This definitive work on Emmanuel Moòr's
double keyboard piano offers evidence that
Moòr's instrument is indeed feasible. The instrument's second keyboard, which is pitched
an octave above the first, is directly behind
and above the lower keyboard, making both keyboards accessible to single hand passages;
octave spans can be played simply with the
thumb placed on one keyboard and the second
finger on the other. There were other refinements, such as an octave coupler, "hummocks,"
etc.. The volume gives the pros and cons of
the invention and offers a rationale for why
the instrument was short-lived; peak of popularity was from the late 1920s to the early
1930s. The instrument was endorsed by many
prominent composers and musicians, and was
used in performance by many fine artists.
Illustrations, schematics, musical examples,
appendixes, name index, proper-name index.

116. Singleton, Esther. "American Pianos; Of Late
Old Pianos Are Highly Prized as Antiques."
The Antiquarian 3 (October 1924): 12-13.

An interesting parallel: the author begins
her article with this remark, "In the age of
victrolas and radios the piano is fast be-
coming a rare article in the ordinary home."
In our day and age the rationale for the prob-
able demise of the piano is television, high
tech instruments, computers, etc.. Times
have not changed that much. Singleton notes
early British and American piano builders.
Illustrations.

117. Solis-Cohen, Lita. "Auctioning Rare Pianos."
Piano Technicians Journal 23 (July 1980):
15-17.

An interesting article on auctions of old
pianos. The author relates auction events
at Sotheby's. In one instance (in June of
1980) 25 musical instruments were put up for
sale. An 1804 John Isaac Hawkins upright
was sold for $16,650, a German Lyraflügel
sold for $7,750 and a small Broadwood sold
for only $2,800. The highest auction price
for a piano at that time (not at Sotheby's)
was $390,000, the sum paid for the "Alma
Tadema Piano," an opulently decorated Steinway which sold in New York. Those interested
in collecting instruments and in selling
them by auction will benefit from this article. Illustrations.

118.   Stewart, Madeau.   "Playing Early Pianos-A
       Lost Tradition?" *Early Music* 1 (April
       1973): 93-95.

A comparison of harpsichord and piano
techniques and tone, in regard to performing
on early pianofortes. The author comments
on fingering techniques, the perfection of
the early pianos, the revival of interest in
old instruments, and the transition period
from harpsichord to piano. Illustrations.

119.   Terse. Paul.   *Studien zur Verwendung des Kon-*
       zertflügels im Opernorchester in der Zeit
       von etwa 1930 bis etwa 1970. [Studies on
       the use of the Grand Piano in the opera or-
       chestra in the time from c.1930 to c.1970]
       Regensburg: Heinrich Hüschen-Gustav Bosse,
       1982. ii, 235 p. ISBN 3-7649-2212-5
       OCLC 8426752   ML 1705 T32 1982

Investigates the use of the concert grand in
the opera orchestra of the twentieth century.
Detailed analysis of specific operas, in regard to manner and method of the use of piano
as an orchestral instrument and the purpose
of its use by the composer. The piano in
this role is viewed: as a single instrument,

continuo instrument, one of several keyboard
instruments, a "short toned" instrument, in
a percussive function, and in combinations of
these uses. Works illustrating Terse's subject are by Schönberg, Berg, Hindemith, Stravinsky, Blacher, Britten, Haubenstock-Ramati,
Zimmermann, Penderecki, and Dallapiccola.
Musical examples, bibliography, appendixes.

120.   Turner, W.J.   "The Passing of the Piano-
        forte." *New Statesman* 25 (29 August
        1925): 549-50.

        Turner laments the passing of the piano
        in the English home. Even in 1925 there
        was an awareness that the piano was losing
        ground, but in this case the reasons given
        are the invention of the wireless and the
        gramophone. In our present day we can lay
        blame for declining piano sales to the popu-
        larity of television and stereo recordings,
        electronic instruments, and spiraling costs.
        The author predicted that in 25 years the
        piano would be a "historical" instrument,
        along with the harpsichord and viols.

121.   United States. Commission to the Paris Ex-
        position, 1867. *Reports of the United
        States Commissioners to the Paris Univer-
        sal Exposition, 1867.* Published under the
        direction of the Secretary of State by Au-
        thority of the Senate of the United States.
        Ed. by William P. Blake. Washington: Govt.
        Printing Office, 1870. 6 v. OCLC 507332
        T 801 E1 U5

        United States Commissioner Paran Stevens re-
        corded his *Report Upon Musical Instruments*,
        subtitled "Pianos and Other Musical Instruments
        at the Paris Exposition," in volume 5 (pages 3-
        18) of the collection of reports by U.S. Com-
        missioners on the *Exposition universelle*
        (Paris), 1867. Musical instruments presented
        at the 1867 Exposition were placed in classi-

fications: church organs, harmoniums, pianos,
stringed instruments, wind instruments, percussion instruments, accessories for manufacture, and editions of musical works. A
sampling of the number of piano manufacturers that exhibited their instruments: from
France (57), Prussia (northern and central
Germany) (29), Austria (26), Italy (13), and
USA (3). It is apparent that the world market in piano construction was dominated by
the Europeans. American piano manufacturers
represented were Steinway & Sons (awarded a
gold medal), Chickering & Sons (gold medal),
and Linderman & Sons. Since the Exposition
was held in Paris, the report by Stevens
seems greatly influenced by the contribution
of the French to the art of piano construction. His report includes units on: the "History of the Invention of the Piano," in which
he states, ("according to some authorities")
that Cristofori added some improvements to
the work of Marius which developed into the
first piano; the "Erard Piano"; "Power in
Pianos"; "Progress in Musical Education in
the United States"; "Manufacture of Pianos
in France"; "Manufacture of Pianos in the
United States"; "Notice of Pianos at the Exposition"; "German, English, and French Pianos"; "Organs"; "List of Awards." A fascinating view of the state of the art and historical opinion of the mid-nineteenth century.
Stevens' report includes a useful tabular
list of the number of exhibitors at the expositions of 1851, 1862 (both in London),
1855, and 1867 (both in Paris).

122.   United States International Trade Commis-
       sion. Washington, D.C.: International
       Trade Commission Publication 721, March
       1975. TC 1.2 P57

       An investigation of the importation and
       domestic sale of certain electronic pianos
       and of alleged unfair methods of competition
       and unfair acts in the importation and sale

of foreign made electronic pianos. Of interest to those delving into import statistics
and the effect imports have on the piano industry in the USA.

123. United States International Trade Commis-
     sion. Washington, D.C.: U.S. Interna-
     tional Trade Commission, 1983. 65 p.
     ITC 1.12: 332-159

     A study on the competition between imported
     and domestically produced pianos; report to
     the Subcommitte on Trade, Commission on Ways
     and Means, U.S. House of Representatives on
     investigation no. 332-159 under section 332(b)
     of the Tariff Act of 1930. Interesting sta-
     tistics. Includes charts, graphs, etc..

124. United States International Trade Commission
     Washington, D.C.: U.S. International Trade
     Commission, 1984. 8, 45 p. ITC 1.12:731-
     TA-204/prelim.

     Grand and upright pianos from the Republic
     of Korea; determination of the commission
     investigation no. 731-TA-204 (preliminary)
     under the Tariff Act of 1930, together
     with the information obtained in the inves-
     tigation. One of many annual government
     reports on the piano industry, this one
     specifically dealing with imported pianos.

125. Warner, Robert A. "Two Early Square Pianos."
     American Music Teacher 12 (July-August
     1963): 21-23,31.

     A detailed descriptive comparison of an
     Erard (1808) and a Broadwood (c.1815) square
     piano, both housed in the Stearns Collection
     of Musical Instruments at the University of
     Michigan. Warner offers historical back-
     ground on the houses of Erard and Broad-
     wood and examines the mechanical character-

istics of both instruments. Illustrations,
action schematic.

126. Wolfram, Victor. *The Sostenuto Pedal.*
      Stillwater, Okla.: Oklahoma State Uni-
      versity Publication (Arts and Sciences
      Studies, Humanities Series No.9), Sep-
      tember 1965. 45 p.   OCLC 190216
      MT 227 W6

      Historical survey of the damper pedal (split
      pedals, etc.), with primary attention to the
      sostenuto pedal. Wolfram attributes the in-
      troduction of the sostenuto pedal to three
      people: Boisselot and Sons (Marseille), who
      exhibited a pedal at the Paris Exhibition of
      1844 that enabled the pianist to sustain tone
      selectively, Alexandre-François Debain, who
      produced a sostenuto mechanism in 1860, and
      Claude Montal, who devised a sostenuto pedal
      (*pédal de prolongement*) in 1862. Wolfram
      states that the improved Steinway sostenuto
      mechanism of 1876 superseded other sostenuto
      devices. Wolfram also describes the use of
      the sostenuto pedal in music of Beethoven,
      Schumann, Chopin, Liszt, Debussy, Poulenc,
      and others. A conclusion notes the rejection
      of the use of the sostenuto pedal (and the
      reasons for it) by various performing artists.
      An informative monograph. Musical examples,
      references.

127. Wood, Ralph W. "The Piano as an Orchestral
      Instrument." *Music and Letters* 15 (April
      1934): 139-46.

      "Piano and orchestra do not mix," states
      the author, and he sets forth to prove his
      point. The piano cannot be played in an or-
      chestral ensemble without being recognized;
      therefore it stands out instead of melding
      with other orchestral tones or textures.
      Basically, Woods stresses the point that the
      piano is a percussive instrument and only

when it is employed as such, as in Stravinsky's
Petrouchka, does it fulfill its rightful
role as an orchestral instrument. The author
feels that piano concerti are not conducive
to producing pleasing sounds. He examines
examples of the piano used as a percussive
orchestral instrument by: Stravinsky, Berlioz,
de Falla, Debussy, Bax, Bartok, and Respighi.

THE INSTRUMENT

II. Historical Studies

Museum Catalogues and Keyboard Collections

128. Boomkamp, C[arel]. van Leeuwen, and J.H. van
     der Meer. *The Carel van Leeuwen Boomkamp
     Collection of Musical Instruments.*
     Amsterdam: Frits Knuf, 1971. 190 p. ISBN
     9-0602-7150-5   OCLC 314547   ML 462 L45 C3

     Pianos represented in the collection are a
     Clementi & Co. grand (1830), Meincke & Pieter
     Meyer square (1808), and a Jean-Henri Pape
     square (1840). Instruments are described in
     detail as to size, range, structure, case,
     finish, etc.. The pianos are illustrated.
     Illustrations, musical examples, no index.

129. Cselenyi, Ladislav. *Musical Instruments in
     the Royal Ontario Museum.* Toronto: Royal
     Ontario Museum, 1971. 96 p. OCLC 262262
     ML 462 T7 R75

     Foreword by H. Hicki-Szabo and introductory
     chapter by L. Cselenyi. Musical instruments
     from the late sixteenth to the nineteenth
     century. Most instruments in the catalogue
     of the exhibit are from the R.S. Williams
     Collection, presented to the museum in 1913
     and later. Keyboard instruments shown in the
     catalogue: Italian virginal (c.1560), Eng-
     lish Harpsichord (Jacob Kirckman c.1770),
     Italian Harpsichord (Johannis Celestini
     1596), English Spinet (Baker Harris 1773),

German Clavichord (c. first half of the
eighteenth century), English Square Piano
(Johannes Zumpe 1768), English Pianoforte
(Joseph Kirckman 1796), French Grand Pianoforte (Ignace Pleyel c.1823-25), English
Upright Piano (John Broadwood c.1810-20).
The instruments are well presented in
a fine setting. Worth visiting. Illustrations, bibliography (33 items on an-
cient instruments), no index.

130. Hollis, Helen R. *Pianos in the Smithsonian
Institution.* Washington, D.C.: U.S.
Government Printing Office, 1973. 47 p.
OCLC 659080   ML 650 H64

Similar to the booklet compiled by Emanuel
Winternitz, *Keyboard Instruments in the
Metropolitan Museum of Art*, in which a
sampling of pianos is discussed to best rep-
resent the stages of keyboard evolution.
The pianos selected from the Smithsonian
Institution holdings and examined in the
Hollis booklet are: square by Zumpe and
Gabriel Buntebart (1770), square by Gottlob
Emanuel Rüfner (c.1780), grand by Johann
Schmidt (1788), grand by André Stein (c.
1825), giraffe by Stein (1810), Broadwood
grand (1794), upright by Hawkins (1810),
upright by Broadwood (1815), Pleyel upright
(1858), square by Culliford, Rolfe, and
Barrow (1790), square by Albrecht (1798),
Babcock square (1835), Chickering squares
(1828 and 1850), square by Steinway (1877),
a Jankó keyboard upright by Decker Bros.
(1790), and the 1903 White House concert
grand by Steinway. The accompanying historical text is well done; it presents a concise overview of the development of the
modern piano from its early beginnings.
Illustrations (including actions), bibliography (24 items), no index.

131. Libin, Laurence. *American Musical Instru-*
      ments in the Metropolitan Museum of Art.
      New York: Metropolitan Museum of Art and
      W.W. Norton & Co., 1985. 213 p. ISBN 0-
      3930-2277-3 (Norton); 0-8709-9379-8 (MMA)
      OCLC 11785223   ML 476 L5 1985

      A lavishly illustrated volume presenting
      American musical instruments of the Metro-
      politan Museum of Art. The unit containing
      pianos is titled "Keyboards and Automata."
      Illustrated pianos are by Dodds & Claus
      (c.1791), Charles Albrecht (c.1798), Ben-
      jamin Crehore (c.1800), Gibson & Davis
      (c.1815), John Geib & Son (c.1816), Adam
      and William Geib (c.1822-27), Babcock (1822-
      23 and 1825), Thomas Loud (c.1815, 1830,
      and 1831), John Tallman (c.1835-38), Chick-
      ering (1829, 1851, and 1868), Henry Kroeger
      (1856), Firth, Hall & Pond (c.1835), Nunns
      & Clark (1853), Steinway (1872), and a cyl-
      inder piano (no keyboard) by George Hicks
      (c.1860). The descriptive text that accom-
      panies the photographs contains a great deal
      of historical information. A good example
      of combining history with pictures of the
      actual artifacts. The *automata* portion in-
      cludes lap organs, melodeons, combination
      piano and reed organs, roller organs, barrel
      organs, etc.. Illustrations, bibliography,
      index of works by accession number, general
      index.

132. ------. "Keynotes: Two Centuries of Piano
      Design." *Clavier* 26 (July-August 1987):
      11-15.

      Libin, curator of musical instruments at
      the Metropolitan Museum of Art, describes
      the special exhibition of pianos displayed
      at the Metropolitan (May 1985-December 1986)
      which commemorated two centuries of piano
      construction and design. Libin states that
      the exhibit was very popular and that over
      670,000 visitors attended the showing.

Thirty-two instruments were displayed, from
the Cristofori instrument of 1720 to an 1872
rosewood Steinway parlor grand. Libin
briefly describes some of the exhibited instruments. Illustrated (nine pianos).

133. Metropolitan Museum of Art (New York, N.Y.).
      *Keyboard Instruments of the Metropolitan
      Museum of Art; A Picture Book by Emanuel
      Winternitz, Curator of Musical Instruments.*
      New York: Metropolitan Museum of Art, 1961.
      48 p.   OCLC 1303714   ML 462 N5 W5

      A keyboard instrument iconography of a
      selection of the instruments in the Crosby
      Brown Collection of the Metropolitan Museum
      of Art in New York (c.1961). This concise
      picture book portrays instruments that best
      reflect the successive stages of the evolu-
      tion of keyboard instruments. The black and
      white illustrations begin with views of a
      monochord and conclude with an example of a
      pianoforte by Nunns and Clark (c.1850). The
      booklet shows details of several clavichords,
      harpsichords, organs, and pianofortes. The
      Cristofori instrument (1720) is shown, with de-
      tails of the action; in addition there are
      photographs of a Stein *Pedalflügel* (c.1778),
      a Zumpe Pianoforte (1767), Broadwood instru-
      ment of 1792, a Giraffe, an elaborate Erard
      (c.1830), and the American Nunns and Clark
      square pianoforte of c.1850. Just a sampling
      of the wealth of musical instruments in the
      Metropolitan. Illustrations, no index.

134. Metropolitan Museum of Art (New York, N.Y.).
      *The Crosby Brown Collection of Musical
      Instruments of All Nations. Catalogue
      of Keyboard Instruments.* New York:
      Metropolitan Museum of Art, 1903.
      313 p.   OCLC 896238   ML 462 N5 M3

      A.J. Hipkins presents an introduction,
      describing the history of keyboard instru-

ments. The Metropolitan Museum of Art has
a formidable collection of keyboard instruments, and the complete inventory of their
1903 holdings will not be listed here.
There are pianos made by: Zumpe (1767),
Stein, Longman & Broderip, George Astor,
Thomas Western, Broadwood, Clementi, Stodart, Evendon, etc.. The prize of the collection, of course, is the Cristofori Pianoforte of 1720. It is one of the three extant
Cristofori pianofortes. The Metropolitan
instrument is the oldest; there is a 1722
Cristofori pianoforte in Rome, *Museo degli
Strumenti Musicali*, and an instrument of
1726 in Leipzig at the Karl Marx University
Musikinstrumenten Museum. The Crosby Brown
collection catalogue is well illustrated,
with many side and back photos of the instruments. It contains a list of actions (of
specific museum instruments), models of actions (schematic drawings), and documents
relating to the Cristofori piano bearing on
its authenticity. Illustrations, appendixes, proper name index, general index.
The *Metropolitan Museum of Art Hand-Book
No.13. Catalogue of the Crosby Brown
Collection of Musical Instruments of All
Nations. I Europe* (OCLC 769200), published
in 1902, offers the same keyboard instruments but without the many photographs of
the instruments. The *Handbook No.13*
does explain the origin, history, and the
arrangement and classification of the collection.

135. Museo degli strumenti musicali (Castello
      Sforzesco, Milano). *Catalogo, a cura di
      Natale e Franco Gallini.* Milano: Comune
      di Milano, 1963. 448 p. OCLC 834259
      ML 462 M44 C3

      This is the second edition of the catalogue
      first published in 1958 (*Milano. Civico mu-
      seo di antichi strumenti musicali. Catalogo
      descrittivo a cura di Natale Gallini.* 1958.

OCLC 4351983   ML 462 M4 C5). The first edition listed 10 pianoforti, whereas in the second edition there are 28 pianoforti. There
are various pianos built by: Del Mela, Zumpe,
Antonio Battaglia, William Rock, Michael Rosem-
berger, Gaetano Scappa, Broadwood, Stodart,
Clementi and Co., Graf, Giuseppe Prestinari,
Jean-Henri Pape, Erard, etc.. Instruments
are illustrated and described, including range
and dimensions. Illustrations, three indexes
(instrument, name, and illustration).

136.   *Museo teatrale alla Scala.* Tomo 1°, Tomo
       2°, Tomo 3°. Chief editor, Carlo Pir-
       ovano. Milano: Electa Editrice, 1975.
       3 v. (885 p.)   OCLC 3033483   PN 1620.M5
       M8 1976

       A catalogue of photos of artistic items,
       including paintings, sculpture, coins, med-
       als, musical instruments, posters, puppets,
       stage settings, etc.. The three volumes
       comprise a selection of items from the city
       of Milan. Various Milanese museums and pri-
       vate collections were chosen to be repre-
       sented in this fine edition. It stands as
       a testament to the artistic heritage of the
       city of Milan. Musical instruments are ex-
       hibited in volume two. The instrument col-
       lection is compiled by Giovanni Pellini and
       contains six piano entries (three are illus-
       trated). Those illustrated are: Fortepiano
       a martelli (*a tavolino*) c.1833; Erard Pi-
       anoforte c.1870 which belonged to Giuseppe
       Verdi; Steinway Pianoforte c.1878 which be-
       longed to Franz Liszt. Illustrations, bib-
       liography (in each volume), name index (in
       volume three).

137.   Sachs, Curt. *Sammlung Alter Musikinstru-
       mente: Bei der Staatlichen Hochschule für
       Musik zu Berlin.* [Collection of old musi-
       cal instruments at the State Conservatory
       of Music in Berlin] Berlin: Julius Bard,

1922. viii, 383 p., 30 pp. of plates
OCLC 2010280   ML 462 B3 S13

Descriptive catalogue of instruments of
the State Conservatory of Music (Berlin).
The unit on the piano describes various
actions in historical perspective (with
schematics) and includes pertinent data on
each instrument. Types illustrated are:
square, grand, pedal *Hammerflügel*, pyra-
mid/giraffe, pianino, Vorsetzer, transposi-
tion piano, Jankó, to name a few. Builders
represented are: Johannes Matthäus Schmahl,
Friedrich Stentzel, Pascal Taskin, Conrad
Graf, Jean Silbermann, Henry Broadwood, etc..
Data includes size, type action, type pedals,
case finish, dates (if known), builder, and
region. Illustrations, museum numbers, instrument index, no builder index.

138.   Stanley, Albert A. *Catalogue of the Stearns
       Collection of Musical Instruments.* 2d ed.
       Ann Arbor, Mich.: University of Michigan,
       1921. 276 p., 40 plates   OCLC 392903
       ML 462 S81

At the time this catalogue was published,
the collection included the following pianos:
Longman & Broderip square (c.1790), Broadwood square (c.1800), Erard square (1808),
F.P. Hale square (n.d.), Allovon (of France)
upright (n.d.), Broadwood grand (c.1800),
Frenzel (of Linz) *Flügel* (1837), Johann
Christian Dietz *Klavierharfe* (n.d.), as
well as unsigned instruments by other builders. Descriptions are brief, primarily noting size, case, and range, along with some
historical background. Illustrations, bibliography, list of donors, list of builders
and inventors represented in the collection,
name index, instrument index.

139. *Gli strumenti musicali nel Museo del Con-
     servatorio di Milano.* [Musical instru-
     ments in the Milan Conservatory Museum]
     Illustrations and descriptions by Eugenio
     de' Guarinoni. Milano: Ulrico Hoepli,
     1908. vi, [7]-109 p. OCLC 3949157
     ML 462 M4 G8

     An illustrated catalogue of musical instru-
     ments housed in the museum of the *Conserva-
     torio di Musica Giuseppe Verdi* [commonly re-
     ferred to as the Milan Conservatory]. The
     volume is in honor of the first centenary
     (1808-1908) of the founding of the institu-
     tion. The collection at this time contained
     a rich array of stringed instruments. Key-
     board instruments are represented by a spinet,
     clavichord by Burkat Shudi (illustrated), and
     two pianoforti *a tavolo* (not illustrated),
     one constructed by Gaspar Katholnig Bürger
     (Vienna) and the other by Kaspar Lorenz
     (Vienna). Unfortunately, instruments are
     not dated; short descriptive commentary in-
     cludes dimension and range of each instrument.
     Illustrations, musical examples, instrument
     index.

140. Victoria and Albert Museum. *A Descriptive
     Catalogue of the Musical Instruments in
     the South Kensington Museum.* Prefaced
     by "An Essay on the History of Musical In-
     struments" by Carl Engel. London: Printed
     by G.E. Eyre and W. Spottiswoode and sold
     by Chapman & Hall, 1874. 402 p. OCLC
     896286 ML 462 S78 E6; Reprint. New York:
     B. Blom, 1971. OCLC 204506 ML 462 L6
     S74 1971

     Engel's essay deals primarily with in-
     struments of antiquity. The catalogue has
     but a few pianofortes: English chromatic
     pianoforte (keys are colored); English
     "Bijou" pianoforte; English pianoforte
     ("Euphonicon") (1840) by John Steward.
     Also included in the catalogue are "note-

worthy" instruments lent for exhibition:
Erard square pianoforte made for Marie
Antoinette; square pianoforte by Johannes
Pohlman (1767); square pianoforte by Zumpe
& Mayer (1776); square pianoforte by Longman
& Broderip (end of the eighteenth century);
and Queen Victoria's Erard grand pianoforte
(n.d.). The catalogue lacks sufficient
descriptive accounts of each of the instruments; information is kept to a bare minimum. Illustrations, musical examples,
general index.

141.   Victoria and Albert Museum. *Catalogue of
       Musical Instruments.* Vol.I *Keyboard In-
       struments.* Raymond Russell. London:
       Her Majesty's Stationary Office, 1968.
       xvii, 94 p., 47 plates.   OCLC 38874
       ML 462 L6 S77

       Since the Victoria and Albert Museum's
       catalogue of 1874 the keyboard collection
       has doubled in size. The catalogue of
       pianos and organs in this volume is com-
       piled by Austin Niland and contains pho-
       tographs and descriptions of 15 piano-
       fortes, including instruments by Zumpe,
       Florez, Longman & Broderip, Taschta,
       Clementi, Van der Hoef, Stodart, Collard
       & Collard, Wornum, Broadwood, Priestly,
       and Chappell. The descriptions of the
       pianos contain historical background and
       pertinent structural data. End material
       includes biographical notes on the instru-
       ment builders represented in the collection;
       "Decoration of Keyboard Instruments" by Peter
       Thornton; bibliography (16 items), addenda,
       name index.

THE INSTRUMENT

II. Historical Studies

Iconographies

142. Bragard, Roger, and Ferdinand Joseph De Hen.
      Musikinstrumente aus Zwei Jahrtausenden.
      Stuttgart: Belser, 1968. 328 p. OCLC 11-
      977026 ML 460 B74

      A pictorial history of musical instruments
      over a span of two thousand years. Beautiful-
      ly illustrated, the volume contains descrip-
      tions and views of several pianos: square
      pianos of Meyncke Meyer & Pieter Meyer (1782),
      Johannes Schmahl, and Johann Gottlob Wagner
      (1783); *Flügel* by Stein (1786), a pianino
      by Goetz equipped with the Jankò keyboard,
      and a grand by Pleyel with a Hans system
      double keyboard. Illustrations, glossary,
      bibliography (by period), name-instrument
      index.

143. Buchner, Alexander. *Musical Instruments
      Through the Ages.* Translated by Iris
      Urwin. London: Spring Books, 1961. xv,
      37 p., 323 plates OCLC 7984238 ML 460
      B89 1961; Also, London: Batchworth Press,
      1961. OCLC 1082884; original, *Hudebni
      nastroje od praveku k dnesku.* Prague:
      Orbis, 1956. OCLC 5519585 ML 460 B88;
      Also in German, *Musikinstrumente im Wandel
      der Zeiten.* Prague: Artia, 1956. OCLC 1-
      0496404 ML 460 B89 1956

144. ------. *Musical Instruments: An Illustrated
      History.* Translated from the Czech by
      Borek Vancura. New York: Crown, 1973. 275 p.
      OCLC 738822   ML 460 B8813 1973

      Musical instrument iconographies. Both
      volumes by Buchner are similar in content.
      They are oversize volumes with color, black
      and white, and sepia-tone illustrations.
      Various keyboard instruments are shown. In-
      cludes concise text on the evolution of mu-
      sical instruments. The piano is represented
      with the following instruments: square piano
      and pyramid by Leopold Sauer, an eighteenth
      century piano (Treviso Museum), a forte pi-
      ano (Prague Museum), a giraffe piano (nine-
      teenth century), a nineteenth century instru-
      ment by Streicher, and a square piano by Gae-
      tano Scappa. Illustrations, list of plates,
      bibliography (extensive), instrument index.

145. Colt, C.F., with Antony Miall. *The Early
      Piano.* London: Stainer and Bell, 1981.
      ISBN 0-8524-9572-2   OCLC 7537092   ML 655
      C64 1981

      Like Hirt's work of 1955, this is an illus-
      trated catalogue of specific period keyboard
      instruments, with pertinent data. Colt's
      earliest illustrated piano is a Matthäus Heil-
      man fortepiano c.1775. Instruments progress
      chronologically until 1868, which is repre-
      sented by an embellished Erard grand. Most
      of the instruments are beautifully photo-
      graphed in color. Text includes a concise
      history of the early piano (Cristofori to
      Broadwood), how to play the instrument (from
      Hummel's Elementary Instructions), and advice
      on stringing, tuning, and maintaining instru-
      ments. Illustrations, musical example, glos-
      sary, no index.

146. Harrison, Frank Llewellyn, and Joan Rimmer.
      European Musical Instruments. New York:

Norton, 1964. vi, 210 p. OCLC 896393
ML 489 H4; London: Studio Vista, 1964.
OCLC 4658206

A musical instrument iconography accom-
panied by concise historical background.
Illustrated pianos include: the Cristofori
1720 instrument in the Crosby Brown Collection of the Metropolitan Museum of Art; a
square piano by Zumpe and Buntebart (1777);
a harpsichord-piano by Joseph Merlin (1789);
a Stein pianoforte (1797); a Broadwood grand
(1820). Illustrations, index of instruments,
name index.

147. Hirt, Franz Joseph. *Stringed Keyboard Instru-
     ments 1440-1880.* Translated by M. Boehme-
     Brown. Boston, Mass.: Boston Book and Art
     Shop, 1968. xxviii, 466 p. OCLC 236394
     ML 650 H56 (1st ed. *Meisterwerke des Klav-
     ierbaus.* Olten, Switzerland: Urs Graf-Ver-
     lag, 1955.); Also, *Meisterwerke des Klavier-
     baus - Stringed Keyboard Instruments.* Trans-
     lated by M. Boehme-Brown. Dietikon-Zürich:
     Urs Graf (distributed in the USA by Da Capo
     Press), 1981. 235 p. ISBN 3-8595-1135-1
     OCLC 9393711 ML 650 H56 1981

     An illustrated catalogue of distinctive
     period keyboard instruments, with a great
     deal of text on history and construction.
     An indispensible volume for keyboard histo-
     rians, collectors of instruments, and re-
     searchers. Artfully done, the book traces
     the history of keyboard instruments, begin-
     ning with an early example of an Italian
     upright harpsichord (*clavicytherium*) up to
     pianos c.1880. There are schematic drawings
     of actions, as well as detailed views of the
     period pieces. The chapter on keyboard,
     stringing, frame and action also offers valu-
     able historical data. Hirt dedicates his
     work to "masterpieces of the keyboard instru-
     ment maker's art," a most fitting testimony
     to the craftsman's diligence. The volume

contains pictures of most of the historic instruments referred to in works that discuss
the instruments of the great masters e.g.,
Mozart, Haydn, Beethoven, Liszt, and others.
An excellent source for research. The 1981
printing contains parallel text in English
and German and the volume is reduced to a
smaller format. Gone are the large photos
of instruments that were present in previous editions. The 1981 edition contains the
identical text, however the illustrations
are smaller. Unfortunately, the new volume
has not been brought up-to-date. Illustrations, charts, list of international keyboard
instrument builders (to 1880), bibliography
(over 200 entries), list of museums and private collections of musical instruments;
lacks an index.

148.   Hollis, Helen Rice. *The Piano: A Pictorial
       Account of Its Ancestry and Development.*
       New York: Hippocrene Books, 1984.   130 p.
       ISBN 0-8825-4711-9   OCLC 8708273

       An iconographic survey of the history of
       the piano. Begins with a description of the
       organistrum (tenth to fourteenth century)
       and follows with precursors of the piano up
       to the modern piano. Most of Hollis' descrip-
       tions are of specific museum instruments.
       She presents a brief survey of the early pi-
       ano craftsmanship in Italy, Germany, Austria,
       England, and France. There is a chapter on
       early American music and keyboard instruments
       in the USA. The work is especially valuable
       for the views of period museum instruments
       and the informative data supplied. Illus-
       trations, bibliography (over 100 entries),
       index.

149.   Michel, Norman Elwood. *Old Pianos.*   Rivera,
       Cal.: N.E. Michel, 1954.   181 p.   OCLC 72-
       2265   ML 650 M623 O4

An iconography of old pianos and a few precursors. Not all data accompanying the illustrations is complete; some items lack
dates of origin, etc.. The volume consists
of black and white photos of squares, uprights,
grands, harpsichords, clavichords, spinets,
giraffes, and more. There are a few interesting, unique instruments in Michel's pictorial exhibit. Illustrations, index (by
builder).

150. Michel, Norman Elwood. *Historical Pianos,*
Harpsichords and Clavichords. Pico Riv-
era, Cal.: Michel, N.E., 1963. 212 p.
OCLC 1575626   ML 650 M48

An illustrated volume showing pianos of
the famous and celebrated. Pianos belonging to the Presidents of this country,
royalty, movie stars, composers, etc. are
shown, as well as views of historical pianos
that are housed in museums. There are pictures of the "Siena Piano." A good representation of the various types of historical
instruments. Illustrations, name index.

III. Construction

General Historical Surveys

151. Anderson, David. *The Piano Makers.* New York: Pantheon Books, 1982. 52 p. ISBN 0-3948-5353-9 OCLC 8431943 ML 657 A5 1982

     The subject of Anderson's volume is not diverse piano manufacturing companies, as the title might imply, but rather the personnel who actually build the instrument in the factory. Anderson's *Piano Makers* is directed towards young people and is a pictorial account of the construction process of the Steinway concert grand. Photographs were taken by the author. Illustrations, no index.

152. Bielefeldt, Catherine C. *The Wonders of the Piano: The Anatomy of the Instrument.* Edited by Alfred R. Weil. Melville, N.Y.: Belwin-Mills, 1984. v, 128 p. ISBN 0-9109-5731-2 OCLC 11881121 ML 652 B53 1984

     An illustrated overview of the construction of the modern piano. A short history of the piano, from its elementary predecessors (e.g., psaltery, dulcimer) to the early years of piano building (1700-1870), is followed by material on piano construction. Construction details are well displayed in numerous photographs. There are many excellent views of the instrument, both in and

outside of the factory, which cannot be seen
elsewhere. Bielefeldt effectively displays
construction procedures. The volume is well
indexed. Illustrations, historical chronology, bibliography (extensive), name-parts-
subject index.

153.   Blüthner, Julius Ferdinand, and Heinrich
       Gretschel. *Lehrbuch des Pianofortebaues
       in seiner Geschichte, Theorie und Technik
       oder Bau und Zusammenfügung der Flügel,
       Pianinos und tafelförmigen Pianofortes,
       nebst einer Darstellung der hierauf bezüg-
       lichen Lehren der Physik und einem kurzen
       Abriss der Entwickelungsgeschichte des
       Pianofortes. Für angehende Pianoforte-
       bauer und Musiker.* [Textbook of Piano-
       building in its history, theory and tech-
       nique or construction and building of the
       grand piano, pianinos and table pianos,
       including a presentation of the theories
       of physics related to the field and a
       short summary of the history of the devel-
       opment of the pianoforte. For prospective
       piano builders and musicians] Weimar:
       Bernhard Friedrich Voigt, 1872. viii,
       238 p. OCLC 6655640 mfm 587 c.2 mht/
       mfm 746 c.2 mht (Smithsonian Institution
       Library)

       Blüthner, who is known for his fine in-
       struments and for his use of *aliquot* scaling
       in his more expensive pianos, presents with
       co-author Gretschel an account of the art of
       piano building as of 1872. The authors ad-
       dress this technical work to young piano
       craftsmen and interested musicians, specifi-
       cally pianists. Chiefly, the principles of
       construction utilized in north Germany are
       described. The volume includes a scientific
       summary of physical aspects of the instrument.
       The authors make note of the great strides
       made in the study of musical acoustics and
       their intent is to convey this information
       to the builder and musician. The volume is

in three parts: "Physical Principles"; "History of the Pianoforte"; "Practice of Piano Building." An illustrated atlas is included, with 17 pages of action schematics, frames, etc.. Material on the history of the piano is primarily drawn from Oskar Paul's *Geschichte des Claviers vom Ursprunge bis zu den modernsten Formen dieses instrumentes* (1868). Illustrations, musical examples, no index.

154. Briggs, Gilbert Arthur. *Pianos, Pianists, and Sonics.* Bradford, Yorks (Eng.): Wharfedale Wireless Works, 1951. 192 p. OCLC 1304128 ML 650 B7; Also, New York: Herman and Stephens, 1951. OCLC 6612630 ML 650 B7

A useful, semi-technical book that delves into the history of the piano, acoustics, tone, touch, construction, tuning, voicing, and other facets of the piano. The author presents many pertinent subjects concerning the piano. A chapter on room acoustics describes proper piano placement in a room and sound absorption properties of various household materials, both of which one should be aware of for optimum sound projection. Briggs includes interviews with several British pianists who describe various learning and performing techniques. Illustrations, action schematics, graphs, glossary, index.

155. Dietz, Franz Rudolf. *Das Intonieren von Flügeln. Grand Voicing. L'harmonisation des pianos à queue. Intonering av flyglar. L'intonazione di un piano a coda.* Frankfurt (a.M.): Das Musikinstrument, 1968. 55 p., 16 plates OCLC 4690145   ML 652 D53

Text is in German, English, French, Swedish, and Italian. Dietz guides the technician step by step through the voicing process. This is the voicing procedure ap-

plied to hammers after a new set of hammers
has been installed. Rough needling, rough
voicing, filing, fine voicing, and voicing
in the shift position (una corda) are the
major topics covered. The needling technique
described by Dietz is the method used in the
Steinway (Hamburg) factory. Illustrations,
no index.

156.   ------. *Das Regulieren von Flügeln bei
        Steinway. The Regulation of the Steinway
        Grand Action. Le réglage du piano à
        queue de Steinway. La registrazione di una
        coda Steinway. Flygelns justering hos
        Steinway.* Frankfurt (a.M.): Das Musik-
        instrument, 1981. 82 p., 38 plates   ISBN
        3-9201-1216-4   OCLC 11373839   ML 694 D5
        1981

        Text is in five different languages. Be-
        cause of the need for descriptive clarity
        of the regulation of the Steinway grand ac-
        tion, piano builder Dietz offers here a de-
        tailed step-by-step explanation of the regu-
        lation. This work is the outcome of two pre-
        sentations on the subject by Dietz in 1961
        and 1962 for the piano industry personnel in
        Braunschweig and Zurich. Illustrations con-
        tained in the volume help to clarify various
        facets of regulation. Illustrations, no in-
        dex.

157.   Fétis, François Joseph. "Improvement in
        the Construction of Pianos." *Harmonicon*
        5 (July 1827): 158-59.

        Belgian musicologist Fétis makes note
        of construction defects in the early piano,
        i.e. short strings, small soundboard, hammer
        striking point variance (square pianos),
        etc., and extols instruments made by Pfeiffer
        and Petzold. The subject of transposing pi-
        anos is also addressed by the author; in ad-
        dition, he comments on the improvements made

by Pleyel and Broadwood in their instruments.
Fétis gives 1718 as the date of Cristofori's
invention.

158. Goebel, Josef. *Grundzüge des modernen
      Klavierbaues; Ein Hand- und Lehrbuch,
      umfassend die Theorie und Praxis des
      Klavier- und Flügelbaues, sowie eine
      Abhandlung über Tropenklaviere.*
      [Fundamentals of modern piano building;
      A textbook covering the theory and prac-
      tice of piano- and grand piano building,
      as well as a treatise on the tropical
      piano] 3d ed., enl. Leipzig: Bernhard
      Friedrich Voigt, 1925. viii, 133 p.
      OCLC 11985344   ML 652 G6 1925

159. ------. *Grundzüge des modernen Klavier-
      baues.* 4th ed., enl. and rev. Leipzig:
      Fachbuchverlag, 1952. vii, 146 p. OCLC
      14989411   ML 652 G6 1952

      A testament to the skill of the German
piano manufacturer. Goebel states that although early piano builders were skillful in
copying fine instruments, present day piano
manufacturers are knowledgeable about the
scientific properties of the building art,
and it is this knowledge that dominates the
building process today. Goebel demonstrates
why the Germans proved to be superior piano
craftsmen and leaders for many years in the
world market. He describes various parts
of the piano, giving scientific support to
his observations. The Steinway, Grotrian-
Steinweg, Pfeiffer, and Ibach are some of
the pianos viewed; in addition, there are remarks on the Renner, Langer, and Feurich actions. Goebel also discusses building pianos for tropical climates. Illustrations,
source and literature directory; lacks an
index.
      Goebel has attempted to include new tech-
nical developments in the field of piano
building in his 4th edition (1952). He has

incorporated the more recent developments
in the individual sections of the volume.
Principal additions were made to the sections
on measurement and the sound board. Illustrations, appendixes, bibliography (source
and literature directory), subject index;
lacks a name index or general index.

160. Hautrive, G.M. "La Facture du piano." *La
      Revue internationale de musique* 1 (Nu-
      méro spécial Avril 1939): 801-11.

      The author briefly describes the complex-
      ity of piano construction. The article is
      divided into units: tone, woods, frame,
      strings, hammers, action, keys, pedals, var-
      nish and glue, and tuning. Hautrive does
      not delve into the actual construction pro-
      cess *per se*, but rather explains the func-
      tion of each of the subjects listed above.
      This is evidently addressed to the lay per-
      son as an introductory view of the parts of
      the piano.

161. Herzog, H[ans].K[urt]., comp. *Europe Piano
      Atlas: Piano-Nummern.* Frankfurt am Main:
      Bochinsky, 1984. 100 p.   ISBN 3-9201-12-
      46-6   OCLC 7619945   ML 652 H48 1984

      Piano serial numbers of about 300 interna-
      tional brands of pianos, including those from
      the USA. Instruments are listed by name of
      piano (not necessarily the builder's name).
      Data provided includes name of piano, firm
      name, year of construction, and serial num-
      ber. The volume is printed in English,
      German, Italian, Spanish, and Norwegian.
      See also *Michel's Piano Atlas* by Norman
      Elwood Michel and S.K. Taylor's *Musician's
      Piano Atlas.*

162. Kennedy, K.T. *Piano Repairs and Maintenance.*
      London: Kaye and Ward; South Brunswick,

N.J.: Barnes and Co., 1979. 101 p. ISBN 0-
7182-1205-3 (UK), 0-498-02402-4 (USA)   OCLC
5140996   ML 652 K45

Kennedy's work is divided into two parts:
Repairs to upright pianos and repairs to
grand pianos. Repairs such as: dismantling,
re-covering, re-facing, re-fitting, re-cen-
tering, re-bushing, re-assembly, regulation,
etc.. Various parts of the piano are explained in easy language. The author fore-
warns the reader that if one does not have a
"natural ability and intelligence" to handle
everyday repair work, one should never attempt
any of the repair work described in the text.
However, he does urge the reader to examine
the book in order to gain insight into the
kinds of work involved in piano repairs. Illustrations, no index.

163.   Mason, Merle H., comp.   *PTG Piano Action
       Handbook.* 2d ed. Seattle, Wash.: Piano
       Technicians Guild, 1971.   55 p.   OCLC 11-
       40089   ML 657 M411 1971

       Action-regulating dimensions of pianos
       from the USA and Canada, and those imported
       to the USA from Europe and Asia. This new
       edition was prompted by changes in brands,
       models and designs. First edition was pub-
       lished in 1958.   Regulating   dimensions
       are   shown   for: key   height,   key dip,
       hammer   blow,   hammer   let-off,   and   back
       check   distance.   Manufacturer's "touch
       weight" and player's "weight touch" are ex-
       plained. Contains names and addresses of
       piano firms. Illustrations, no index.

164.   ------., comp.   *Piano Parts and Their Func-
       tions.* Seattle, Wash.: Piano Techni-
       tions Guild, 1977.   xi, 98 p.   OCLC 3607-
       824

       This valuable volume came into being pri-

marily because of the manufacturers' lack of
uniformity in naming parts of the piano.
Having conflicting names for identical parts
can be bothersome for the technician and con-
fusing for the layman, though the reason for
the differing names is easily seen: historically, the art of building pianos was borrowed
from several widely differing crafts, and the
process developed at about the same time in
different countries. Mason's work is an important contribution to a movement towards
standardization of piano nomenclature. Schematic diagrams are displayed, with part names
of modern grands and verticals. Antique,
square, player, and electrical pianos are not
considered in this work. Diagrams, parts index, glossary, glossary appendixes (winking
and rails). See also Klaus Schimmel and H.K.
Herzog's volume on piano nomenclature of six
different countries *Piano Nomenclatur* [1983]).

165.   Michel, Norman Elwood. *Michel's Piano Atlas.*
       Rivera, Calif.: N.E. Michel, 1957.   243 p.
       OCLC 4125865   786.1 M582 1957

       The author alphabetically lists 6107 names
       of pianos (4506 American firms and 1601 for-
       eign companies). Dates of manufacture and
       serial numbers follow entry of piano name.
       Many small piano firms are listed without
       dates and serial numbers. Dates are through
       1957. Useful in placing the date of a speci-
       fic instrument. Illustrations. See also
       The Musician's Piano Atlas by S.K. Taylor
       and H.K. Herzog's *Europe Piano Atlas: Piano
       Nummern.*

166.   Piano Technicians' Conference. *Secrets of
       Piano Construction: proceedings of the
       Piano Technicians' Conference, Chicago,
       1916, 1917, 1918; New York, 1919.* (Pre-
       viously published: *Piano Tone Building.*
       American Steel and Wire Co.)   Vestal,
       N.Y.: Vestal Press, 1985.   292 p. ISBN

0-9115-7215-5   OCLC 12079151   ML 652
P5 1985

Highly technical material on diverse subjects: "Composition of Tone," "Effects of
Hammer Felts and Tension," "Height of Keyboard, Hammer Felts," "Peculiarities of
Wound Strings," "Engineering Problems in
Piano Construction," "Varnish," "Qualities
and Uses of Wood," "Wood and the Piano
Builder's Art," "Problems of the Piano Action Maker," "Mysteries of Glue," "Meeting
of Hammer and Wire," "Treatment of the Piano after Leaving the Factory," "Trade-in
Pianos," "Effect of Hammer Wire Resiliency
Upon Tone Quality," and more. Of interest
to skilled technicians. One might compare
contemporary building practices with those
outlined here. Illustrations, no index.

167. Reibeholz, Lutz. *Das Regulieren von Steinway
      & Sons-Klaviermechaniken und deren Reparatur:
      Eine Arbeitsanleitung für Werkstatt und Ser-
      vice.* [The regulating of Steinway & Sons Pi-
      ano mechanism and its repair: A guide for
      workshop and service] Frankfurt am Main:
      Verlag Das Musikinstrument, 1981. 73 p.
      ISBN 3-9201-1281-4   OCLC 8530755   ML 694
      R44

      An illustrated manual noting functions, es-
      pecially the repetition apparatus, of the
      Steinway piano. The manual is designed for
      the experienced technician, although the prac-
      tical information will benefit anyone inter-
      ested in piano construction. Individual func-
      tions, i.e., dampers, pedals, touch, weight,
      intonation etc., as well as the preparation
      of the keyboard, hammers, and action parts for
      repair and adjustment are described. Illus-
      trations, no index.

168. Schimmel, Klaus [Nikolaus], and H.K. Herzog.
      Piano-Nomenclatur. Deutsch, English, Fran-

çais, Italiano, Norsk, Español. 2d ed.,
rev. and enl. Frankfurt, A.M.: Das Musikinstrument, 1983. 127 p. ISBN 3-9201-1219-9
OCLC 10170706   ML 102 P5 S35; 1st ed. titled,
Piano Nomenclatur. Ein Bildwörterbuch der
Teile von Klavier und Flügel: Deutsch, Eng-
lisch, Französisch, Italienisch und Norweg-
isch. [A picture dictionary of the parts of
the piano and grand piano: (in) German, English, French, Italian, and Norwegian] Frankfurt, A.M.: Das Musikinstrument, 1966. 70 p.
OCLC 1194331   ML 102 P5 S3

The second edition of *Piano Nomenclatur*
differs from the first edition in several aspects: another language is added (Spanish),
the parts listed in English are now based on
the British-American terminology instead of
solely on American usage, and an appendix
containing piano-manufacturing terminology
in the different languages has been added.
Piano Nomenclatur does not compete with
Merle Mason's fine work, *Piano Parts and
Their Functions* (1977) but instead com-
plements it. A person armed with both volumes will have a better comprehension of the
complexities of the industry's nomenclature.
Schimmel and Herzog's work names and describes
(via schematic illustrations) parts of the
piano, both uprights and grands, of six different countries, and the entire work is in
those languages (German, English, French,
Italian, Norwegian, and Spanish). The authors
have realized a service to the piano industry
in attempting to untangle the perplexing problem of properly identifying parts of the piano. *Piano Nomenclatur* is a valuable work.
Illustrations, appendix, bibliography (annotated), indexes (in the different languages).
See also Merle Mason's work on nomenclature,
Piano Parts and Their Functions.

169.   Smith, Fanny Morris. *A Noble Art: Three Lectures on the Evolution and Construction of
the Piano.* New York: Charles F. Tretbar

[Steinway Hall], 1892. xii, 160 p. OCLC
8253156   ML 652 S64 1892a

A good approach to the evolution and construction of the piano. Smith's lectures
were first presented to students of the
"Misses Masters' School." In consultation
with Steinway builders and technicians, Smith
compiled this information to express her ad-
miration for the art of piano construction.
Despite its dated predilection towards flowery prose, the work offers an easy-to-understand view of the evolution of construction
methods. The attention to the development
of wood bracing and the iron plate are of
particular interest. There is also information on the history of the piano, as well
as basic acoustical peculiarities. Illustrations, schematics; lacks an index.

170. Taylor, S.K. *The Musician's Piano Atlas.* Mac-
      clesfield, Cheshire, Eng.: Omicron Publish-
      ing, 1981. 216 p. ISBN 0-9075-0700-X   OCLC
      8114741   ML 652 M87

A listing of piano manufacturers' serial
numbers and production dates for over 300
brands from 23 countries. Some pianos that
are manufactured in the USA and Canada primarily for home use are not in the directory.
The volume does contain serial numbers and
production dates for a few American pianos:
Baldwins (1890-1981), Hamiltons (1900-81),
Howards (1895-1968), Kimballs (1888-1980),
Steinways (1856-1980), Wurlitzers (1903-80),
and Sohmers (1872-1979). A handy guide for
determining the year in which a particular
instrument was produced. Includes a capsule
history of the piano by David S. Grover titled
"A History of the Piano from 1709 to 1980."
Illustrations, index. See also *Michel's Pi-
ano Atlas* by Norman Elwood Michel and H.K.
Herzog's *Europe Piano Atlas: Piano-Nummern.*

171. Uchdorf, Hans-Jürgen. *Klavier: praktisches Handbuch für Klavierbauer und Klavier-spieler.* Wilhelmshaven: Heinrichshofen, 1985. 240 p. ISBN 3-7959-0431-5 OCLC 13244238 ML 652 U25 1985

The two structural details of this volume that are immediately apparent are the well-organized layout and the handsome illustrations. Starting from the monochord, the volume covers forerunners of the piano while placing major attention on the modern piano. Construction details are observed: upright pianos, grand pianos, tuning, intonation, industrial production of pianos, pianos in various surroundings, philosophy of modern pianism, care and upkeep of the piano, developmental tendencies i.e., self-playing pianos, electronic pianos, synthesizers; and the art of playing (awareness on the performer's part of the qualities of the instrument). The volume proves helpful in its descriptive and technical account of the instrument. Of interest to the pianist as well as the nonmusician piano owner. Literature, builder, and subject indexes, bibliography, illustrations, tables.

172. "What's Inside a Piano." *Design* 83 (July-August 1982): 18-23.

A historical overview, with attention to building innovations and functional descriptions. Adapted from *The Book of the Piano* edited by Dominic Gill. Illustrations.

173. White, William Braid. *Theory and Practice of Pianoforte Building.* New York: E.L. Bill Publisher, 1906. 160 p. OCLC 1923762 ML 652 W58; Reprint. as *Theory and Practice of Piano Construction: With a Detailed Practical Method for Tuning.* New York: Dover, 1975. ISBN 0-4862-3139-9 OCLC 1363621 ML 652 W58 1975

Interesting for its historic value, this
work stresses the theoretical aspects of
tuning and construction. Not a very practical manual for the handyman. Examines
acoustics, intonation, temperament, action,
sound-board, etc.. Diagrams, no index.

174. Wolfenden, Samuel. *A Treatise on the Art of*
      Pianoforte Construction. Reprint of the
      original 1916 edition (Unwin) with the sup-
      plement of 1927. Old Woking, Surrey: Unwin,
      1975. 274 p. ISBN 0-9502-1213-X   OCLC 220-
      2617   ML 657 W66 T7 1975

      Wolfenden's classic work on piano construc-
      tion is reprinted for historical purposes.
      The industry has radically changed since 1916,
      yet his work reflects the practical and exper-
      imental commitment of that period. The 1916
      edition includes scale calculations, pattern
      making, the sound-board, bearings, actions,
      tuning, hammer covering, gluing, etc.. The
      1927 supplement to this edition contains ma-
      terial on quality of tone, pitch, scale cal-
      culations, covered strings, sound-boards,
      and other construction data. Illustrations,
      charts, indexes.

THE INSTRUMENT

III. Construction

Builders and Companies

175. "Ain't It Grand: Steinway & Sons Celebrates
      135 Years of Celestial Sound by Building
      Its 500,000th Classic Piano." *Life* 11
      (June 1988): 99-103.

      Concise pictorial account of Steinway's
      years in piano building. Various construc-
      tion aspects are highlighted. Text gives
      historical background of the Steinway dynas-
      ty as well as an overview of production sta-
      tistics. One is given a glimpse of a newly
      designed, modern Steinway grand. Illustra-
      tions.

176. Bonaventura, Arnaldo. "Domenico Del Mela e
      il primo pianoforte verticale." *Bollet-
      tino della Società mugellana di studi
      storici* 4 (1928): 416-22.

      Bonaventura, then director of the museum
      and library of the *Conservatorio di Musica
      "L. Cherubini" di Firenze*, describes and
      gives credit to the story of the Del Mela
      vertical pianoforte, invented in 1739. The
      inscription on the instrument reads *D. Dom-
      inicus Del Mela inventor fecit anno 1739.*
      Del Mela, a gentle priest, lived and worked
      in Mugello (Galliano, Tuscany). His verti-
      cal pianoforte was conserved by the Del Mela
      family for almost two hundred years before
      it was offered to the State (*Ministero*

95

della Pubblica Istruzione), to be housed
in the *Conservatorio di Musica di Firenze*.
Bonaventura points out that Del Mela's invention of the vertical pianoforte preceded
Isaac Hawkins' upright piano by 60 years.
Illustrations. (Del Mela's instrument is also illustrated and described in Franz Josef
Hirt's *Stringed Keyboard Instruments*.)
Note: Del Mela's vertical pianoforte resem-
bled the *clavicytherium*, a vertical harpsichord popular in the seventeenth and eighteenth centuries. This type of harpsichord and
Del Mela's pianoforte were placed upright on
a table, with the strings rising from the
keyboard. Isaac Hawkins' upright instrument
of 1800 (concurrent with Matthias Müller's
upright in Vienna) placed the strings below
keyboard level all the way to the floor. The
Del Mela and Hawkins' instruments were very
different from each other. One might say
that Del Mela was one of the first to construct the vertical pianoforte and Hawkins
was one of the first to construct the modern
upright piano. The subject of early verti-
cal/upright pianos is controversial because
of construction differences. Compare research on the *clavicytherium*, vertical pianoforte, pyramid/giraffe piano, and the upright piano for conflicting opinions concerning historical preeminence.

177.   Bradley, Van Allen. *Music for the Millions:*
       The Kimball Piano and Organ Story (1857-
       1957). Chicago: Henry Regnery Co., 1957.
       334 p.   OCLC 906473   ML 661 B7

       One-hundred-year history of the Kimball Pi-
ano Company from its beginning, when William
Wallace Kimball founded the company in Chicago in 1857, to 1957, when the company moved to
its new two-million-dollar factory and home
office in Melrose Park, Illinois. An interesting account of the Kimball family and the
development of the Kimball Piano Company.
Illustrations, name index.

178. Challis, John. "New: A 20th Century Piano."
      American Music Teacher 12 (July-August
      1963): 20.

      Challis discusses his experimentation in
      adapting a metal bridge and soundboard to
      a modern-size instrument equipped with light
      hammers and a cast aluminum frame. The idea
      of applying metal parts to a piano came from
      Challis' experience in building both a clavi-
      chord and harpsichord with metal bridge and
      soundboard in 1957.

179. Chickering and Sons. *Achievement: An
      Ascending Scale.* Boston: Chickering and
      Sons, Div. American Piano Co., 1920.
      30 p. ML 694 C53 A2

      The history of the House of Chickering.
      On 15 April 1823 Jonas Chickering estab-
      lished himself in business with James
      Stewart, a Scotsman, and under the name of
      Stewart & Chickering, the House of Chick-
      ering was born. The volume does not do jus-
      tice to the firm; its language is dated, and
      historical coverage is cursory. Illustra-
      tions, historical chronology, no index.

180. Doerschuk, Bob. "Bösendorfer Celebrating
      150 Years of Piano-Building Excellence."
      Contemporary Keyboard 5 (1979): 8-14.

      History of the Bösendorfer piano, from
      the time that Ignaz Bösendorfer received
      his permit to build pianos in Vienna on 25
      July 1828, up to 1978. The firm's high and
      low points are observed; wars and the De-
      pression had damaging effects on the company,
      as did postwar inflation and a corporate
      takeover (Jasper Corporation) when business
      improved. Attention is given to materials in
      the Bösendorfer piano and to the production
      process. The Garrick Ohlsson incident is re-
      lated, in which the pianist switched alle-

giance from the Steinway piano to the Bösendorfer. The problem of piano endorsements is
examined. Illustrations.

181. Doerschuk, Bob, and Dominic Milano. "In-
      side Roland: Visionaries in Action."
      Keyboard Magazine 13 (August 1987):
      14-16.

      Concise history of the Roland Corporation.
      Musician and engineer Ikutaro Kakehashi and
      six colleagues founded the company in Japan
      in 1972. Roland helped introduce advances
      in technology, developing synthesizers, se-
      quencers, rhythm machines, and signal pro-
      cessors. The authors describe the advances
      made by the firm and their plans for the
      future. Illustrations.

182. Drake, Kenneth. "Behind the Fallboard."
      American Music Teacher 12 (July-August
      1963): 16-17.

      A comparison of two Beethoven-period grand
      pianos: a Broadwood (1817) and a Streicher
      (1816). The action, damper system, string
      length and striking point, downbearing, and
      use of metal for structural support are de-
      scribed. Schematic drawings.

183. Franz, Gottfried von. "Mozarts Klavierbauer
      Anton Walter." [Mozart's Piano Builder Anton
      Walter] in *Neues Mozart-Jahrbuch: im auf-
      trage des Zentralinstituts für Mozart-
      forschung am Mozarteum Salzburg.* edited
      by Erich Valentin. Regensburg: Gustav Bosse,
      1941. 224 p. OCLC 2201215   ML 410 M9 N25

      Not much was written on Anton Walter dur-
      ing his time, therefore it is difficult to
      observe him historically. Franz's article
      quotes several letters regarding Walter's
      life as a piano builder. Mozart's widow

Constanze writes from Vienna to her son Karl
that she will send him his father's piano,
which had been newly renovated by Walter.
The author quotes Ferdinand von Schönfeld
regarding the Walter instruments "Seine Pianoforte haben einen vollen Glockenton,
deutlichen Anspruch und einen starken vollen Bass..." [his (Walter's) pianos have a
full bell-tone, clear attack, and a strong
bass]. Beethoven is also associated with
the Walter piano, having played Walter instruments for a time. Franz investigates
the genealogical background of Anton Walter.
Walter was eventually surpassed in popularity
by the well-known Johann Andreas Streicher.
A useful overview of piano builder Anton
Walter. The volume contains illustrations
and musical examples.

184. Fuller, Richard A. "Andreas Streicher's
     Notes on the Fortepiano, Chapter 2:
     'On tone.'" *Early Music* 12 (Novem-
     ber 1984): 461-70.

Biographical material on Andreas Streicher
and his wife Anna Maria (Nanette) Stein.
Streicher was a pianist, composer and teacher;
thus he knew the capability of the piano in
all three roles. Fuller reproduces here Chapter Two of Streicher's *Kurze Bemerkungen
über das Spielen, Stimmen und Erhalten der
Fortepiano, welche von [Nannette Streicher]
[geborne] Stein in Wien verfertiget werden.
Ausschliessend nur für Besitzer dieser In-
strumente aufgesetzt, [von Andreas Streicher]*
[Brief remarks on the playing, tuning, and
maintenance of the fortepianos manufactured
in Vienna by (Nanette Streicher) (née)
Stein. Written exclusively for the owners
of these instruments (by Andreas Streicher)].
The booklet, published in 1801, was probably
meant to be given to each new owner of a
Streicher instrument. The chapter reproduced
also appears in English translation. The
text is colorfully written, offering advice

on how to play the piano, including tips on
hand position and technical style of the time.

185. Grafing, Keith G.   "Alpheus Babcock's Cast-
      Iron Piano Frames." *Galpin Society Journal*
      27 (April 1974): 118-24.

      Grafing presents the dispute between Thomas
      Loud and Alpheus Babcock concerning Babcock's
      claim to be the first to apply a cast-iron metal
      frame to the pianoforte.   The heated dialogue
      between the two builders appeared in Philadel-
      phia's *Daily Chronicle*, beginning 26 July
      1833.   Several subsequent rebuttals were
      printed.   Babcock was protecting his patent,
      whereas Loud wrote that the iron-framed pi-
      ano existed many years before Babcock's ver-
      sion and that the iron frame negatively al-
      tered the tone of the piano.   Author Grafing
      includes the text of the two builders' con-
      troversy, originally written in their news-
      paper advertisements.   An example of the cli-
      mate of the time.   Grafing states that at
      first, Babcock's invention was not seen as
      important to the industry, but that even-
      tually the importance of the cast-iron frame
      became evident.   A valuable article.

186. Greenfield, Jack.   "Cristofori's Initial
      Piano Design." *Piano Technicians Journal*
      28 (September 1985): 22-24.

      A detailed description and explanation of
      Scipione Maffei's schematic drawing of Cris-
      tofori's action (originally published in
      Giornale de' Letterati d'Italia [1711]).
      Greenfield explains each segment of the
      Cristofori action and also describes the
      pinblock.   Includes the first portion of
      Maffei's article (English translation);
      final segment of the article is in the sub-
      sequent issue of the *Piano Technicians Jour-
      nal* in a continuing article by Greenfield.
      Schematic drawing.

187. ------. "Cristofori's Soundboard Design;
      Cristofori Becomes Curator of Medici In-
      strument Collection." *Piano Technicians
      Journal* 28 (October 1985): 21-23.

      A continuation of Greenfield's examination
      of Cristofori's piano (first part in the Sep-
      tember 1985 issue of *Piano Technicians Jour-
      nal*). Includes the second half of Scipione
      Maffei's article of 1711 (English translation)
      describing Cristofori's pianoforte (*Grave-
      cembalo col piano, e forte*). Greenfield
      describes the Cristofori soundboard and dis-
      cusses the tuning of instruments at that time.
      The historical sketch of Ferdinando dei
      Medici's death and the Medici succession is
      of interest because of Cristofori's contin-
      uing work with the Medicis. Greenfield re-
      lates that Cristofori was put in charge of
      the Medici instruments in 1716 and mentions
      an inventory of Medici instruments of that
      same year.

188. ------. "Politics and Music in Florence
      During the Latter Part of Cristofori's
      Career." *Piano Technicians Journal*
      28 (November 1985): 16-18.

      A historical panorama of the political
      life in Florence during Cristofori's career.
      Greenfield traces the ruling line in Florence
      from the time of Ferdinando dei Medici's
      death in 1713 to the reign of Grand Duke Gian
      Gastone in 1723. Included in the article is
      a list of Cristofori instruments that are ex-
      tant, including pianos, harpsichords, and
      spinets. Also listed are dubious instruments
      that are attributed to Cristofori. Important
      for the historical survey of the Medici line.
      Bibliography (three items on the Medicis).

189. ------. "Cristofori's Last Work and His
      Successors." *Piano Technicians
      Journal* 28 (December 1985): 15-17.

A continuation of Greenfield's study of
Cristofori and his work. The series presented in *Piano Technicians Journal* began
in September 1985 with articles every month
through January 1986. Here Greenfield notes
evidence of possible Cristofori instruments
in Portugal and in Spain. Drawing on sources
such as Ralph Kirkpatrick's *Domenico Scarlatti*
(1953) and Charles Burney's *The Present State
of Music in France and Italy* (1773), Greenfield effectively points out why the Florentine piano found its way to Portugal and
Spain. Cristofori's assistants, Giovanni
Ferrini, Geronimo di Firenza, and Gherardi
di Padua are noted. The upright piano is
briefly discussed. Useful study of the
Cristofori piano and its influence in other
countries.

190.   ------. "Cristofori Piano Use - Dropped
       in Italy, Continued in Iberian Region."
       Piano Technicians Journal 29 (January
       1986): 24-26.

This issue concludes Greenfield's series
of articles on Cristofori, his work, his
influence, and the Medicis. The series began in September 1985, with articles presented every month. Greenfield continues
his historical overview of the Medici lineage and political life in Florence after
Cristofori's death. He uses sources from
Ralph Kirkpatrick's *Domenico Scarlatti*
(1953), noting the discovery of Florentine
pianos in the royal court of Spain (mid-
eighteenth century). Greenfield speculates
that the pianos there were obtained during
the period of 1731-1737, when Spanish troops
were garrisoned in Florence. Scarlatti's
Essercizi are discussed as to performance
on the harpsichord or piano. The Greenfield
series on Cristofori is well done. Anyone
studying the musical and political climate
of Florence at the time of Cristofori, and
those interested in Cristofori's work, should

examine all five installments (September 1985-
January 1986). Illustration. See also Beryl
Kenyon de Pascual's article "Francisco Pérez
Mirabal's Harpsichords and the Early Spanish
Piano." *Early Music* 15 (November 1987):
503-13.

191. Grossmann, John. "Grand Pianos." *Horizon*
      25 (March 1982): 50-57.

An overview of the Steinway company, with
attention to construction methods, Steinway
heritage, and artists' influence. There are
pointers offered for purchasing a new piano.
Illustrations.

192. Joppig, Gunther. "Petrof - der Begründer
      der tschechischen Klavierbauschule." [Pe-
      trof - founder of the Czech school of pi-
      ano construction] *Das Musikinstrument*
      11 (November 1987): 49-54.

Historical survey of the Czechoslovak piano firm of Petrof, founded by Antonin Petrof
(1839-1915), who apprenticed in Vienna and
whose first pianos were constructed in the
Viennese style. In 1874 Petrof left Vienna
to settle in Brno. At the same time, he
phased out the manufacture of Viennese-style
instruments. Three sons joined the firm, and
by the turn of the century (1900) 13,000 pianos had been manufactured. In 1948 the firm
became state-operated and by 1963 had produced
100,000 pianos. The company prides itself on
its training program for builders, training
some 180 students at a time for a three-year
term of apprenticeship. Illustrations.

193. Kammerer, Rafael. "The Steinway Dynasty: The
      Story of the Modern Piano." *Musical Amer-
      ica* 81 (June 1961): 6-8,56.

A view of the Steinway Company and the pi-

ano industry up to 1961. Kammerer presents
a concise history of the Steinway Company
to that date, noting stylistic changes in
the instrument prompted by economic and social patterns. Illustrations.

194.   Kiraly, William and Philippa. "Sébastien
       Erard and the English Action Piano." *Pia-
       no Quarterly* No.137 (Spring 1987): 49-53.

       The authors offer a concise history of
       the Erard firm, pointing out innovations
       and patents that Sébastien Erard developed.
       The Viennese and English actions are com-
       pared, and the development of the "English
       action" and the Erard double escapement are
       traced. The early work of Zumpe, Stein and
       Silberman, in relation to Erard's construc-
       tion practices, is noted. A helpful summa-
       tion of the achievements of the house of
       Erard. Bibliography (15 entries).

195.   Lenehan, Michael. "The Quality of the Instru-
       ment." *Atlantic Monthly* 250 (August 1982):
       32-58.

       The author describes the beginning of life
       for specific Steinway piano model D K2571.
       He takes the reader on an absorbing journey
       through the Steinway factory, following the
       piano from its earliest stage to the finished
       product. Piano K2571 starts in the Steinway
       wood pile, then on to other stages e.g., bend-
       ing the rim, the "belly" department, string-
       ing, action, the action "banger," and the
       tone regulator. Lenehan offers an intimate
       view of the Steinway shop workers and their
       functions, the Steinway family heritage, ear-
       ly years, and the CBS takeover. The author
       and the Steinway tone regulator attended
       K2571's public debut, held in Alice Tully
       Hall. Lenehan presents an informative glimpse
       into the inner workings of the Steinway fac-
       tory. Illustrations.

196. [Maffei, Scipione.] "Nuova invenzione d'un Gravecembalo col piano, e forte; aggiunte alcune considerazioni sopra gli strumenti musicali." [New invention of a harpsichord with piano and forte; also some remarks on musical instruments] *Giornale de' Letterati d'Italia,* Tomo V, Venezia, MDCCXI [1711], p. 144-59.

The first published description of Cristofori's keyboard invention "the harpsichord [that plays] with soft and loud." This description, as well as a drawing of the action, appeared in the cultural Italian periodical *Giornale de' Letterati d'Italia,* published in Venice. The journal published theological and scientific studies, along with reports on findings (ergo the description of Cristofori's instrument), as well as book reviews. A valuable document in the history of the piano. From this published account of the innovative work of Cristofori, the date of his invention subsequently appears in historical works i.e., encyclopedias, dictionaries, etc., as anywhere from 1709 to 1711. Recently, Mario Fabbri's research on the subject (in *L'alba del pianoforte*) proves that Cristofori started working on his novel instrument in 1698 and completed it in 1700. Several current reference works e.g., *New Groves Dictionary of Music and Musicians,* reflect this new data. The entire Maffei article presented in the *Giornale de' Letterati d'Italia* appears in English translation (by W. Chappel), along with the original Italian, in Edward Francis Rimbault's *The Pianoforte, Its Origin, Progress, and Construction* (1860).

197. Pascual, Beryl Kenyon de. "Francisco Pérez Mirabal's Harpsichords and the Early Spanish Piano." *Early Music* 15 (November 1987): 503-13.

Descriptions of Cristofori (Florentine)-

style pianos built by Seville builder Pérez
Mirabal as early as 1745. An instrument
probably built by Mirabal in Seville that
year, now privately housed in Madrid, is used
as an example of early Spanish piano workman-
ship. The author states that there are still
in existence at least two early Portuguese
pianos inspired by Cristofori's design; one
in the Lisbon Conservatoire Collection (signed
Henrique van Casteel, dated 1763) and one in
London (anonymous) which belongs to Harold
Lester. Pascual describes the construction
details of the 1745 Spanish piano presently
in Madrid, comparing it with Cristofori's
surviving pianos, and also includes historical background on the early Spanish pianoforte.
A worthwhile study. Illustrations. See also
Jack Greenfield's articles "Cristofori's Last
Work and His Successors," and "Cristofori Piano Use - Dropped in Italy, Continued in
Iberian Region" in *Piano Technicians Journal*
28 (December 1985): 15-17 and 29 (January
1986): 24-26.

198.   Pollens, Stewart. "The Pianos of Bartolomeo
        Cristofori." *Journal of the American
        Musical Instrument Society* 10 (1984):
        32-68.

        Detailed descriptions of the three surviv-
        ing Cristofori pianos: the 1720 instrument
        at the Metropolitan Museum of Art (New York);
        the 1722 piano at the *Museo degli Strumenti
        Musicali* (Rome); the 1726 piano at the *Musik-
        instrumenten-Museum der Karl Marx Universität*
        (Leipzig). Pollen offers a full, comparative
        study of the three instruments, examining
        structure, actions, stringing, hammers, keys,
        levers, soundboard ribbing, etc.. He also
        traces past restorations of the instruments,
        noting types of work done. Historical back-
        ground supplied is based on recent research
        e.g., the discovery of 1700 and 1716 inven-
        tories of Prince Ferdinando de' Medici's in-
        struments. The many fascinating illustra-

tions show the instruments as they have never
been publicly seen before (hammers, key levers,
wrestplank, case buttresses, key frames, plan
views, etc.). Comparative tables examine:
string lengths and striking points, dimensions
of hammer mechanisms, distance from bridge to
the bentside (designated strings), diameters
of strings (not original), and case dimensions.
The article is documented. A highly informative and important study.

199.   Reid, Graham. "European Pianos Analyzed."
        Piano Quarterly No.136 (Winter 1986-87):
        34-38 and continued in No.137 (Spring
        1987): 41-44.

        Contemporary Bösendorfers, Schimmels,
        and Steinways (Hamburg and New York) are
        described as to tone and touch; construction
        practices of the three firms are noted as
        well. Reid also attempts to explain the
        differences between the Hamburg Steinway
        and the New York Steinway. Part Two of
        Reid's survey of contemporary pianos ex-
        amines the Bechstein, Ibach, Grotrian-Stein-
        weg, Blüthner, and Feurich. Tone, action,
        case work, durability, are aspects that the
        author covers in his comparative survey.
        The appraisals have some merit but are rath-
        er cursory. This may be because Reid is
        presently completing a book on pianos, and
        the articles presented here are condensed
        versions of his findings.

200.   Rhodes, Lucien. "Piano Man." *Inc.* 9 (Jan-
        nuary 1987): 52-56.

        Informative article on the birth and growth
        of the Falcone Piano Company (Haverhill, Mass.).
        Santi Falcone founded the firm in January 1983.
        The Falcone piano has received recognition as
        a fine instrument. Difficulties in breaking
        into the piano business in this fiercely com-
        petitive age are described by Rhodes. The

fledgling Falcone firm evidently is flourish-
ing, despite the current fragility of the piano industry. It reaffirms one's conviction
that if one builds a fine product people will
eventually hear about it and purchase the
product. The "better mousetrap" syndrome.
Illustrations.

201. Rolle, Günter. "Marktübersicht: Klaviere
      & Flügel." [Market survey: uprights and
      grands] *Keyboards* 12 (1987): 79-83.

      A useful list of about 187 grands and up-
      rights, including electronic and acoustic in-
      struments, with data regarding: model name or
      type, overall size, keyboard size, type of
      wood and finish of case, general price range
      (in Fed. Rep. of Germany DM), MIDI specifi-
      cations (built-in or adaptable), firm's
      self-evaluation of each instrument (categor-
      ies as: 1. instrument for beginners of all
      ages, 2. instrument for advanced students,
      3. instrument for music conservatories, 4.
      solo instrument for concert pianists), and
      other points of information, such as types
      of pedals, etc.. The list includes pianos
      by Bechstein, Euterpe, Kawai, Samick, Sauter,
      Schimmel, Seiler, Steingraeber, Steinway (Ham-
      burg), Taiyo, Thürmer, Yamaha, Young-Chang,
      Fazer, Matthaes, May, and Wurlitzer. Larry
      Fine's book *The Piano Book: A Guide to Buying
      a New or Used Piano.* Jamaica Plain, Mass.:
      Brookside Press, 1987 also offers piano eval-
      uations.

202. Rothstein, Edward. "At Steinway, It's All
      Craft." *New York Times* (22 February
      1981): 8E.

      A quick run-down of Steinway's factory
      rigors and a description of materials used
      in the Steinway piano. The article appears
      adjacent to an article "On Yamaha's Assembly
      Line" by Henry S. Stokes. The two contrast-

ing articles are juxaposed for comparison
purposes. Illustration.

203. [Silverman, Robert Joseph] "A Talk With
John Steinway." *Piano Quarterly* 30
(Winter 1981-82): 15-21.

A conversation held at the Steinway factory
between the editor of *Piano Quarterly*, Robert
Joseph Silverman, and John Steinway. Topics
such as: the CBS takeover, teflon bushings,
traditional building versus automated construction methods, Steinway family involve-
ment in the company, recent improvements in
the Steinway piano, research and development
procedures, and artist endorsements. John
Steinway mentions that by far the largest cost
of manufacturing is labor, guessing that materials cost approximately 25%; the rest is
labor, overhead, advertising, etc..

204. Steinway, Theodore E. *People and Pianos: A
Century of Service to Music.* New York:
Steinway, 1953. 122 p. OCLC 685863 ML
424 S76

A centenary volume commemorating the history of the Steinway Company from its formation in 1853. A pictorial account of the
firm's progress. There are photographs of
the manufacturing process, as well as a vis-
ual parade of the many artists who performed
on the Steinway piano. Illustrations, no index.

205. Stokes, Henry Scott. "On Yamaha's Assembly
Line." *New York Times* (22 February
1981): 8E.

A quick run-down of Yamaha's assembly-line
piano factory methods. This article is
meant to be compared with an adjacent article titled "At Steinway, It's All Craft"

written by Edward Rothstein.   Illustration.

206.   Wainwright, David.   *Broadwood, By Appointment:*
       A History. London: Quiller Press, 1982.
       360 p.   ISBN 0-9076-2110-4   OCLC 9286144
       ML 678 W32 1982; Also, New York: Universe
       Books, 1983.   ISBN 0-8766-3419-6   OCLC 99-
       34690   ML 678 W32

       A handsomely designed volume with many full-
       color illustrations.   This Broadwood history
       book commences with the Shudi workshop (1728)
       and traces the family growth and the develop-
       ment of the John Broadwood & Son piano firm
       to its 250th anniversary in 1978.   The text
       has important data regarding innovations to
       the instrument, as well as detailed informa-
       tion about the family commitment and involve-
       ment.   Included is the Broadwood family tree
       and a technical appendix containing descrip-
       tions and data of various Broadwood instru-
       ments and their integral parts.   A useful
       work.   Illustrations, charts, appendix, bib-
       liography (keyboard, biography, general),
       name index (compiled by Elma Forbes).

207.   ------.   "John Broadwood, the Harpsichord
       and the Piano." *Musical Times* 123
       (October 1982): 675-78.

       An excerpt from Wainwright's volume *Broad-*
       wood by Appointment. The author relates
       important events in Broadwood's career as
       builder and manager of his piano firm, be-
       ginning with the year 1776.   The author
       notes, from entries in the *Broadwood Journal*
       for the years 1772-84, that from 1783 the
       pianoforte began to overtake the harpsichord
       in popularity.   This observation was deduced
       from the rise in the company's piano transac-
       tions at this time.   Wainwright relates that
       many musicians came to London at that time
       and eventually purchased Broadwood pianos.
       Illustrations.

208.   "Wie entstehen Hammerköpfe?" [How are ham-
       mer-heads made?] *Das Musikinstrument*
       11 (November 1987): 66-67.

       Descriptions of hammer manufacturing, se-
       lection of felt, glue, etc.. The Renner
       firm of Stuttgart is renowned for its piano
       action; its actions are the standard of the
       industry. This article deals with the pro-
       cess of buiding Renner hammers; it discloses
       what type of felt is the best to use, that
       white beach or mahogany is the best wood for
       the hammer head, etc.. The Renner firm has
       been producing its own hammers since 1906.
       Illustrations.

209.   Wythe, Deborah. "The Pianos of Conrad Graf."
       Early Music 12 (November 1984): 446-60.

       Biography of Conrad Graf and data concern-
       ing the 40 known extant pianofortes of the
       builder. The Graf instruments which were
       entered in the 1835 Austrian Industrial Pro-
       ducts Exhibit (*Gewerbs-Produkten-Ausstel-
       lung*) are described. Graf's construction
       techniques are examined. An appendix lists
       the surviving Graf pianos and their locations.
       The "Bonn" piano owned by Beethoven and a
       Graf that was owned by the Schumanns and by
       Brahms are described in detail. A useful
       study, helpful in understanding the man Con-
       rad Graf and his works of art. Thoroughly
       documented. Illustrations (Graf and his in-
       struments). Note: Photographs and descrip-
       tions of the Beethoven and Schumann Grafs
       are contained in Franz Josef Hirt's *Stringed
       Keyboard Instruments 1440-1880* (1955).

THE INSTRUMENT

III. Construction

Tuning - Temperament

210. Bliven, Jr., Bruce. "Profiles: Piano Man."
      New Yorker 29 (May 9 1953): 39.

      The story of Steinway technician William
      Hupfer, Rachmaninoff's personal Steinway
      technician, who traveled with him on tour
      for 13 years. The end of the era of trav-
      eling personal technicians was about 1943;
      this is the story of what it was like to
      travel with an artist: the tuner's job,
      talent of the technician, Steinway methods,
      etc.. Fascinating account of an exciting
      era and of the life of a traveling techni-
      cian/tuner of that time.

211. Dyer, Daniel L. *How to Tune a Piano in One
      Hour - Electronically.* Bronxville, N.Y.:
      Daniel Dyer, 1975. iv, 25 p. OCLC 1529616
      MT 165 D98

      A tuning manual for using the electronic
      "Tune-master" tuning device. As the author
      states, it may take a first-time user of an
      electronic tuning aid seven hours to tune a
      piano, but after considerable experience it
      can be done in one hour. Contains step-by-
      step directions for tuning with the "Tunemas-
      ter." Illustrations, no index.

212. Feaster, C. Raymond. *The Dynamic Scale and
      How to Tune It.* Louisville, Ky.: C. Ray-

mond Feaster, 1958. 47 p. OCLC 7619934
MT 165 F3

Feaster sets out to construct and delineate
a standard system for piano tuners, based on
the fact that technicians do not tune in
strict equal temperament. His "Dynamic Scale"
is a compromise of the equal temperament
scale. The author refers to William Braid
White's works, which seem to be a motivating
factor in his system. Feaster's guide to
tuning is theoretically based and practically explained. Includes various charts, e.g.,
temperament patterns, string hysteresis, octave partials tuned to the "Dynamic Scale."
Illustrations, no index.

213.   Fischer, Jerry Cree. *Piano Tuning, Regulat-
       ing and Repairing: A Complete Course of
       Self Instruction in the Tuning of Pianos
       and Organs.* Philadelphia: Presser, 1907
       viii, 7-219 p. OCLC 3537330   MT 165 F52
       F529p

Designed as a piano tuning text book; contains problems for students to solve, along
with short quizzes at the end of each unit.
The work is dated e.g., detailed information
on maintaining the square piano and repairing
reed organs; current tuning fee reported as
$2.50 to $5.00! Includes information on all
aspects of tuning and minor repair. Illustrations, action schematics, index.

214.   Funke, Otto. *The Piano and How to Care for
       It: Piano Tuning in Theory and Practice.*
       Frankfurt am Main: Das Musikinstrument,
       1961. 66 p. OCLC 8049830   ML 650 F8513

Available in German (*Das Klavier und seine
Pflege*) since 1940. Also available in
French (*Le piano - son entretien et son ac-
cord*). A good general guide for the piano
owner and for the novice piano tuner; the

book offers an easy non-technical course in
tuning, although Funke stresses the importance
of proper care by a qualified technician. A
fine all-round book for the pianist and mu-
sically inclined handyman, ready to understand the refinements of his/her instrument.
Illustration, no index.

215.   Hardin, Donald C. *A New Method for Electron-*
           ic Piano Tuning.   Stockton, Calif.: Hardin
           Piano Service, 1982. 43 p. OCLC 10996397
           MT 165 H25 1982

           A tuning manual designed for the electron-
        ic "Hale Sight-O-Tuner." Explains the con-
        trol settings and contains step-by-step pro-
        cedures. Hardin calibrates the tuner with
        a tuning fork before tuning and charts his
        method systematically. Includes several
        charts: rough-tune, tuning curve, etc..
        The text is intended for experienced tuners.

216.   Meffen, John. *A Guide to Tuning Musical*
           Instruments. London: David & Charles,
           1982. 160 p. ISBN 0-7153-8169-5   OCLC 98-
           77737   MT 165 M44 1982

           Meffen offers useful information regarding
        tempered tuning ("why and how to"). The unit
        on tuning keyboard instruments is exception-
        ally good (it includes pointers on tuning
        early pianos, clavichords, harpsichords,
        etc.). Other units examine the tuning of
        brass and woodwind instruments, stringed in-
        struments, and percussion instruments. The
        chapter on the history of temperament is
        valuable for understanding the total scheme
        of tempered tuning. Illustrations, musical
        examples, appendixes, glossary, bibliography
        (extensive), index.

217.   Reblitz, Arthur A. *Piano Servicing, Tuning,*
           and Rebuilding: For the Professional, The

Student, The Hobbyist. Vestal, N.Y.: Vestal Press, 1976. viii, 179 p. ISBN 0-9115-7212-0   OCLC 2332179   ML 652 R3

A well-illustrated piano servicing book, with excellent schematic diagrams of actions. The author offers practical tuning exercises, lists theoretical intervallic beat rates, and covers many aspects of repair and reconstruction. Directions are in easy language and begin with fundamental operations, e.g., to remove the action, first remove the music rack. Includes tuning and mechanical servicing of electronic pianos (Baldwin Electropiano, Rhodes, and Wurlitzer). Illustrations, bibliography (33 entries), conversion tables, appendix, index.

218. Smith, Eric. *Piano Care and Restoration.* Guildford, Surrey: Lutterworth Press, 1980. 192 p. ISBN 0-7188-2436-6   OCLC 7902858 ML 652 S62 1980; Also, Blue Ridge Summit, Penn.: Tab Books, 1981. 192 p. ISBN 0-8306-9723-3; 0-8306-1168-1 (pbk.)   OCLC 7172582 ML 652 S62

This volume considers only "straight" pianos, omitting electronic, player, and mini pianos. There are chapters on tools and materials, tone and touch, tuning and toning, structure and resonant parts, and actions and keyboards. Many useful diagrams and oscillograms aid the potential handyman in servicing his own piano. A useful piano care manual that is a bit more sophisticated than others. Illustrations, glossary, bibliography (16 entries), index.

219. ------. *Pianos in Practice: An Owner's Manual.* London: Scolar Press, 1978. 100 p. ISBN 0-8596-7393-6; 0-8596-7394-4 (pbk.) OCLC 5750927   ML 652 S59

The author provides guides to tuning, ad-

justment, and care; describes the mechanics
of the instrument e.g., production of tone,
pedals, action. Includes historical data,
points on action regulation, tuning and
toning, etc.. An aid in determining mechanical faults in a piano and how to go about
fixing these problems and in understanding
the general function of the instrument. Illustrations, bibliography, index.

220.   Stevens, Floyd A. *Complete Course in Profes-*
       sional Piano Tuning, Repair, and Rebuilding.
       Chicago: Nelson-Hall Co., 1972. 216 p. ISBN
       0-9110-1207-9   OCLC 286800   ML 652 S75

A nontechnical presentation of piano-tuning,
repairing, and rebuilding techniques. Also
offers instruction in tuning and repairing
electronic organs and pianos. Schematics
list nomenclature of action parts (Baldwin
grand; Hamilton upright; Acrosonic; Howard
"402"; Wood & Brooks grand, drop, inverted
sticker; and 90-degree action). Chapters
dealing with the use of the Strobotuner, repairing a piano to sell (complete overhaul),
developing a successful business, and tuning
of electronic pianos give this work a different aspect from the usual piano tuning/main-
tenance guide. Illustrations, schematics,
index.

221.   ------. *Complete Course in Electronic Piano*
       Tuning. Chicago: Nelson-Hall Co., 1974.
       xiv, 257 p.   ISBN 0-9110-1224-9   OCLC 90-
       0892   MT 165 S8

A tuning text dealing exclusively with electronic tuning aids. Stevens encourages people
to investigate tuning as a profession and in-
forms the reader that learning how to tune
with the help of electronic tuning aids can
appreciably shorten the learning time. Opening chapters describe piano construction and
operation. Explanations of tuning methods

are given, using: Peterson Chromatic Tuner
Model 320, Peterson Strobe Tuner Model 400,
Conn Strobotuner Model ST-6, Yamaha Portable
Tuning Scope Model PT-3, Tune Master, and the
Hale Sight-O-Tuner. Additional chapters de-
scribe the advantages of tuning electronically
and how to develop a tuning business. Illus-
trations, action schematics, index.

222. White, William Braid. *Piano Tuning and Allied
      Arts.* 5th ed., rev. and enl. Boston, Mass.:
      Tuners Supply Co., 1946. vii, 295 p.   OCLC
      832190   MT 165 W4 1970M

      First and second editions of White's trea-
tise, published in 1917 and 1927 respectively,
had the title *Modern Piano Tuning and Allied
Arts.* An indispensable volume of scientific
and practical information. White has revised
the fifth edition, clarifying obscure passages,
simplifying and condensing some of the explanations, and correcting errors. He describes
mean-tone and equal temperament, tuning methods, piano repair, actions, etc.. For the
layperson the volume is useful simply as a
dictionary of parts and scientific data pertinent to the piano. Illustrations, musical
examples, action schematics, glossary, bibliography (15 items based on acoustics, piano history and construction), index.

THE INSTRUMENT

III. Construction

Acoustics

223. Blackham, E. Donnell. "The Physics of the
Piano." *Scientific American* 213 (December 1965): 88-99.

"Most musical instruments produce tones
whose partial tones, or overtones, are harmonic: their frequencies are whole-number
multiples of a fundamental frequency. The
piano is an exception," states Blackham.
Blackham and his colleagues experimented
with piano tone and frequency in their
Brigham Young University laboratory. They
included a series of tests in which a jury
of musicians and non-musicians were asked
to distinguish between recordings of real
piano tones and synthetic ones. Their
findings are documented. In this article,
Blackham reviews the history of the piano,
especially regarding the tone-producing
mechanism of the clavichord, harpsichord,
and piano. The article also appears in reprint in *Musical Acoustics, Piano and Wind
Instruments* (1977) edited by Earle L. Kent.
Illustrations, graphs.

224. Bosquet, Jean. "Quelques éléments de
l'acoustique du piano." *Revue internationale de musique* 1 (Numéro spécial
Avril 1939): 813-21.

A brief overview of acoustical fundamentals to be utilized in understanding the piano. Tone, its amplitude and intensity, frequency, interferences, beats, combination and difference tones, harmonics, piano timbre and touch are some of the acoustical properties identified. Bosquet's conclusion: "*le piano moderne est une 'somme' artistique, scientifique et technique, simple en son principe, extraordinairement complexe en ses détails, bref, une grande oeuvre humaine.*"

225. Campbell, Murray, and Clive Greated. *The Musician's Guide to Acoustics.* New York: Macmillan (Schirmer Books), 1987. x, 613 p. ISBN 0-0287-0161-5   OCLC 15316728   ML 38-05 C24 1987

This work should be especially interesting to performing musicians, as the authors have constructed a volume that examines the science of sound and conveys the information in relatively easy-to-understand language. It examines the nature of sound, the generation of musical sound, and the historical development of the modern instrument. The basic creation and transmission of musical sounds, playing in tune (mean tone and equal temperament), the musical environment (hall, auditorium, etc.) are a few of the subjects covered. Each group of instruments i.e., woodwinds, brass, percussion, bowed/plucked, keyboard, is examined as to sound production. The piano parts are described in terms of sound production, especially noting the strings, soundboard, and tuning. Illustrations, musical examples, charts, diagrams, bibliography (extensive), general index (name, instrument, subject).

226. "Fingertip Control and Piano Tone." *Science News* 125 (16 June 1984): 376.

A presentation of the theory that the tone of a piano can be altered by how the pianist

presses down on the key. Asami T. Alberti
and Ramon A. Alba, of the Philosonic Institute
of New York, state that the impact of the key
upon the keybed also adds to the tone quality of the instrument.

227.   Hill, William G. "Noise in Piano Tone, A
       Qualitative Element." *Musical Quarterly*
       26 (April 1940): 244-59.

       A theoretical study of piano tone. Hill
       compares the "aural aesthetics" of tone with
       the "visual aesthetics" (illusions) of the
       Greeks. He notes that intensity can alter
       frequency; tone not only includes overtone
       patterns but noise also; noise is a char-
       acteristic element of an instrument's tone;
       the performer controls the amount and nature
       of the piano's noise. Hill explains and
       describes his theory on piano tone. Illus-
       trations.

228.   Junghanns, Herbert. *Der Piano- und Flügel-
       bau.* 6th ed., rev. and enl. by H.K.
       Herzog. Frankfurt am Main: Erwin Bochinsky/
       Das Musikinstrument, 1984. 382 p. ISBN
       3-9236-3960-0   OCLC 12367178   ML 652 J64
       1984

       A valuable collection of studies on various
       physical and scientific properties of the pi-
       ano, pertinent to modern construction methods
       and written by recognized authorities in the
       field. Authors include: Klaus Fenner, Otto
       Funke, Hermann Jedele, Martin F. Jehle, Karls
       Jung, Herbert Junghanns, Herbert A. Kellner,
       Earle L. Kent, J. Engelhardt, Ulrich Liable,
       Emile Leipp, Edgar Lieber, Max Matthias,
       Hanns Neupert, Walter Pfeiffer, Heinrich
       Riedel, Lothar Thomma, and Klaus Wogram. An
       introductory chapter on the history of the
       piano is followed by units investigating (not
       a complete list): acoustics and sound patterns
       of the piano, soundboard resonance, pitch,

tone, piano sonagrams, voicing, tone-color,
Siegfried Hansing's measuring theories and
criticism, physical properties of the piano
(i.e., plate-brace stress, resistance, etc.),
and piano manufacturing details: hammers, actions, stringing, iron frame casting, acoustical examinations of tone/sound, historic tun-
ings. Also included is information on various
nomenclatures, the SI-System (international
uniform system), requirements in the trade
education of the piano/cembalo builder as of
December 1982, requirements of the Master Exam
for piano-builder craftsman, and vocation test
rules for the piano tuner. An important collection of scientific monographs on the construction of the instrument and its various
acoustical properties. The volume is considered the standard scientific work on piano
construction. Illustrations, charts, action
schematics, bibliography, subject-name index.

229. Kent, Earle L., ed. *Musical Acoustics, Pi-
     ano and Wind Instruments.* Stroudsburg.
     Penn.: Dowden, Hutchinson & Ross, 1977.
     xiii, 367 p. ISBN 0-8793-3245-X   OCLC
     2900989   ML 3805 M885

     A collection of published articles on the
     physics of the piano and wind instruments.
     All papers reprinted are of twentieth cen-
     tury origin. The studies on the piano are:
     E. Donnell Blackham's paper on the "Physics
     of the Piano" (see entry under Blackham, E.
     Donnell for description); "The Vibrating
     String Considered as an Electrical Trans-
     mission Line" by Winston E. Kock (uses the
     knowledge gained concerning the character-
     istics of electrical circuits as a basis for
     understanding the characteristics of the pi-
     ano string); R.S. Shankland and J.W. Coltman's
     "The Departure of the Overtones of a Vibrating
     Wire From a True Harmonic Series" (presents
     a study of stretched, vibrating strings on a
     monochord); "Observations on the Vibrations
     of Piano Strings" by O.H. Schuck and R.W.

Young (a study of the partial frequencies
and the decay characteristics of piano tone
partials); Harvey Fletcher's "Normal Vibration Frequencies of a Stiff Piano String"
(reviews theoretical aspects of solid strings
and modifies equations so that they will ap-
ply to wrapped bass strings); "Influence of
Irregular Patterns in the Inharmonicity of
Piano Tone Partials Upon Tuning Practice"
by Earle L. Kent (examines string-to-string
patterns of partial inharmonicity and the
practical implications for the tuner and the
musician). An important collection of scientific studies on piano tone. Illustrations,
bibliography (extensive), author index, subject index.

230. McFerrin, W.V. *The Piano - Its Acoustics.*
      Boston: Tuners Supply Co., 1972. v,
      193 p.   OCLC 11026417   ML 3805 M2y

      Designed for the tuner-technician, useful
      to all those interested in the science of
      piano sound and tone. Includes historical
      material on the nature of sound, brief his-
      tory of the piano, string vibration, harmon-
      ics, overtones, tone quality, beats, vector
      forces, and many more highly scientific
      topics pertinent to piano sound. McFerrin
      also includes some non-scientific or partly
      scientific subjects such as, the piano and
      humidity, tuning fork, room acoustics, the
      ear and hearing, etc.. The author often re-
      lates topics to the structural elements of
      the piano, which emphasizes the point that
      the total instrument is a sound-producing
      unit. A useful study. Illustrations
      (charts, diagrams, graphs), appendixes
      (sources, glossary, measurements, etc.),
      index.

231. Weinreich, Gabriel. "The Coupled Motions of
      Piano Strings." *Scientific American* 240
      (January 1979): 118-27.

Physicist Weinreich describes why the trip-
ling and pairing of strings on the modern piano affects the quality of tone. Slight differences of frequency for each string ("mis-
tuning") contribute to the sound of the instrument. Sound decays ("prompt sound and
aftersound") are examined, as well as vertical and horizontal string motion. Weinreich
states that prompt sound is the effect of
vertical string motion, and aftersound is the
effect of horizontal string motion. He investigates conflict of string motion. Graphs
and charts demonstrate Weinreich's findings.
An effective and useful study in understanding the physical properties of piano tone.
Illustrations.

THE INSTRUMENT

IV. Pianos of Specific Composers

232. Badura-Skoda, Eva. "Mozart's Piano." *Ameri-
      can Music Teacher* 12 (July-August 1963):
      12-13.

      Some of the subjects in Badura-Skoda's de-
      scriptive article are: Mozart's first pur-
      chase of a pianoforte (Anton Walter) in
      Vienna; Haydn's recommendation to a patron
      to purchase a Schantz pianoforte; differ-
      ences of sound of various instruments. Read-
      ers are also urged to visit the *Kunsthis-
      torisches Museum* in Vienna. Illustration.

233. Frimmel, Theodor von. "Von Beethovens
      Klavieren." *Die Musik* 2/14 (1903):
      83-91.

      Extant Beethoven pianos are discussed.
      The Broadwood presented to Beethoven in 1818
      is described and historically traced to its
      ultimate location in the Budapest National
      Museum. Beethoven's Graf is given similar
      examination. Frimmel contends that the
      Erard of 1803, which Beethoven subsequently
      gave to his brother Johann, was given to
      Beethoven by Prince Lichnowski. The author
      considers the sound and character of these
      instruments in regard to the composer's
      temperament and musical style.

124

234. Gabry, Gy[orgy]. "Das Klavier Beethovens
      und Liszts." *Studia Musicologica Aca-
      demiae Scientiarum Hungaricae* 8 (1966):
      379-90.

      Gabry traces the path of the Beethoven
      Broadwood from the time the Broadwood firm
      chose the instrument for Beethoven and pre-
      sented it to him, to its position in the
      Ungarishe Nationalmuseum [Hungarian Nation-
      al Museum] in 1887. A fascinating histor-
      ical account of the Beethoven Broadwood.
      Briefly, according to Gabry and his find-
      ings, the Broadwood firm presented the piano
      to Beethoven in 1818, and after his death
      the instrument was sold to C.A. Spina, who
      eventually gave it to Liszt as a gift in
      1845; Liszt, in turn, (as a patriotic duty)
      gave the Beethoven Broadwood and many other
      important items from his private holdings to
      the Hungarian National Museum c.1873. Gabry
      includes several Liszt letters pertinent to
      this piano, as well as the announcement of
      Liszt's donation to the museum, published
      in *Vasárnapi Ujság* on 25 September 1887,
      titled "*Liszt-Reliquien im Museum.*" Illus-
      trations.

235. Hipkins, Edith J. *How Chopin Played, From Con-
      temporary Impressions Collected from the
      Diaries and Note-books of the Late A[lfred].
      J[ames]. Hipkins, S.A.F..* London: J.M.
      Dent and Sons, 1937. viii, 39 p. OCLC 15-
      48973   ML 410 C54 H44

      Contains recollections of Chopin's associa-
      tion with the Broadwood piano in London (1848)
      and includes a chapter in which there are
      many references to Alfred James Hipkins' work
      of 1896 on the art of the early piano (*A De-
      scription and History of the Pianoforte and
      of the Older Stringed Instruments*). Hip-
      kins (A.J.) notes a transference of clavi-
      chord playing techniques to the piano, where
      a legato tone is produced by the sliding mo-

tion of the fingers. There are descriptions
of pianos played at the time of Chopin. Illustrations, no index.

236.   Hollis, Helen Rice.   *The Musical Instruments*
       of Joseph Haydn.   Washington, D.C.: Smith-
       sonian Institution Press, 1977.   vi, 33 p.
       OCLC 2427638   ML 410 H4 H59

       Hollis examines various types of musical
       instruments used by Haydn. Keyboard instru-
       ments include a Shudi-Broadwood harpsichord,
       Johann Bohak clavichord, Broadwood piano
       (1775), Johann Schantz piano, Erard grand
       (1801), as well as keyboard instruments by
       other builders. Illustrations.

237.   Kinsky, Georg. "Mozart-Instrumente." *Acta*
       Musicologica 12 (1940): 1-21.

       Kinsky traces keyboard instruments owned
       by the Mozart family, as well as those per-
       formed on or simply examined by Wolfgang
       Amadeus during his lifetime. At one time
       the family instruments included a large
       clavichord by Friederici and a piano by
       Walter, among other keyboard instruments.
       Kinsky traces the history and describes many
       of the instruments, noting changes of owner-
       ship and ultimate residence. Of interest
       is the disposition of the instruments after
       Mozart's death.

238.   Melville, Derek.   "Beethoven's Pianos."
       in *The Beethoven Companion*, edited by
       Denis Arnold and Nigel Fortune. London:
       Faber & Faber, 1971. 542 p. ISBN 0-57-
       10-9003-6   OCLC 154784   ML 410 B4 A75

       An investigation into the pianos of
       Beethoven and a study of dynamics, ranges,
       and textures in his piano music in associa-
       tion with specific instruments. *Una corda*

and *sordini* indications are examined and
explained. There are conflicting opinions
about the *sordini* or *senza sordini* mark-
ings in Beethoven, which Melville addresses.
Melville includes segments of Beethoven letters in which the composer refers to the piano in general or to his own instruments.
Portions of letters to: Johann Andreas
Streicher, Nanette Streicher, Matthäus Andreas Stein, Thomas Broadwood, *et al* are
quoted by Melville. Includes illustrations
of several Beethoven pianos: Erard (1803),
Broadwood (1817), Graf (1825), as well as
an example of a Walter grand (1785). Illustrations.

239. Newman, William S. "Beethoven's Pianos Versus His Piano Ideals." *Journal of the
American Musicological Society* 23 (Fall
1970): 484-504.

A well-presented study of Beethoven's pianos and their mechanical/tonal influence
on his writing. Newman's research contra-
dicts the belief that the Broadwood was the
composer's favorite instrument. Beethoven
remained faithful to the Viennese instruments, and the pianos issuing from Stein
and Streicher remained his unquestionable
favorites, affirms Newman. Beethoven's many
pianos are examined as to their range, pedals, actions, and tone, in relation to the
composer's likings and creative force. A
valuable monograph.

240. Sievers, Heinrich. "Clara und Robert Schumanns Klavier." *Neue Zeitschrift für
Musik* 128 (September 1967): 385.

A bit of background on the Schumanns' Graf
pianoforte, which was made by Conrad Graf as
a wedding gift to Clara Wieck on the occasion
of her marriage to Robert Schumann (12 September 1840). Sievers traces the instrument

after Schumann's death. The instrument is
now in the Vienna *Kunsthistorisches Museum.*
Note: A photograph of the Schumanns' Graf
piano, with descriptive data, is in Franz
Josef Hirt's *Stringed Keyboard Instruments
1440-1880* (1955).

241. Steglich, Rudolf. "Studien an Mozarts Ham-
      merflügel." in *Neues Mozart-Jahrbuch*
      edited by Erich Valentin. Regensburg:
      Gustav Bosse, 1941. 224 p. OCLC 2201215
      ML 410 M9 N25

      An excellent narrative account of Mozart's
      pianoforte of the early 1780s built by Anton
      Walter. Steglich traces the history of this
      instrument from Mozart's home to its place-
      ment in the Mozarteum in Salzburg. Mozart
      owned the Walter during the last decade of
      his life. Steglich also notes that Mozart
      was very attached to the family clavichord
      and often wrote music at this instrument and
      practiced on it. The author traces the Wal-
      ter pianoforte after Mozart's death: his wid-
      ow kept the piano for twenty more years, then
      son Carl cared for it and subsequently gave
      the instrument to the *Mozarteum* on the oc-
      casion of the 100th anniversary of his father's
      birth. An important part of Steglich's mono-
      graph is his account of the restoration of
      the instrument. A detailed description fol-
      lows. A useful study. Illustrations, musi-
      cal example.

242. Wegerer, Kurt. "Beethovens Hammerflügel
      und ihre Pedale." *Österreichische Musik-
      zeitschrift* 20 (April 1965): 201-11.

      Wegerer examines the three extant Beethoven
      pianos: Erard of 1803, now on loan to the
      Kunsthistorisches Museum in Vienna by the
      Oberösterreichischen Landesmuseum of
      Linz; Broadwood of 1817, housed in the *Un-
      garisches Historisches Nationalmuseum*; and

the Graf of c.1823, now in the *Beethovenhaus*
in Bonn. The article specifically deals with
the pedals of these three instruments. The
Erard has four pedals (lute, damper, *Pianozug* [strip of felt between hammers and
strings], and una-corda); the Broadwood has
two pedals (una-corda, and a split damper
[right half lifts treble dampers and the left
half lifts bass dampers]); the Graf has three
pedals (una-corda, *Pianozug*, and damper).
The author offers descriptive data regarding
the instruments as well as explanations of
the functions of the diverse pedals. Useful
study. Illustrations.

THE INSTRUMENT

V. Piano Automata

243. Bowers, Q. David. *Put Another Nickel In: A
      History of Coin-Operated Pianos and Orches-
      trions.* Vestal, N.Y.: Vestal Press, 1966.
      viii, 248 p. OCLC 907430   ML 1050 B63

      An illustrated volume for *aficionados* and
      collectors of player pianos and other pneumat-
      ic-operated instruments manufactured in the
      nineteenth and twentieth centuries. Bowers
      begins his survey with Johann Maelzel's "Pan-
      harmonicon," built c.1812, and coin-operated
      player pianos constructed around 1898 (Roth
      & Englehardt). There are numerous illustra-
      tions and advertisements of instruments manu-
      factured by companies such as: J.P. Seeburg
      Piano Co., Monarch Musical Instrument Co.,
      and the Rudolph Wurlitzer Co. The machines
      grew larger and larger, always becoming more
      complex in construction. The elaborate Wur-
      litzer "PianOrchestras" (imported from Phi-
      lipps of Germany) of 1903-1914 were ornate
      and expensive (from $1200 to $7500). Illus-
      trations, no index.

244. ------., ed. and comp. *A Guidebook of Auto-
      matic Musical Instruments.* 2 vols. in one.
      Vestal, N.Y.: Vestal Press, 1967. 697 p.
      OCLC 1309442   ML 1050 B62

      Contains some of the same photographs and
      information as in Bowers' later and more

extensive work, *Encyclopedia of Automatic
Musical Instruments* (1972). The major difference between the two volumes is that in
A Guidebook of Automatic Musical Instruments
Bowers includes pointers on grading the condition of coin pianos and orchestrions and
related instruments, and includes the rela-
tive worth of many instruments (in 1967 dol-
lars) in two categories: good condition and
fine condition. Useful data for collectors
and dealers. For more historical information,
consult Bowers' *Encyclopedia*. Illustrations, name index, revised price list (December 1967).

245. ------. *Encyclopedia of Automatic Musical
Instruments.* Vestal, N.Y.: Vestal Press,
1972. 1008 p. ISBN 0-9115-7208-2 OCLC 39-
4157 ML 1050 B6

An informative and useful iconographic
survey of automatic musical instruments, including cylinder and disk music boxes, player and reproducing pianos, coin operated pianos and orchestrions, organettes and player
organs, and fairground organs (e.g., barrel
organs, calliopes). Units are prefaced by
explanatory introductions, written by several
authors, noting historical aspects of the instrument. There follows a pictorial account
of the instruments during the period of their
heyday. The unit on "Player Pianos" includes
introductory remarks by Harvey Roehl. Illustrations include advertisements and photographs
of various manufacturers' instruments. There
is some historical text interspersed with the
illustrations. David L. Saul writes the introduction for the unit on the "Reproducing
Piano" and contributes other portions of the
text in the unit. The unit on "Coin-Operated
Pianos and Orchestrions" includes an interview
with automatic piano manufacturer Edwin A.
Link (of more recent repute for his aviation
Link Trainer system) and text material by Art
Reblitz, David L. Junchen, Brian Williams,

and Larry Givens. The *Encyclopedia of Automatic Musical Instruments* is a must for those
interested in the genre, as well as for re-
searchers in automata. Illustrations, dictionary of automatic musical instrument terms,
bibliography, name index (manufacturers, pianists, composers, etc.).

246.   Givens, Larry. *Re-Enacting the Artist: A
       Story of the Ampico Reproducing Piano.*
       Vestal, N.Y.: Vestal Press, 1970. vii,
       136 p. ISBN 0-9115-7204-4   OCLC 103245
       ML 1050 G59

       A historical perspective of the reproduc-
       ing piano, focusing specifically on the Am-
       pico from the time of its invention by
       Charles Fuller Stoddard (c.1910). A de-
       tailed account of the reproducing process,
       with illustrations and examples of Ampico's
       advertisement campaign. An informative vol-
       ume on possibly the finest instrument of its
       genre. Illustrations, index.

247.   Herbert, L. "Patent Self-Acting and Keyed
       Upright Grand Piano Fortes by Rolfe &
       Sons. *Register of Arts [London] and
       Journal of Patent Inventories* New Ser-
       ies, 5 (1831): 23-24.

       Rolfe's self-acting pianoforte (1829) was
       an improved barrel-type mechanical piano.
       He was able to enhance the transition of the
       forte and piano of the instrument by regulat-
       ing the length of the barrel pins, as well
       as altering the volume of the tone by devis-
       ing an independent set of mechanical dampers.
       This early mechanical piano could also be
       played as a normal instrument. The patent
       description by Mr. Herbert explains in detail
       the mechanical improvements made by William
       and Thomas Hall Rolfe.

248. Ord-Hume, Arthur W.J.G. *Player Piano: The
      History of the Mechanical Piano and How
      to Repair It.* London: Allen and Unwin,
      1970. 296 p. ISBN 0-0478-9003-7   OCLC
      138159 ML 1050 O73; South Brunswick and
      New York: A.S. Barnes, 1970. ISBN 498-
      07484-6   OCLC 111906   ML 1050 O73

      This is the author's first book on the
      subject. See also his most recent volume
      on the subject, titled *Pianola* (1984).
      Player Piano is a history of the player
      piano and allied mechanical keyboard instru-
      ments. The barrel piano, various pneumatic
      action instruments, player piano, reproducing
      piano, and player organs are described and
      illustrated with schematics and photographs;
      in addition, functional aspects of each are
      noted. Chapters on rebuilding and repairing
      will benefit the handy or adventurous person.
      Illustrations, schematics, list of principal
      makers and patentees (see revised list in the
      author's 1984 volume, *Pianola: The History
      of the Self-Playing Piano*), player piano
      serial numbers, bibliography, index.

249. ------. *Restoring Pianolas and Other Self-
      Playing Pianos.* London: Allen and Unwin,
      1983. xv, 143 p. ISBN 0-0478-9008-8
      OCLC 10352536   ML 1051 O65 R5 1983

      A companion volume to Ord-Hume's *Pianola:
      The History of the Self-Playing Piano.* Di-
      rections for rebuilding/repairing barrel pi-
      anos, player pianos, and the reproducing pi-
      ano are offered by the author. There are
      many helpful schematic diagrams and photo-
      graphs. Illustrations, appendixes (music
      roll makers and brand names, trade names,
      and player piano serial numbers), bibliog-
      raphy (65 entries), index.

250. ------. *Pianola: The History of the Self-
      Playing Piano.* London: Allen and Unwin,

1984. xx, 395 p. ISBN 0-0478-9009-6
OCLC 10559124   ML 1050 O728 1984

Because the author's first book on the subject, *Player Piano* (1970), was soon out of
print, a proposed second edition was planned;
however, because of the renewed interest in
the player piano (which no doubt can be partly
attributed to Mr. Ord-Hume) Ord-Hume created
this up-dated volume on the subject, with new
text and many new illustrations. It is a valuable work on the history of the player piano.
Ord-Hume surveys the rise and fall of the
mechanical piano, from early beginnings in
the form of a barrel organ (c.1502) to the
1978 computerized Superscope Marantz Piano-
corder. He traces the instrument through its
development: mechanical to pneumatic, reproducing piano, nickelodeon, and the post-war
revival. There are also chapters on how the
mechanisms work, music for the player piano,
and how to play the player piano. Ord-Hume
has effectively encompassed the history of
the player piano and its related instruments
in this comprehensive survey of the genre.
Illustrations, list of makers, patentees and
agents, appendixes, bibliography (extensive),
index. (Lacks the player piano serial numbers
that are present in the author's first book
on the subject [*Player Piano: The History of
the Mechanical Piano and How to Repair It*].)

251. Reblitz, Arthur A. and Q. David Bowers.
      Treasures of Mechanical Music. Vestal,
      N.Y.: Vestal Press, 1981. 630 p. ISBN 0-
      9115-7220-1   OCLC 7204960   ML 1050 R4

An iconography of mechanical music makers,
covering various instruments from disc music
boxes, player and reproducing pianos to the
monstrous orchestrions and band organs. Dis-
tinct period instruments are illustrated and
described. There are also chapters on music
roll making, coin pianos, and various automat-
ically-played organs. A fascinating tour of

dated ephemera. Illustrations, musical examples, dictionary of terms, bibliography
(36 entries), name index.

252. Roehl, Harvey N. *Player Piano Treasury: The
Scrapbook History of the Mechanical Piano
in America as Told in Story, Pictures, Trade
Journal Articles and Advertising.* Vestal,
N.Y.: Vestal Press, 1961. 251 p. OCLC 907-
443 ML 1050 R6; 2d ed., Vestal Press, 1973.
iv, 316 p. ISBN 0-911-57200-7 OCLC-7033-
39 ML 1050 R6 1973

Roehl's book on the player piano represents
a dedication to keep alive the spirit of a by-
gone era. He takes the reader from the time
of the advent of the player piano (Forneaux's
"Pianista" in 1863), via explanatory text,
photos, and advertisements, through the de-
cades of its greatest activity, until the period when the radio and phonograph superseded
its popularity (c.1925). Those not familiar
with the history of the player piano will be
amazed at the variety of instruments manufactured in its heyday. Roehl documents the
thriving industry of the player piano in this
iconography of the history of the instrument.
Illustrations, no index.

THE INSTRUMENT

VI. Piano Manufacturing in Specific Countries

253. Arnold, Janice M. "American Pianos: Revolution and Triumph." *Clavier* 26 (July-
August 1987): 16-22.

History of piano manufacturing in the USA.
The success story of three major American
piano firms is traced: Chickering, Steinway,
and Baldwin. Innovations and specific patents are noted. Illustrated.

254. Barli, Olivier. *La facture française du
piano, de 1849 à nos jours.* Préface de
Pierre Chaunu. Paris: La Flûte de Pan,
1983. 411 p. OCLC 11088937 ML 674 B35
1983

Historical survey of piano production in
France from mid-nineteenth century to c.1980.
Background as to French piano production and
legislation of inventions and patents from
1791. Contains a chronological list of
French invention patents concerning the piano, from 1849 to 1979, with data as to:
name of inventor, region/occupation, type of
invention, and patent number. Many of the
inventions of the late nineteenth century
reflect the innovative minds of the time,
such as concern for novelty e.g., "*piano-
billard*" [billiard table piano], transposing pianos, and various automatic instruments. Unit on quantitative analysis of in-

vention patents includes various pertinent
data: total by year, graphs, types of inventions, etc.. Production figures for the in-
clusive years contain output of foreign piano
firms as well as French firms. Other topics
covered in the volume: cause of the decline
of French piano manufacturing, piano technicians' association, current piano firms in
France, etc.. The volume is an important
compendium of information on the French piano
industry. A useful survey. Illustrations,
charts, appendixes, bibliography, name index,
index of graphs.

255. Clay, Reginald S. "The British Pianoforte
Industry." *Journal of the Royal Society
of Arts* 66 (18 January 1918): 154-63.

Clay traces the beginning of the British
piano industry, with attention to various
founding builders, mainly: John Zumpe, Americus Backers, John Geib, Kirkman, Tschudi-
Broadwood, Collard & Collard-Clementi, etc..
The report indicates a healthy industry with
a very optimistic future. At the time of
publication Clay states that there were over
130 piano manufacturing firms in England. He
gives various statistics concerning the industry, indicating its growth and stability.
Developmental innovations in the English piano are noted. As a means of improving production output, Clay suggests standardization
of manufacture and an apprenticeship program.
A useful study of the British piano industry.

256. Closson, Ernest. *La facture des instruments
de musique en Belgique.* [The manufacture
of musical instruments in Belgium]
Bruxelles: [Presses des établissements
degrace à Hov] 1935. 109 p. OCLC 204-
7117 ML 496 C5 F3

A qualitative summation of the importance
of Belgium in the manufacturing of musical

instruments, especially written for those
visiting *L'exposition international de 1935*.
After a short sketch of the history of the
piano, Closson surveys the contributions made
by Belgian piano craftsmen to the advancement
of the instrument. Pascal Taskin, Hermann
Lichtenthal, La Coste, Joseph Florence, H.
Sternberg, Van Casteel, and Jacques Gunther
are some of the important names in the history of the Belgian piano industry. Pascal
Taskin is given substantial coverage. In
Belgium, the piano was played for the first
time in Liège in 1769 by Jean-Noël Hamal.
Belgians participated in *L'exposition universelle de Paris* in 1867 and 1878, with
10 representative pianos for each *Exposition.* Illustrations, bibliography, name
index.

257.   Cole, Warwick Henry. "The Early Piano in
       Britain Reconsidered." *Early Music* 14
       (November 1986): 563-66.

       Cole offers a rebuttal to statements made
       in Virginia Pleasants' article in *Early Mu-
       sic* 13 (February 1985): 39-44 titled "The
       Early Piano in Britain (c1760-1800)." Cole
       questions data used by Pleasants, mainly:
       validity of the term "12 Apostles" (early
       builders who settled in England); J.C. Bach's
       choice of piano for his 2 June 1768 London
       concert; and the reaction of English harpsi-
       chord makers to the pianoforte. A differing
       opinion. Illustration.

258.   Dannemiller, Joanne Dilley. "The Development
       of the Importance of the Piano in America."
       Master's thesis, Kent State University, 1959.
       vi, 84 p.   OCLC 2007680   ML 650 D24x

       Study begins with the advent of the piano in
       the USA c.1771, includes its development in
       this country through American composers and
       performing artists, notes improvements to the

instrument, views Americanism in music via
quotations from American composers, e.g., Ives,
Gershwin and Cowell, and concludes with an account of the piano industry in this country to
c.1925. Good coverage of early American piano
music and pioneer piano performance in the
USA. Appendixes, bibliography (31 entries),
no index.

259.   Dolge, Alfred. *Men Who Made Piano History.*
       [original title, *Pianos and Their Makers
       Vol.II: Development of the Piano Industry
       in America Since the Centennial Exhibition
       at Philadelphia, 1876*] Covina, Cal.:
       Covina Publishing Co., 1913. Reprint. Ves-
       tal, NY: Vestal Press, 1980. xxii, 242 p.
       ISBN 0-9115-7218-X   OCLC 5777108   ML 404
       D64 1980

       Dolge pays honor to American piano manufac-
       turers of the late nineteenth to the early
       twentieth century. An alphabetical listing
       of founders of American piano companies, de-
       scribing their backgrounds, their firms,
       highlights of their manufacturing process,
       and other historical information. Dolge does
       not go into great depth but rather gives an
       overview of the state of the American piano
       industry at this time. It is interesting to
       note how many founders of American piano com-
       panies have Germanic origins. Illustrations,
       appendix, name index.

260.   Flood, Grattan W.H.   "Dublin Harpsichord and
       Pianoforte Makers of the Eighteenth Cen-
       tury." *Journal of the Royal Society of
       Antiquaries of Ireland* 39 (1910): 137-45.

       Description of the harpsichord-piano tran-
       sition in Ireland. Flood points out the im-
       portance of Dublin piano builder William
       Southwell, who constructed pianos in the
       years 1787-93. Flood credits Southwell with
       inventing the upright piano (1793). (Opin-

ions on this subject vary: Italians claim
that Domenico Del Mela constructed the first
upright in 1737 [Piero Rattalino in *Storia
del pianoforte*], A.J. Hipkins in his *Description and History of the Pianoforte*
states that John Isaac Hawkins invented the
upright in 1800). Besides describing various instruments and builders, Flood offers
colorful views of the history of keyboard
instruments in relation to Dublin, noting
visits to the city by Handel, Haydn, and
Southwell. Illustrations.

261. Jehle, Martin Friedrich. *Württembergische
    Klavierbauer des 18. und 19. Jahrhunderts.*
    [Württemberg piano builders of the 18th
    and 19th centuries] Frankfurt am Main:
    Das Musikinstrument, 1982. 120 p. ISBN 3-
    9201-1295-4   OCLC 9571886   ML 726 B2 J4
    1982

    A survey of eighteenth and nineteenth cen-
    tury klavier builders of the Württemberg
    region (southern Germany). This area was
    blessed with many fine cabinetmakers who
    turned their skills to building keyboard in-
    struments. The many names include Andreas
    Silbermann, Johann Andreas Stein, the
    Schiedmayer family, Elias family, Adolph
    Mörike, Joseph Anton Pfeiffer, and Franz
    Anton Kaim and descendants. The author
    traces family legacies, describes building
    influences, offers historical background,
    and notes construction innovations. Name
    index.

262. Loest, Roland. "American Pianos: Evolution
    and Decline." *Clavier* 26 (July-August
    1987): 34-39.

    A summary of the piano industry in the
    USA, followed by a perceptive rationale for
    why the American piano industry has faced
    a backslide since the turn of the century.

Many reasons for the decline are given e.g.,
the Depression, takeovers, proliferation of
inferior builders, and Asian competition.
Loest predicts the demise of the acoustic
piano. A useful overview of the problems
and state of the American piano industry.
The author is curator of instruments at the
Museum of the American Piano in New York
City. Illustrations.

263. Parton, James. "The Piano in the United
     States." *Atlantic Monthly* 20 (July
     1867): 82-98.

     250,000 pianos were made in the USA in
     1866; there were 60 makers in New York, 30
     in Boston, 20 in Philadelphia, 15 in Balti-
     more, 10 in Albany, etc.. These are some of
     the statistics revealed by Parton. He also
     quotes the average price of pianos, ranging
     from $450 to $1500. Parton reflects on the
     popularity of the instrument, discusses pi-
     ano rental, piano production in England,
     France, and Germany, and piano music publi-
     cation. There is a short history of the pi-
     ano, drawn from Rimbault and Burney, and at-
     tention given to the history of piano con-
     struction in the USA, noting particularly the
     Chickering and Steinway piano firms. An in-
     formative article.

264. Pleasants, Virginia. "The Early Piano in
     Britain (c1760-1800)." *Early Music*
     13 (February 1985): 39-44.

     Traces early piano builders in Britain
     e.g., Zumpe, Burkat Shudi, Jacob Kirkman,
     Gabriel Buntebart, John Broadwood, and the
     use of the pianoforte in Britain during the
     years 1760-1800. Illustrations. See also
     Warwick Henry Cole's rebuttal of this arti-
     cle in "The Early Piano in Britain Reconsid-
     ered" *Early Music* 14 (November 1986):
     563-66.

265.   Pollens, Stewart.   "The Portuguese Piano."
       Early Music 13 (February 1985): 18-27.

       Looks at the Italian influence on the pi-
       ano in Portugal and notes several influ-
       ential Italian musicians who resided in that
       country for a period of time e.g., Domenico
       Scarlatti and Carlo Broschi Farinelli.   Early
       pianos in Portugal were modelled after those
       of Cristofori.   The author describes in detail
       the construction of two eighteenth century
       Portuguese pianos: an Henrique Van Casteel
       (1763) and an unsigned piano, and compares
       them with Cristofori's three extant pianos.
       Illustrations.   See also Jack Greenfield's
       article "Cristofori Piano Use - Dropped in
       Italy, Continued in Iberian Region" *Piano
       Technicians Journal* 29 (January 1986):
       24-26.

266.   Rindlisbacher, Otto.   *Das Klavier in der
       Schweiz; Klavichord, Spinett, Cembalo, Pi-
       anoforte; Geschichte des Schweizerischen
       Klavierbaus 1700-1900.* [the clavier in
       Switzerland; clavichord, spinet, harpsi-
       chord, pianoforte; History of Swiss piano
       construction] Bern und München: Francke,
       1972.   268 p.   OCLC 771559   ML 690 R55

       A significant contribution to the under-
       standing of the instrument-building skills
       of the Swiss.   Over 70 Swiss craftsmen are
       noted, along with biographical sketches,
       photographs of their instruments (with de-
       scriptive data), and other pertinent infor-
       mation.   Earliest instruments shown are
       clavichords/spinets from early eighteenth
       century.   Additional instruments displayed
       are tafelklaviers [square pianos], hammer-
       klaviers [grands], and pianinos [uprights]
       of the nineteenth century.   Majority of in-
       struments shown are tafelklaviers; it is
       evident that the Swiss excelled in instru-
       ments of this type, for the variety and
       elegance of the illustrated tafelklaviers

exemplify the artistic skills of the Swiss
piano builders. End material includes: technical (construction) explanations i.e., action, dampers, keyboard, strings, soundboard,
etc., with illustrations; chart showing Swiss
builders' dates and locations; Swiss builders
of whom no instruments have been found; list
of published keyboard advertisements; Swiss
builders who presented instruments in Swiss
industry expositions of the nineteenth century; photo index; chronology of illustrated
instruments.

267. Spillane, Daniel. *History of the American
      Pianoforte; Its Technical Development, and
      the Trade.* New York: D. Spillane, 1890
      xii, 369 p.   OCLC 1157198   ML 661 S85;
      Reprint. (with new introduction by Rita
      Benton) New York: Da Capo Press, 1969.
      xv, xii, 369 p.   OCLC 21361   ML 661 S85
      1969

      History of piano manufacturing in the USA.
      Spillane draws his information from direc-
      tories, patent data, journals, works by Rim-
      bault, Brinsmead, Fétis, etc. and his own
      expertise in piano construction and in the
      piano trade in the USA. Contains chapters
      pertaining to the origin of the piano, but
      primary focus is on the history of the in-
      strument in several American cities: Boston,
      New York, Philadelphia, Charleston, Balti-
      more, and Albany; New York and Boston receive
      the most historical coverage. There is at-
      tention to the Great Exhibition of 1851 in
      London and the Centennial Exhibition (1876)
      in Philadelphia, which showcased American
      manufacturers of the piano. Spillane adds
      chapters dealing with outside suppliers of
      piano parts, e.g., actions, plates, varnish,
      etc. and the influence of musical and trade
      journalism on piano manufacturing. The work
      is the first history of the American piano.
      The new introduction in the reprint offers
      background on Spillane and his work. Illus-

trations, appendixes, name index.

268. Uchitel', Ĭakov Moiseevich. *Sovetskoe Forte-
     piano: Kratkiĭ Istoricheskiĭ Ocherk.* [The
     Soviet Fortepiano: A Short Historical Essay]
     Moskva-Leningrad: Muzyka, 1966. 80 p. OCLC
     4233866   ML 734 U3

     An examination of piano manufacturing in
     the Soviet Union from pre-Revolutionary time
     to the year 1966. A very informative study.
     The piano industry in the USSR had a rela-
     tively late beginning (period of 1924-34);
     during those years, scientific and technolo-
     gical research on piano manufacturing was
     accelerated in order to eliminate the depend-
     ency of the industry on foreign imports.
     Prior to the First World War, piano produc-
     tion in Russia did not have a native base and
     could not compare to other nations in output
     and quality. Pre-Revolutionary Russian pian-
     os were built largely by German immigrants
     who marketed their instruments under their
     family names, e.g., "Bekker," "Shreder,"
     "Mĭul'bakh," "Renish," "Diderikhs," "Ratke,"
     "Offenbakher," "Tsimmerman" (Russian trans-
     literations). At the time of publication
     (1966), the USSR maintained 60 piano-build-
     ing companies and was purportedly second to
     the USA in output. Bibliography (25 entries),
     no index.

269. Villanis, Luigi Alberto. *L'arte del Piano-
     forte in Italia (da Clementi a Sgambati).*
     Torino; Fratelli Bocca, 1907. 253 p.
     OCLC 6698876 ML 730 V54; [Reprint]
     Bologna: Forni, [1969]. 253 p. OCLC 24-
     79113   ML 730 V71 1969

     History of the pianoforte in Italy from
     Clementi to Sgambati. Covers Cristofori's
     invention (with short biography), the harp-
     sichord-piano transition, early musical
     styles and forms, the "Italian School," etc..

Identifies Italian "methods," Italian composers of the period, surveys Clementi and
his followers, and compares Liszt and Sgambati. Presents a general overview of the
early period of the piano in Italy, with
attention to its music and composers. Musical examples, list of Italian composers
(from 1750 to after 1850), no index.

270. Wainwright, David. *The Piano Makers.* London: Hutchinson, 1975. 192 p. ISBN 0-
0912-2950-2 OCLC 2120008 ML 678 W34

Largely a history of the British piano industry. Wainwright effectively traces the
evolution of the piano and its construction
in England. English piano manufacturers
are historically observed and Clementi's
varied career in that country is covered.
Units on virtuosi, foreign competition, electronic instruments, and post-war renewal of
the industry add to the interest of Wainwright's historical overview. Excellent photographs of historical instruments. Illustrations, bibliography (31 entries), discography (performances on historical instruments),
name index.

THE INSTRUMENT

VII. Electronic Piano

271. Aikin, Jim. "Electronic (Synth, Sampler,
      Sequencer, Drum Machine, MIDI Technical
      Terms) Music Glossary." *Keyboard Maga-
      zine* Pt.1: 13 (February 1987): 77-80;
      Pt.2: 13 (March 1987): 93-95.

      Helps fill a communication gap between
      instrument designer and consumer. Defini-
      tions of electronic music/instrument terms,
      from "additive synthesis" to "zero cross-
      ing." A handy glossary for referral when
      investigating an electronic keyboard instru-
      ment or other electronic equipment for pur-
      chase. An aid in understanding the "hi-
      tech" wording in advertisements of the many
      new keyboard instruments.

272. Friedman, Dean. *Synthesizer Basics.*
      NY; London; Sydney: Amsco Publications,
      1986. xiii, 135 p.   ISBN 0-8256-
      2409-6 [USA];   0-7119-1022-7 [UK pbk.]
      OCLC 15664315   ML 1092 F7

      Friedman offers a relatively easy-to-read
      technical description of the mechanics of
      the synthesizer. Avoiding complex terminol-
      ogy in explaining diverse features of dif-
      ferent makes of synthesizers, Friedman uses
      a "composite" synthesizer as a basis for his
      examination. This "typical" synthesizer is
      used in diagrams, to give the reader an exam-

ple of the kinds of features likely to be
found in most synthesizers. The volume includes some historical background, basic data on sound waves, elements of sound, harmonics, voltage-controlled synthesizers,
components, performance controls, MIDI, etc..
Keyboard instruments such as, Yamaha DX7 Digital Synthesizer, Casio CZ101, Synclavier,
Fairlight, E-MU Systems' Emulator II, etc.
are used in the explanatory text. A good
general introduction to the world of synthesizers. Illustrations, glossary, index.

273. Milano, Dominic. "Really, A Synthesizer is
Just Like a Piano (Well, Almost)." *Keyboard* 13 (January 1987): 110.

Step by step, Milano describes the synthesizer in relation to the acoustic piano. He
employs an analogical approach in comparing
the sound-producing aspects of both instruments. An aid to understanding the musical
and scientific technology of our age.

274. Silverman, Robert J. "The Clavinova CLP-
50." *Piano Quarterly* No.138 (Summer 1987):
61-62.

A description and evaluation of the Yamaha
Clavinova CLP-50. The full-size (88 keys)
electronic instrument has pressure sensitive
keys (for touch and tone), stays in tune,
has two pedals (damper and soft), can trans-
pose, and has a MIDI interface, allowing the
instrument to be hooked up to a systhesizer,
computer/printer, etc.. Silverman was im-
pressed by the sound and versatility of the
Clavinova CLP-50.

275. Vail, Mark. "NAMM." [National Association of
Music Merchants] *Keyboard Magazine* 14
(April 1988): 34-46.

Survey of electronic products exhibited at
the annual National Association of Music Mer-
chants Winter Trade Show (1988) held in Ana-
heim, California. Listed here are just a
few of the electronic items mentioned in
Vail's review of the trade show: Samplers/
Sample Players (Dynachord ADS, Yamaha TX16W,
Roland S-330, Casio FZ-10M, etc.), synthesizers (Roland D-20, D-110, Oberheim Matrix-
1000, Casio VZ-1, Yamaha DX11, etc.), MIDI
Gear (Gambatte, Korg tuner DT-1, etc.), Drum
Machines (Yamaha RX7, etc.), Macintosh Software, Atari Software, IBM PC/Compatible
Software, and other electronic units. Several keyboard instruments were introduced
e.g., Yamaha Disklavier, Casio digital piano
CDP-3300 and CDP-3000, Roland digital HP-
6000C, Korg Concert Series Pianos C-7000,
C-7100, C-7500, Technics SX-K700. Competition is very keen in the industry. Vail's
survey offers short descriptions and current
prices. Illustrations.

THE INSTRUMENT

VIII.   Purchase and Care of the Piano

276.   Bezdechi, Adrian. *Pianos and Player Pianos:*
       An Informative Guide for Owners and Prospec-
       tive Buyers. Portland, Ore.: Player Piano
       House, 1979. 63 p. OCLC 5679876 ML 657 B5

       Contains descriptions of various parts of
       the piano and player piano; diagnoses of func-
       tional problems; suggestions on maintenance,
       tuning, buying new instruments, etc.. Appen-
       dixes include information on several "Vorsetz-
       ers" [push-up player pianos], care of piano
       rolls, and refinishing. A basic, descriptive
       booklet. Illustrations, schematics, no index.

277.   Fine, Larry. *The Piano Book: A Guide to*
       Buying a New or Used Piano. Jamaica
       Plain, Mass.: Brookside Press, 1987.
       xiii, 186 p. ISBN 0-9617-5121-5; 0-9617-
       5120-7 (pbk.) OCLC 15521584   ML 650 F46
       1987

       The best "how-to" book currently available
       on the subject of purchasing pianos. The au-
       thor, who writes a regular column in *Keyboard*
       Magazine, has compiled a handy, easy-to-
       understand volume containing: the art of buy-
       ing a used or new piano, reviews of various
       brand-name pianos, sales gimmicks to be wary
       of, descriptions of integral parts of the
       instrument, special attention to Steinways,
       care and servicing, and much more. The book

makes an excellent introduction to the piano
for shoppers as well as dealers and pianists
of all levels. It is in non-technical language, written by an experienced and candid
technician who gives the reader straightforward information. Of special interest is
the appraisal of approximately 200 pianos
manufactured by leading firms. The foreword
by Keith Jarrett offers the pianist's view of
the technician. The only item missing is a
bibliography, which would be helpful for in-
depth study. Illustrations, glossary/index,
index to trade names. Günter Rolle's article "Marktübersicht: Klaviere & Flügel."
Keyboards 12 (1987): 79-83 also offers piano evaluations.

278. McCombie, Ian K. *The Piano Handbook.* New
      York: Scribner, 1980. 176 p. ISBN 0-6841-
      6444-2   OCLC 5239547   ML 652 M3

      A very good general guide to the purchase
of a piano, its maintenance, repair, tuning,
re-stringing, voicing, etc.. The author also includes a chapter on reconditioning player pianos. The action schematics are well
drawn, showing the action both in rest position and in strike position. McCombie offers
the novice technician a step-by-step practical tuning procedure and also describes other
maintenance techniques. Glossary, appendixes
(piano manufacturers, piano data [wire sizes,
pin sizes], metric conversion tables), illustrations, bibliography (12 entries), index.

279. Miller, Harold. *The Rise and Decline of the
      Piano: Care and Use of the Piano.* Toronto:
      Harold Miller, n.d.(c.1975). 106 p. OCLC
      876079   ML 652 M54

      Miller's title, "Rise and Decline of the
Piano" does not imply that the piano's popularity or production output have declined,
but rather it is a statement on the deterio-

ration of quality in the instruments of today in comparison to the quality of older
instruments. Miller is candid in his criticism of the newer instruments, especially
the small uprights. The work gives a short
history of the piano, tips on care of the piano, descriptions of actions, pointers on
purchasing an instrument, and other practical
information. Illustrations, bibliography
(14 entries), index.

280. "Pianos: Fine-Tune Your Choices." *Changing
Times* 40 (January 1986): 70-74.

Current (1986) average price of various
pianos; information on shopping for a new
or used instrument; description of major
parts of the piano; suggestions on proper
care and upkeep of pianos in the home. Illustration.

281. Schmeckel, Carl D. *The Piano Owner's Guide:
How to Buy and Care for a Piano.* Chicago:
Adams Press, 1971. 114 p. OCLC 220431 ML
652 S35; Also, Sheboygan, Wis.: Apex Piano
Pub., 1972. OCLC 826814 ML 652 S35 1972;
Also, rev. ed., New York: Scribner, 1974.
xiii, 127 p. ISBN 0-6841-3869-7 & 0-6841-
3872-7 (pbk.) OCLC 1116972 ML 652 S35 1974

Schmeckel offers practical information for
both the future piano purchaser and the present piano owner. Content is in four parts:
"General Information" (historical sketch, piano sizes, major piano parts, etc.); "Purchasing a New Piano" (warranty, electronic pianos,
organs, quality, brand, etc.); "Purchasing a
Used Piano" (from private owner, dealer, re-
conditioned piano, old upright, player-piano,
etc.); "Piano Care and Service" (tuning, technicians, action regulating, moving the piano,
location in the home, etc.). Handy basic information for the layman. Illustrations, index.

282. Wood, Lawrence Robert. *Pianos, Anyone?* New
      York: Vantage Press, 1977. 48 p. ISBN 0-
      5330-2931-7   OCLC 3481967   ML 652 W78

      A simple, general, descriptive guide to pur-
      chasing a piano and to the care of the instru-
      ment. No index.

Plate 1. PIANO FORTE (1720) by Bartolomeo Cristofori. Metropolitan Museum of Art. The Crosby Brown Collection of Musical Instruments, 1889, No. 1219, New York City.
(Courtesy Da Capo Press [New York], agent for Franz Josef Hirt's *Stringed Keyboard Instruments*, 1981. ISBN 3-8595-1135-1)

Plate 2. PYRAMIDENFLÜGEL [Pyramid Piano] (1745) by Christian
Ernst Friederici. Musée insturmental du Conservatoire Royal de
Musique, No. 1631; Bruxelles.
(Courtesy Da Capo Press [New York], agent for Franz Josef Hirt's
Stringed Keyboard Instruments, 1981. ISBN 3-8595-1135-1)

Plate 3. SQUARE PIANO (1840) by Jean-Henri Pape. Germanisches
nationalmuseum, Klavierhistorische Sammlung Neupert,
MINe211; Nürnberg.
(Courtesy Da Capo Press [New York], agent for Franz Josef Hirt's
Stringed Keyboard Instruments, 1981. ISBN 3-8595-1135-1)

Plate 4. (top illustration) PIANINO (c. 1835) by A. Flohr.
Historisches Museum, No. 24773; Bern. (bottom illustration)
PIANINO (early 19th century) by Andreas Marshall. Norsk
Folke Museum, No. 88; Oslo.

(Courtesy Da Capo Press [New York], agent for Franz Josef Hirt's *Stringed Keyboard Instruments*, 1981. ISBN 3-8595-1135-1)

Plate 5. PLAYER PIANO (1920s) by Smith & Barnes. (Courtesy of Vestal Press [Vestal, N.Y.], *Treasures of Mechanical Music* [1981] ISBN 0-9115-7220-1 by Arthur A. Reblitz and Q. David Bowers)

Plate 6. CONCERT GRAND (contemporary) by Steinway & Sons (New York, N.Y.).

Connecting Parts for Wippens and Hammers, in Grands

1. Main action rail; main rail; action rail; other names at V 10
1a. Auxiliary wippen spring loop (Kawai)
2. Wippen flange screw; whip etc. (Wurlitzer); support etc. (Steinway)
2a. Auxiliary wippen spring (Kawai)
3. Wippen flange; whip etc., support etc.
4. Wippen flange pin; whip etc., support etc.
5. Wippen flange bushing; whip etc., support etc.
6. Hammer outer felt
7. Hammer under felt
8. Hammer molding (Schimmel); hammer wood
9. Hammer rest rail; hammer rail; hammer shank rail or stop
10. Hammer rest rail felt; hammer rail felt; hammer shank rail felt
11. Hammer rest rail hook; hammer rail hook; hammer shank rail hook
12. Hammer shank; hammer stem
13. Knuckle buck skin; knuckle skin; roller skin (Yamaha)
14. Knuckle wood; roller wood (Yamaha); knuckle strip (Wurlitzer, Schimmel); knuckle insert (Baldwin); rosewood, let-off knuckle wood
15. Knuckle felt; roller core (Yamaha)
16. Hammer shank pin bushing
17. Hammer shank center pin
18. Drop screw
19. Hammer shank flange screw
20. Spring lock washer
21. Plain lock washer
22. Hammer flange
23. Hammer flange rail (Kimball); top deck rail (Scheer)
24. Let off, or regulating, prop screw
25. Let off**prop; let off rail support hook; let off rail bracket

26. Let off screw
27. Let off rail
28. Let off butten; let off dowel (Kawai, Kimball)
29. Let off punching or punch
30. Action bracket
31. Capstan screw
32. Capstan screw keyblock
33. Key
34. Back check (with back check accessories: wire, base, on key; block at top; buckskin; inner felt)
35a. Back rail cloth; key cloth
35b. Key end felt; under lever pick-up felt (Steinway)
36. Key stop rail (Steinway); key stop strip (Baldwin, Aeolian); and for each of these: felt, prop, and prop nut
37. Key stop rail prop base; key stop prop block (Baldwin)
38. Key sharp
39. Key covering. Detail: VI 18, 19
40. Keyframe
41. Key button bushing
42. Glider bolt; see VI 9a
43. Balance rail pin, balance pin
44. Key button; chase (Schimmel)
45. Balance rail punching (felt)
46. Balance rail
47. Front key bushing
48. Front rail pin
49. Front rail punching (felt)
50. Front rail paper punchings
51. Front rail; keyframe front rail

footnote:

Where **let off occurs in numbers 25-29 the word **regulating** is in equally wide usage though **let off** is more closely definitive.

(Diagrams are from Merle H. Mason's *Piano Parts and Their Functions* (1977), courtesy of Piano Technicians Guild [Kansas City, Mo.]. Since Mason's work deals with nomenclature of piano parts, the illustrated parts are given multiple names as used by various companies.)

XV

Grand Piano

Wippen and Hammer Connecting Parts
Top Half of Page

Key and Connecting Parts
Bottom Half of Page

(After Wurlitzer with additions from Steinway and Kawai)

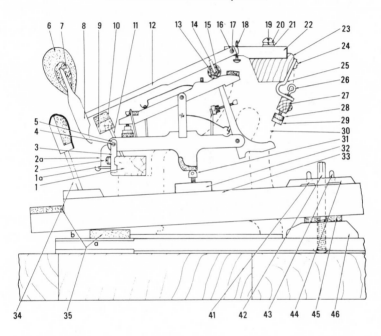

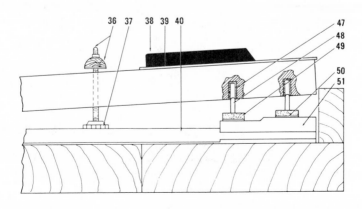

Action-related Parts in Vertical Pianos

1. Damper wire; damper lever wire; damper stem wire
2. Damper block with set screw
3. **a** - Damper head back
   b - Damper felt (see XXIV for damper wedges)
4. Overdamper felt with wire
5. Pressure bar screw
6. V-bar; vee bar
7. Pressure bar (and see III 25)
8. Damper lift rods and levers (Steinway, Kawai); sustain damper rods and levers (Wurlitzer); full and bass damper lifter rods and tongues (Schimmel)
9. Jack; fly; fly jack (Sohmer)
10. Main action rail; main rail; action rail; hammer beam rail (Kimball, Schwander); hammer rail beam (Schimmel); wippen flange rail
11. Jack stop rail; jack check rail; with rail positioning screw at **a**
12. Jack stop rail (etc.) felt
13. Back stop; catcher; butt check; butt heel. With back stop (etc.) skin or leather
14. Back stop shank; catcher shank (Yamaha); hammer butt heel stem (Baldwin)
15. Hammer butt spring; butt spring; with butt spring cord; hammer butt cord; loop cord; spring loop (Kawai)
16. Hammer shank
17. Half-blow rest rail
18. Hammer rest rail; hammer rail
19. Half-blow rail back cushion
20. Hammer rail cushion
21. Hammer rail cloth
22. Hammer molding; hammer wood or head
23. Wedge end of molding
24. Hammer felt (under)
25. Hammer head staple; hammer felt staple or fastener; twisted wire (Steinway)
26. Hammer felt (outer)
27. Hammer rail cloth
28. Same as 18
28a. Hammer-blow-distance shim (felt)
29. Felt for damper stop rail (etc. as in 30)
30. Spring rail; hammer spring rail (Baldwin); hammer butt spring rail (Steinway); damper check rail when minus springs (Schwander); damper stop rail (Yamaha, Kawai)
31. Hammer spring; spring rail spring (Sohmer)
32. Hammer rail swing (Wurlitzer); hammer rail hinge (Yamaha); hammer rail hook (Baldwin)
33. Damper lever spring; damper spring; damper flange spring (Sohmer)
33a. Damper lever spring punching
34. Hammer butt; butt (For butt felt, skin, cloth, undercloth, covering, see butt detail, diagram XXIV)
35. Damper lever flange; damper flange; damper stem flange; with damper lever flange screw at **a**
36. Hammer flange; hammer butt flange; butt flange; brass flange, in certain pianos; also, flange screw
37. Damper lever; damper stem (Schwander); with damper lever (etc.) felt, cushion, covering at **a**
38. Regulating rail; let-off rail; jack rail; set-off rail (Schwander); with regulating screw at **a**
39. Regulating button and punching
40. Spoon; damper spoon; damper lever spoon (Baldwin)
41. Wippen flange; lever flange; screw at **a**
42. Jack (or fly) flange; jack (or fly) spring at **a**
43. Wippen; rocker; whip (Wurlitzer); lever (Schwander). Also, at **a**, wippen cushion; rocker cushion; wippen cloth (Yamaha); capstan screw felt (Baldwin)
44. Bridle strap; bridle tape; with tip or tab attached to bridle wire. Also action tape
45. Bridle wire; stirrup wire
46. Back check block with **a**; back check felt, and **b**; back check wire
47. Action bracket bolt nut
48. Action bracket bolt
49. Action bracket
50. Action bracket pivot
51. Action bracket leg

(Diagrams are from Merle H. Mason's *Piano Parts and Their Functions* (1977), courtesy of Piano Technicians Guild [Kansas City, Mo.]. Since Mason's work deals with nomenclature of piano parts, the illustrated parts are given multiple names as used by various companies.)

V

Action-Related Parts in Vertical Pianos

After Schwander, Wurlitzer

After Steinway

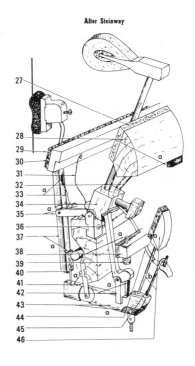

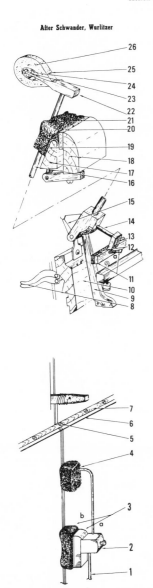

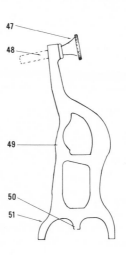

XVI
Dampers and Associated Parts, in Grands

1. Key
2. Keybed
3. Keyframe
4. Back rail cloth (or strip)
5. Key and felt (on key); under lever cushion (beneath damper under lever)
6. Lead weight for damper lever
7. Damper lever wire flange center pin (Baldwin); under lever top flange center pin (Steinway); damper lift flange center pin
8a. Damper lever; under lever
8b. Sostenuto tab center pin & bushing
9. Damper lift felt and capstan cushion; swing (lift) rail capstan cushion; under lever capstan cushion; damper lever capstan cushion
10. Damper lift rail; swing rail (Wurlitzer); lifting rail (Yamaha); under lever frame (Steinway); damper lever frame (Schimmel); damper tray; damper table; damper lever board (Baldwin)
11. Damper lift rail cushion; under lever frame cushion (Steinway); lifting rail cushion, under (Yamaha)
12. Damper pitman cushion; swing rail dowel cushion; damper lift rail bumper
13. Damper lift pitman; swing rail pedal dowel
14. Damper lift rail flange and hook; swing rail flange and hook (Wurlitzer)
15. Damper lift rail cushion; swing rail cushion
16. Damper lever flange, center pin, and screw; under lever flange, etc. (Steinway)
17. Damper lever spring
18. Dag (Steinway); and see other names at XIII 4a
19. Damper rail; damper lever board; damper lever flange rail; and see XIII 6
20. Keybed trim; keybed rail (Schimmel)

* * *

21. Damper lift rail spring; under lever frame spring (Steinway)
22. Damper upstop rail and felt; liberty strip (Aeolian)
23. Damper wire; damper lever wire
24. Middle belly bar; cross block head; and see XIII 9
25. Cross bar; soundboard support or molding (Schimmel)
26. Soundboard (sometimes called **belly**)
27. Damper guide rail; guide rail block at **a**
28. Damper guide rail bushing
29. Damper felt; damper head felt
30. Damper head trim felt (Baldwin, Schimmel); damper lining felt (Yamaha)
31. Damper head; damper wood (Yamaha); damper head molding
32. Damper lift flange; damper lever wire flange (Baldwin); damper lever flange (Schimmel); damper wire block; damper block; damper drum
33. Damper wire screw & socket (Baldwin); damper block screw (Wurlitzer, Yamaha)

* * *

34. Damper lever
35. Key
36. Damper lever key-end felt
37. Damper lever spoon
38. Damper lift flange; universal (or double swing) damper flange as shown here (Schimmel, Euterpe)

* * *

39. Sostenuto tab cushion
40. Sostenuto tab and tab cloth
41. Sostenuto rod, and lip at **a**
42. Sostenuto rod bracket spring and screw
43. Sostenuto tab spring
44. Sostenuto bracket screws
45. Sostenuto bracket (attached to action bracket)
46. Action bracket

(Diagrams are from Merle H. Mason's *Piano Parts and Their Functions* (1977), courtesy of Piano Technicians Guild [Kansas City, Mo.]. Since Mason's work deals with nomenclature of piano parts, the illustrated parts are given multiple names as used by various companies.)

XVI

The Damper and Its Associated Parts

A composite drawing using parts of diagrams from
Baldwin; Steinway; Pratt, Read and Co; Schimmel; etc.

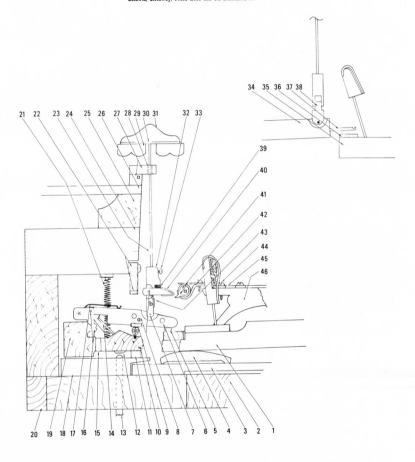

Plate with Strings and Dampers, in Grands

1. Horn (underneath) and see XI 14
2. Diagonal bar
3. Cross bar; cross brace; plate bar; compression bar. Also, bass over arm (O.S. Kelly Co.)
4. Bass bar; bass under arm (O.S. Kelly Co.)
5. Center bar
6. Bass registry hole; locating hole
7. Flange
8. Hitch pins
9. Web
10. Lower treble bar
11. Lightening holes (for heat relief in the casting); plate opening
12. Treble bar
13. Rear duplex scales
14. Treble registry hole; locating hole
15. Treble end bar
16. Capo d'astro bar (Steinway); pressure bar; V-bar; capotaster (Schimmel)
17. Plate screw holes; lag screw holes
18. Front duplex scales
19. Wrest plank web; tuning block web
20. Plate center section with bass section at left, lower treble and upper treble sections at right
21. Tuning pin holes
22. a. Agraffe; stud
    b. Agraffe shelf (Pratt, Read & Co.)
23. Front flange; head bar (Booth and Brookes)

• • •

24. Plate set screw; lag screw or lag bolt; oval head screw (Baldwin)
25. Stringrest and accompanying part as in footnote at ##
26. Bass button (Yamaha)
27. Dampers and damper covers (Schimmel)
28. Soundboard molding; quarter round molding (Baldwin); reflector bar (Wurlitzer)

29. Bass string (#1)
30. Nose bolt (Baldwin, et al.); bearing rod; bearing bolt; plate set-bolt (Yamaha)
31. Soundboard
32. Stringing felt; string tape (Baldwin) or bass hitch pin felt (Baldwin); stringing braid (Kawai)
33. Plate screw (Steinway); plate lag bolt (Kawai); lag screw and washer (Baldwin); lag bolt (Schimmel)
34. Hitch pin
35. Bridge
36. Bridge pin
37. Bass bridge apron
38. Bass bridge base
39. Rear duplex scales
40. Down bearing adjustment (Schimmel, model 190 only)
41. Treble bridge
42. Treble string #88
43. Serial number (Schimmel)
44. Tuning pins; wrest pins
45. Front(al) bar; and for other names see XIII 21 and explanations in GLAP under **Front rail**
46. Lock
47. Crevice felt (Yamaha, et al.); bellyman felt (Steinway, et al.)
48. Keyslip
49. Shield or seal (Schimmel); plate mark (Kawai)
50. Keyboard
51. Agraffe; stud
52. Keyblock; cheekblock

footnote:

##Associated with stringrest is the string rest felt (Kawai); string bearing felt (Schimmel); or stringing pillow felt (Yamaha)

(Diagrams are from Merle H. Mason's *Piano Parts and Their Functions* (1977), courtesy of Piano Technicians Guild [Kansas City, Mo.]. Since Mason's work deals with nomenclature of piano parts, the illustrated parts are given multiple names as used by various companies.)

XII

Plate in Grand Piano

Plate (Frame, Harp) in Grand Piano
with drawing
after Steinway

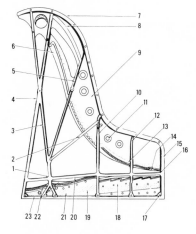

Plate with Strings and Dampers
composite drawing
After Baldwin, Schimmel, Yamaha, etc.

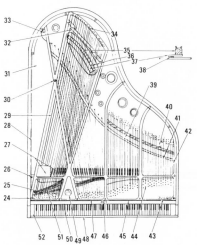

IX. Historical Studies

General Surveys

283. Aguettant, Louis. *La musique de piano, des origines à Ravel.* [Piano music, from its beginning to Ravel] Paris: Albin Michel, 1954. 447 p.   OCLC 2096884   ML 700 A3; Reprint. Paris: Editions D'Aujourd'hui, 1981. ISBN 2-7307-0269-5   OCLC 9790110   ML 700 A3 1981.

Aguettant bases his work on lectures he presented at the *Conservatoire de Lyons* beginning in 1924. He imparts his colorful and exuberant impressions of major composers and their piano works. He notes influences and compares works and styles of various composers. Of special interest are units on *"Les clavecinistes," "César Franck," "L'école de César Franck," "Gabriel Fauré, et Les élèves de Fauré."* The author also includes very short sketches of selected composers of Russia, Scandinavia, and Spain. Portrait, name index.

284. Alekseev, Aleksandr Dmitrievich. *Klavirnoe Iskusstvo: ocherki i materíaly po istoriĭ pĭanizma.* [Keyboard Art: essay and material on the history of pianism] Moskva: Gos. Muzykal'noe Izd-vo, 1952. 252 p.   OCLC 10545025   ML 700 A394 1952

Designed as a text for piano students. The work was written largely at the *Konser-*

vatoriĭa Imeni P.I. Chaikovskogo [Tchaikovsky
Conservatory] in Moscow. The study primarily
centers on early (sixteenth to eighteenth century) pedagogical guides, e.g., C.P.E. Bach's
essay *Versuch über die wahre Art das Clavier zu
spielen*. The work surveys practical literature that would be useful to Soviet piano
students, offering historical background, interpretative suggestions, and pedagogical support. J.S. Bach, Clementi, Mozart, C.P.E.
Bach, and Haydn are represented, as well as
several pre-Bach composers. A large part of
the volume centers on composers of the clavi-
chord/harpsichord era. Illustrations, musical
examples, bibliography; lacks an index.

285.   ------. *Istoriĭa fortepĭannogo iskusstva.
        chast'II.* [History of pianoforte art.
        Vol.2] Muzyka, 1967. 285 p. OCLC 95353-
        99   ML 700 A39 1967

        Designed as a text book for schools of music
and specifically directed towards pianists.
An international general historical overview
of the development of piano literature from the
period of 1789-1870, covering styles, interpretation, virtuosi, and pedagogical practices of
composers of piano music. Selected works of
various composers (from Clementi to Tchaikovsky) are analyzed as to style, interpretation
and form. Illustrations, musical examples,
errata, bibliography (over 100 entries); lacks
an index.

286.   Apel, Willi. *Masters of the Keyboard: A
        Brief Survey of Pianoforte Music.* Cam-
        bridge, Mass.: Harvard University Press,
        1947. 323 p. OCLC 406526   ML 700 A6

        Apel's book is based on material from his
series of lectures given at the Lowell Institute of Boston in 1944. The author's principal emphasis is on compositional evolution
and forms of characteristic works of the pe-

riod. He begins his survey with an example
from the Middle Ages (1300), from the *Roberts-*
bridge Codex, and continues through to Im-
pressionism and "New Music," with examples
from Stravinsky and Hindemith. Most musical
examples are complete pieces. The Roccoco
period (1725-1775), which is usually slighted
in historical works, is given proper coverage
by Apel in a chapter of its own. A useful,
easy-to-read, musicological survey of keyboard music. Illustrations, musical examples, name index.

287. Bücken, Ernst. *Die Musik des 19. Jahr-*
     hunderts bis zur moderne. [Music of the
     19th century to modern times] Potsdam:
     Akademische Verlagsgesellschaft Athenaion,
     1932. OCLC 1289221 ML 160 B9 B92; Al-
     so, New York: Musurgia OCLC 6958607 ML
     160 B9 B92

     A handsomely illustrated volume which sur-
     veys the Romantic epoch from Beethoven to
     Tchaikovsky and Smetana. The work does not
     deal exclusively with piano works; however,
     it observes a great number of compositions
     for piano. Biographical material is not
     present here, rather the book chronological-
     ly surveys Romanticism, often reflecting on
     influences, style, and nationalistic develop-
     ment. Illustrations, musical examples, por-
     traits, letters, bibliography (at the con-
     clusion of each unit), name index.

288. Dale, Kathleen. *Nineteenth-Century Piano Mu-*
     sic: A Handbook for Pianists. Preface by
     Dame Myra Hess. London: Oxford University
     Press, 1954. 320 p. OCLC 405050 ML 706
     D3; Reprint (corrected). New York: Da Capo
     Press, 1972. ISBN 0-3067-1414-0 OCLC 297-
     530 ML 706 D3 1972

     Critical survey of the standard nineteenth
     century piano literature, with attention to

historical background, style, form, and content. Compositions are arranged into categories determined by structure (sonatas, rondos etc.); type (études, dances, duets,
etc.); or style (Impressionistic, abstract,
Romantic, etc.). Some sections explore material in more depth than others. The units
on sonatas and variations are quite informative. Includes a chapter on piano duets.
Musical examples, bibliography (38 entries),
appendixes (3), name-composition index, general index.

289. Fillmore, John Comfort. *Pianoforte Music: Its
      History, With Biographical Sketches and Crit-
      ical Estimates of its Greatest Masters.*
      Chicago: MacCoun, 1883; Philadelphia: Pres-
      ser, 1888. viii, 245 p.   OCLC 906488
      ML 700 F48

      A critical survey of the history of piano
      music, from J.S. Bach and D. Scarlatti to the
      "successors of romanticists" e.g., Gottschalk,
      Tchaikovsky and Grieg. Not only is Fillmore's
      survey of historic value, it reflects a well-
      constructed format. The history opens with
      an introduction to polyphony, which is direct-
      ly followed by a chapter on J.S. Bach, Handel,
      and D. Scarlatti. An introduction to the so-
      nata form is then followed by a chapter on
      C.P.E. Bach, Haydn, and Mozart. "Emotion and
      Content in Music" is followed by a unit on
      Beethoven, and so on. Forms of music precede
      the exponents of those stylistic techniques.
      Fillmore includes material on piano technique
      and contemporary pianists. Name index.

290. Ganz, Rudolph. *Rudolph Ganz Evaluates Mod-
      ern Piano Music: A Guide for Amateur and
      Student.* Evanston, Ill.: Instrumentalist
      Co., 1968. vi, 54 p. OCLC 40746   MT 140
      G2

      An outgrowth of Ganz's revision work done

on Ernest Hutcheson's book *The Literature of the Piano*. The material presented in *Rudolph Ganz Evaluates Modern Piano Music* was meant for inclusion in the revised edition of Hutcheson's volume (published in 1964) but because of its length was not appended to that work. Ganz mainly investigates solo piano works, with less attention to duets, two piano-four hands, and concerti. Most works are dated after 1950 but many earlier compositions are also included. Annotations are rather brief, usually illustrating the character of the work. Illustrations, no index.

291. Gemmellaro, Carla. *Storia e letteratura del pianoforte*. Catania: Libreria S. Urzi, c.1967. 182 p. OCLC 492210   786.4 G284s

A general survey of keyboard literature, designed as a text book. Information as to composers and their literature is arranged according to schools and styles. It is advised to check composers' dates as there are errors. Material is very concise and devoid of biographical data. Short descriptions of the history of the piano and a survey of keyboard literature are oriented towards quick assimilation by students. Each chapter concludes with a summation. Of particular interest is the coverage of Italian composers of the late nineteenth century and of the present time, and the inclusion of piano course requirements for the Conservatory of Barcelona and the Conservatory of Vienna. Illustrations, errata, mnemonic charts, name index.

292. Gillespie, John. *Five Centuries of Keyboard Music: An Historical Survey of Music for Harpsichord and Piano*. Belmont, Cal.: Wadsworth, 1965. xiii, 463 p. OCLC 4150-56   ML 700 G5; Reprint. New York: Dover, 1972. ISBN 0-486-22855-X   OCLC 549403

A broad historical overview of keyboard
music, commencing with examples from 1320
and progressing to the twentieth century,
with musical examples by representative composers. Gillespie presents minor composers
as well as major composers in his survey.
Chapters are based on regions and different
musical periods, with primary importance
given to individual composers. Each composition's form and background are described.
Illustrations, musical examples, glossary,
bibliography (85 entries), name index.

293. Glennon, James. *Making Friends With Piano
Music; The History and analytical notes
on over a hundred piano compositions with
short notes on the composers.* Adelaide:
Rigby Limited, 1967. 68 p. OCLC 656958
MT 140 G58

Critical annotations of selected solo piano compositions by Beethoven, Brahms, Chopin, Debussy, Franck, Granados, Grieg, Liszt,
Mendelssohn, Mozart, Rachmaninoff, Schubert,
and Schumann. The author touches on historical background and adds colorful descriptive commentary. Glossary, no index.

294. Hamilton, Clarence Grant. *Piano Music, Its
Composers and Characteristics.* Boston:
Oliver Ditson; New York: Charles H. Ditson; London: Winthrop Rogers, 1925.
v, 235 p. OCLC 1308531   ML 650 H16 1925

A rather thorough, though selective and concise, survey of piano literature up to 1925.
The author discusses: the evolution of the
piano; early keyboard works in Italy, England,
France, and Germany; creators of the sonata;
and various periods of music. Hamilton
stresses form throughout his work and points
out influences of past composers. Includes
biographical sketches, lists of representative literature, and books for further read-

ing. Illustrations, musical examples, bibliography (lacks complete data), name-subject index.

295. Kentner, Louis. *Piano.* London: Macdonald and Jane's, 1976. xi, 204 p. ISBN 0-3560-4713-0 OCLC 2307122 MT 220 K3 1976; New York: Schirmer Books, 1976. ix, 210 p. OCLC 2310721 MT 220 K3

The major portion of Kentner's work describes selected piano compositions by Beethoven, Chopin and Liszt, along with interpretative suggestions. Other units are on chamber music, history of the piano, structure of the instrument, art of piano performance, temperament, technique, fingering, pedaling, etc.. An artist's contribution to the study of the piano. Musical examples, illustrations, discography (general literature), bibliography (29 entries), index.

296. Kirby, F.E. *A Short History of Keyboard Music.* New York: Free Press, 1966. xviii, 534 p. OCLC 223935 ML 700 K47

Historical survey of music composed for all keyboard instruments, primarily covering solo literature and excluding music for keyboard and orchestra and chamber music. Kirby briefly describes the history and construction of the organ, harpsichord, clavichord, and piano, then continues with a general descriptive overview of keyboard music, beginning with an example from the *Robertsbridge Codex* (fourteenth century) and concluding with music of the twentieth century, with examples of Copland and Barber. Like Weitzmann's work of 1897, Kirby's book covers a wide span of music history, touching on many important aspects but not often probing in great depth into any one of them. Kirby's work serves as a general survey of keyboard literature. Includes an extensive bibliogra-

phy containing critical editions, reproductions of music, treatises and secondary literature; composition-index, name-index.

297. Matthews, Denis. ed., *Keyboard Music.* New
      York: Praeger; Hamondsworth: Penguin;
      Newton Abbot: David & Charles, 1972.
      383 p. ISBN (Penguin) 0-1402-1250-7
      OCLC (Penguin) 663158; OCLC (Praeger)
      364044; ISBN (David & Charles) 0-7153-
      5612-7 OCLC (David & Charles) 515155
      ML 650 M25 K47

      A collection of monographs which survey
      keyboard literature, by various authors:
      "Early Keyboard Music" by Howard Ferguson
      examines pre-piano literature, from the
      Robertsbridge Fragment (c.1320) to works
      of Georg Philipp Telemann. Ferguson divides
      his work by countries; a useful bibliography
      is included. "Bach and Handel" by Charles
      Rosen examines style in the literature of
      Bach and Handel. "Haydn, Mozart and Their
      Contemporaries" by Eva Badura-Skoda regards
      the advent of the piano, styles, descrip-
      tions of various works, and includes a list
      of the Haydn sonatas with differing enumera-
      tion in current editions. "Beethoven, Schu-
      bert, and Brahms" by Denis Matthews examines
      the music of these three giants in an intro-
      spective manner. "The Romantic Tradition"
      by John Ogdon traces Romanticism, starting
      with J.B. Cramer and Clementi before settling
      in on Chopin, Schumann, Mendelssohn, Liszt,
      et al. "The Growth of National Schools"
      by James Gibb views other composers (some
      minor) via the classification of national
      schools. "The Twentieth Century" by Susan
      Bradshaw examines the contemporaries (Bartók
      to Cornelius Cardew). Historical viewpoints
      of renowned performers and musicologists.
      Musical examples, name index.

298. Nimitz, Daniel. *Keyboard Masters; Study
      Guide.* [Prepared by the State University
      of New York in Cooperation with the State
      University of New York at Albany and the
      Office of Continuing Education] Albany,
      N.Y., 1968. xv, 168 p.   OCLC 7961
      ML 390 N62

      Designed as a keyboard literature survey
      course (excluding works for organ). Nimitz's
      compilation of information largely focuses
      on historical aspects of periods, style, and
      composers. A small number of compositions
      by representative composers of a period are
      chosen and analytically described. The his-
      torical information is especially valuable
      for students and for teachers who instruct
      similar courses. Bibliography (11 entries),
      musical examples, no index.

299. Plantinga, Leon. *Romantic Music: A History
      of Musical Style in Nineteenth-Century
      Europe.* New York; London: Norton, 1984.
      xiii, 523 p. ISBN 0-3939-5196-0   OCLC 13-
      667439   ML 196 P6 1984

      Plantinga's excellent work, which primarily
      deals with the history of Romanticism, also
      explores the piano and piano music in sub-
      stance. Plantinga fully analyzes a few pi-
      ano compositions e.g., Beethoven's *Sonata*
      Op.31, No.2, *Diabelli Variations*, and par-
      tially analyzes and comments on many works
      of major composers; he also regards many com-
      positions of minor composers. Units on
      Beethoven, Schubert, Chopin, Liszt, Schumann,
      Mendelssohn, and Brahms outline many of their
      works for piano. Plantinga's musical obser-
      vations are pertinent. Contains an excellent
      bibliography and is well-indexed. Illustra-
      tions, musical examples, bibliography (exten-
      sive, by chapters), name-composition-subject
      index.

300. Schünemann, Georg. *Geschichte der Klavier-musik.* Zweite Auflage, bearbeitet und erweitert von Herbert Gerick [History of keyboard music. 2d ed., revised and enlarged by Herbert Gerick]. Münchberg: Bernhard Hahnefeld, 1953. 141 p. OCLC 50-95652   ML 700 S3 G4 1953

Designed as a study aid for the piano student and the practical musician. Encompasses the entire range of keyboard literature, though concentrating largely on German composers. Material is presented in a very concise form. Begins with Antonio Squarcialupi and closes with Paul Hindemith. Schünemann's work is a broad overview of keyboard literature and includes only the bare minimum of information on any one composer. Data on J.S. Bach, Haydn, Mozart, Beethoven, Chopin, and Liszt outweighs the coverage given other composers. There is attention shown to many minor German composers, mentioned in relation to their more important contemporary composers. The volume is of interest primarily to German piano students (as it was intended) and to those delving into the numerous minor composers who were surpassed by the musical giants of the period. Illustrations, name index.

301. Unger-Hamilton, Clive. *Keyboard Instruments.* Minneapolis, Minn.: Control Data Pub., 1981. 124 p. ISBN 0-8989-3505-9   OCLC 7596420 ML 549 U54; Toronto: Wiley, 1981. ISBN 0-4717-9876-2   OCLC 14341883   ML 549 U54; Oxford: Phaidon, 1981. ISBN 0-7148-2177-2 OCLC 8236076   ML 549 U57 K44 1981

Although Unger-Hamilton's volume deals with the history of keyboard instruments, its primary thrust is keyboard literature. The volume is lavishly illustrated. Music of the virginalists to music of the twentieth century is surveyed, with pictorial supplement. Illustrations, glossary, index.

302. Weiser, Bernhard D. *Keyboard Music.* Dubuque, Iowa: Brown, 1971. xi, 151 p. ISBN 0-697-03407-0 OCLC 114883 ML 500 W40

Pianist Weiser surveys keyboard music from Byrd and Bull to Carter and Barber. Designed as a text, this small volume views the important regions and periods of music in a concise manner. Chapters describe characteristic works of the period and examine major composers. A select bibliography accompanies each chapter. Illustrations, bibliography (96 entries), index.

303. Weitzmann, Karl Friedrich. *A History of Pianoforte-Playing and Pianoforte-Literature.* Reprint of first American edition (1897), New York: Da Capo Press, 1969. xix, 379 p. OCLC 57767 ML 700 W432 1969; 1st ed., *Geschichte des Klavierspiels und der Klavierliteratur.* Leipzig: Breitkopf und Härtel, c.1897. x, 461 p. OCLC 10734573 ML 700 W433; Also reprint of the Leipzig ed. (c.1897), Hildesheim: G. Olds, 1966. OCLC 768703

Violinist and music theoretician Weitzmann offers a historical perspective of the field of keyboard literature, with attention to its composers (including many minor composers), beginning with examples from the fourteenth century through to Saint-Saëns and Tchaikovsky. The author often interjects pertinent theoretical data into the historical text. A supplementary chapter on the history of the pianoforte refers back to the monochord and concludes with innovations made by Jankó, Logier (Hand-guide), and Debain (sostenuto pedal). An appendix contains selected keyboard music from the sixteenth, seventeenth, and eighteenth centuries. Weitzmann covers a wide span of music history, touching on many important aspects but not delving into any subject in great depth. The theoretical material offered by Weitzmann gives the work a unique twist. Illustrations, music, appendixes, errata, index.

304. Westerby, Herbert. *The History of Pianoforte
      Music.* London: Kegan Paul, Trench, Trub-
      ner and Co.; New York: Dutton and Co., 1924.
      xxii, 407 p.   OCLC 413364   ML 700 W47

      The author's aim is to extend and up-date
      the scope of literature that Weitzmann pre-
      sented in his work of 1897 (*Geschichte des
      Klavierspiels und der Klavierliteratur*).
      Early music i.e., for clavichord and harpsi-
      chord, is concisely reviewed. The main por-
      tion of Westerby's overview of piano litera-
      ture encompasses classicists to the moderns.
      In this case, modern composers are MacDowell,
      Cyril Scott, H.H.A. Beach, etc.. Many minor
      composers who were prominent at the time of
      publication are given inordinate coverage.
      Literature described is selective, at times
      not reflecting the total output of the com-
      poser. Topics as: national "schools," the
      sonata, composers of études, and piano
      methods are addressed. Westerby's attempt
      to improve previous works on the subject (by
      including numerous minor composers) has only
      made the volume appear archaic today. Musi-
      cal examples, bibliography (grouped under
      various subjects), publishers, composer in-
      dex, subject index.

305. Wier, Albert Ernest. *The Piano: Its History,
      Makers, Players and Music.* London: Long-
      mans, Green and Co., 1940. 467 p. OCLC 9-
      88028   ML 652 W63 P5

      Major portion of Wier's book is concerned
      with the development of piano music. Mate-
      rial on the history of the instrument is ra-
      ther limited. Harpsichord music (François
      Couperin) is Wier's starting point for illus-
      trating the development of piano music. Be-
      sides a relatively short history of the piano
      and a survey of piano literature, Wier explores

piano teaching, technique, interpretation,
piano ensemble music, etc.. Wier attempts
to survey too broad a scope of the instrument,
resulting in a lack of comprehensive depth in
any one subject. List of two-piano works,
biographical dictionary of pianists, discography, bibliography (over 100 entries, including 13 works by Matthay), name index.

306. Wolff, Konrad. *Masters of the Keyboard: Individual Style Elements in the Piano Music
of Bach, Haydn, Mozart, Beethoven, and
Schubert.* Bloomington, Ind.: Indiana
University Press, 1983. xi, 206 p. ISBN 0-
2533-3690-2   OCLC 9441424   ML 705 W64 1983

A scholarly work, emphasizing the individ-
uality of five major keyboard composers: Bach,
Haydn, Mozart, Beethoven, and Schubert. Wolff
refrains from comparing each composer's music
to that of the others; instead, he observes particular traits, styles, idioms, forms, key re-
lationships, thematic treatments, and other musical elements that best represent each individual composer. Units on Bach and Beethoven
are more extended, delving into notational elements and performance practices. A very informative work, documented and written in a
personable style. Musical examples, bibliography (general sources; material on each composer), name-composition index.

307. Yates, Peter. *An Amateur at the Keyboard.*
New York: Pantheon (Random House), 1964.
xiv, 300 p.   OCLC 946427   MT 220 Y4

Yates offers a history of keyboard music
interpolated within various chapters dealing with keyboard instruments and allied
subjects. He uses Antonio de Cabezón as a
springboard for the units on the history of
keyboard music, and continues his overview
to composers of the twentieth century. Yates
addresses his volume primarily to amateurs,

and in doing so makes his comments in general terms. His observations are interesting and effective in whetting the appetite for further examination. At times, his comments express an opinionated view. The unit on twentieth century piano music begins with Debussy and Satie and concludes with John Cage. An appendix includes material on temperament and tuning. Bibliography (various subjects e.g., anthologies, composers, books, publishers), appendixes, name-subject index.

THE MUSIC

IX. Historical Studies

Specialized Topics

308. Alekseev, Aleksandr Dmitrievich. *Frantŝuz-skaiâ fortep'iânnaiâ muzyka kontŝa XIX-nachala XX veka.* [French piano music: end of 19th and beginning of 20th century] Moskva: Akademîâ Nauk SSSR, 1961. 220 p. ML 270 A4

Essays on French piano music, covering Saint-Saëns, Franck, Debussy, and Ravel. Alekseev delves into the development of French piano music, stressing the importance of Saint-Saëns in this role. He includes biographical material, gives descriptive analyses of selected compositions, notes French-Russian influences, and generally comments on genres and style. Illustrated, musical examples, errata, bibliography, no index.

309. ------. *Russkaiâ fortepiânnaiâ muzyka. Konets XIX-nachalo XX Veka.* [Russian piano music from the end of the 19th century to the beginning of the 20th century] Moskva: "Nauka," 1969. 391 p. OCLC 3531726 ML 734 A37

Deals with the development of Russian piano music from the end of the nineteenth century to c.1930. The work is a continuation of a monograph by the author covering early Russian piano music (up to the nineteenth century)

167

titled *Russkaia fortepiannaia muzyka. Ot
istokov do vershin tvorchestva* [Russian piano music from its beginning to its zenith],
published by the Akademiia Nauk SSSR [USSR
Academy of Science], Moskva, 1963. The present volume examines characteristics, style,
influences, etc. in the piano works of Tchaikovsky, Liadov, Glazunov, Liapunov, Taneev,
Arenskii, Rachmaninoff, Scriabin, Medtner,
Miaskovskii, Prokofiev, Stravinsky, and Stan-
chinskii. A fine stylistic survey of Russia's
great composers of piano music. Illustrations, musical examples, appendix (children's
piano music), bibliography (55 entries primarily based on composers), errata; unfortunately,
lacks an index.

310.   ------. *Sovetskaia fortepiannaia Muzyka
        (1917-1945).* Moskva: Muzyka, 1974.
        246 p.   OCLC 7254587   ML 734 A43

Descriptive comparative survey of piano
music written by Soviet composers from c.1920
to 1945. The following list mentions a few
of the composers covered: N. Miaskovskii,
A.N. Aleksandrov, S.E. Feinberg, A.V. Zat-
aevich, V.S. Kosenko, A.M. Balantsivadze,
V. Sofronitzky, S.S. Prokofiev, D.D. Shosta-
kovitch, A.I. Khachaturian, D.B. Kabalevskii,
B.N. Liatoshinskii. There are many more composers in the survey. Illustrations, musical
examples, list of composers and their piano
works, no index.

311.   Apoian, Shushanik Arutiunovna. *Fortepiannaia
        muzyka Sovetskoi Armenii.* [Fortepiano music
        of Soviet Armenia] Erevan: "Aiastan," 1968.
        246 p.   ML 734 A66

Survey of the historical development of
Armenian piano music from its beginning in
1822, with examples by founders Komitas and
A. Spendiarov (c.1894), progressing to c.1964,
noting Levon Astvatsatrian and Tigrana Man-

surian and other contemporary composers.
Aram Il'ich Khachaturîan is given ample coverage. Piano music is very important to Ar-
menians. Apoîan asserts that Armenian musical characteristics are based on folk music
and dance, which often change meters, contain jumps, impulsive dynamics, and variations in repetitions. The work emphasizes
the richness and variety of Armenian piano
music and notes its influence on Soviet music in the larger sense. An effective survey of Armenian piano music and its composers.
Illustrations, musical examples, list of composers (71) and selected works, no index.

312.   Augustini, Folke. *Die Klavieretüde im
       19. Jahrhundert: Studien zu ihrer Entwick-
       lung und Bedeutung.* [The piano étude in
       the 19th century: Studies on its develop-
       ment and significance] Duisburg, Germany:
       Giles & Francke, 1986. xii, 548 p. ISBN 3-
       9253-4800-X   OCLC 14365983   ML 706 A93
       1986

       Traces the historical development of the
       étude, including the English School (Cle-
       menti and his pupils), Viennese School (Hum-
       mel and his contemporaries), Beethoven's in-
       fluence, the French School (Kalkbrenner and
       the virtuosi), Chopin, Brahms, etc.. Analyt-
       ical survey of selected examples of études
       by Clementi, Cramer, Brahms, Schumann, etc..
       Notes influences (Paganini) and observes var-
       ious aspects of the étude genre e.g., étude
       in teaching, in performance, and its position
       in the history of music literature. Musical
       examples, bibliography, appendix, list of
       works by composer, composition-title index,
       various lists.

313.   Cortot, Alfred. *La musique française de
       piano.* 3 vols. Paris: Presses univer-
       sitaires de France, 1930-1932. Vol.1   253 p.,
       Vol.2   253 p., Vol.3   293 p.   ML 724 C6 M8

1948; Also, vol.1 in Italian. *La musica
pianistica francese.* Milano: Curci, 1957.
264 p. OCLC 15174346; Also vol.1 in English.
French Piano Music. Translated by Hilda
Andrews. London: Oxford University Press,
1932. Reprint. New York: Da Capo Press,
1977. viii, 208 p. OCLC 2875381   ML 724
C713 1977

La musique française de piano was first
published in Paris in 1930, and subsequent
volumes covering other French composers appeared in 1932 and 1944. The work is based
on a series of essays originally written for
the *Revue musicale.* Cortot shares his impressions of some of France's greatest composers and their piano works: Vol.1 covers
Claude Debussy, César Franck, Gabriel Fauré,
D'Emmanuel Chabrier, and Paul Dukas; Vol.2
views Maurice Ravel, Camille Saint-Saëns,
Vincent D'Indy, Florent Schmitt, Déodat de
Séverac, and Maurice Emmanuel; Vol.3 covers
les "Six," Albert Roussel, Igor Stravinsky
(in a unit titled "*Le piano et les pianistes*"),
Erik Satie, Gabriel Pierné, and Gustave
Samazeuilh. Cortot's comments are vivid,
very descriptive, and often colored by Gallic
pride in his gifted countrymen. Comments do
not cover analytical aspects but rather historical background, interpretation, and aes-
thetic qualities. Cortot's remarks reflect
the same sensitivity that one feels in his
piano performance. Lacks indexes.

314. Dorfmüller, Joachim. *Studien zur norweg-
      ischen Klaviermusik der ersten Hälfte
      des zwanzigsten Jahrhunderts.* [Studies
      on Norwegian Piano Music of the First Half
      of the Twentieth Century] Marburg: Mar-
      burger Beiträge zur Musikforschung, band
      4, 1969. 239 p. OCLC 1699547   ML 736 D67

      A study of the tonal, homophonic period of
      late-Romantic piano music of Fartein Valen
      (1887-1952), Harald Saeverud (b.1897), and

Klaus Egge (b.1906), also noting nationalism
in the piano works of Saeverud and Egge and
examining the atonal and dodecaphonic music
of Valen. It is the author's purpose to
demonstrate the characteristic elements and
strengths displayed by Norwegian piano music
of the last half-century. Forty-eight compositions of Valen, Saeverud, and Egge are
cited. Pianist Dorfmüller toured Norway
with baritone Helge Birkeland, and while
there realized the need for this study.
Thoroughly documented. Musical examples,
bibliography, chronological conspectus of
works studied, list of other composers' works
cited, name index.

315. Ellis, Mildred Katharine. "The French Piano
    Character Piece of the Nineteenth and Early
    Twentieth Centuries." (Volumes I and II)
    Ph.D. diss., Indiana University, 1969.
    Ann Arbor, Mich.: University Microfilms
    Inter., 1970. 1022 p.

Purpose of this dissertation, states Ellis,
is to create interest in the revival and performance of the nineteenth/early twentieth
century French character piece. This lengthy
in-depth study analyzes the piano character
pieces written by representative French composers of this period (1770-1920), stylistic
features relating to this genre of piano literature, its cultural milieu, and the Romantic
movement in France. Ellis gives attention to
composers who are usually neglected e.g., Léon
Boëllmann, Alexandre Boëly, etc.. Some of
the better-known composers are Charles Henri-
Valentin Alkan, Georges Bizet, Charles Gounod,
Francis Thomé. The character piece is defined, and compositions are categorized and
described. There are numerous tables, musical examples, appendixes, bibliography (extensive), etc.; the entire work is on a large
scale.

316. Erlebach, Rupert. "Style in Pianoforte Con-
      certo Writing." *Music and Letters* 17
      (April 1936): 131-39.

      A critical examination of the piano con-
      certo from Bach to Rachmaninoff. Stylistic
      change in piano concerti is brought about
      primarily because of the evolution of the
      instrument, states Erlebach. "The style of
      keyboard concertos is closely associated
      with this question of sustaining-power."
      Differences in style, technical as well as
      compositional, of composers as, Bach, Mozart,
      Beethoven, Brahms, Chopin, Liszt, and Rach-
      maninoff are observed and compared. Musical
      examples.

317. Gibson, Nora. "Women Composers of Keyboard
      Music: An Historical Overview." *American
      Music Teacher* 35 (November-December 1985):
      51-54.

      A historical survey of women keyboard com-
      posers, using six composers as subjects.
      Earliest composer in the study is Elisabeth
      Jacquet de la Guerre (1669-1729); the latest
      is Thea Musgrave (b.1928). Other composers
      are: Fanny Mendelssohn, Clara Wieck Schumann,
      Amy Cheney Beach, and Ruth Crawford Seeger.
      Biographical sketches and descriptions of
      selected compositions are included. These
      are the women keyboard composers who are best
      known. Unfortunately, the list does not in-
      clude any lesser-known ones. Bibliography
      (19 entries, including four recordings).

318. Hinson, Maurice. *The Piano Teacher's Source
      Book: An Annotated Bibliography of Books Re-
      lated to the Piano and Piano Music.* 2d ed.,
      rev. Melvill N.Y.: Belwin Mills, 1980.
      187 p. OCLC 6973836   ML 128 P3 H55 1980

      An annotated bibliography listing diverse
      literature (including theses and disserta-

tions) on the piano. Entries are listed in
12 categories: accompanying, aesthetics, a-
nalysis, biographies, church music, class
piano, construction and design, history, list
of piano music, ornamentation, pedagogy, and
performance practices. Only books in English
are reviewed. Indexes, list of publishers.

319.   ------.   *The Pianist's Reference Guide: A*
        Bibliographical Survey. Los Angeles,
        Cal.: Alfred Publishing Co., 1987. xi,
        336 p. ISBN 0-8828-4358-3   OCLC 15489-
        638   ML 128 P3 H54 1987

        An enlargement and revision of the author's
        volume of 1980 *Piano Teacher's Source Book:*
        An Annotated Bibliography of Books Related
        to the Piano and Piano Music. There are
        almost 1,000 annotated entries of books and
        dissertations on diverse literature dealing
        with the piano and piano music. The subjects
        listed in his 1980 volume are present (church
        music is not indexed), plus a few more, name-
        ly: "Performance Anxiety - Stress and Ten-
        sion," "Piano Duets, Transcriptions," and
        "Two or More Pianos." The volume contains
        only works in English and does not include
        articles. Good source of pertinent litera-
        ture, especially of dissertations. Subject
        index, composer index, list of publishers.

320.   Krueger, Wolfgang. *Das Nachtstück; ein*
        Beitrag zur Entwicklung des einsätzigen
        Pianofortestückes im 19. Jahrhundert.
        [The nocturne; a lecture on the develop-
        ment of the single-movement piano piece in
        the 19th century] München: Musikverlag
        E. Katzbichler, 1971. 210 p. ISBN 3-
        8739-7007-0   OCLC 597457   ML 706 K78

        Originally presented as the author's thesis
        (University of Kiel), this is a history and
        criticism of the nocturne, tracing various
        musical "night-pieces" from ancient times

to the twentieth century. Krueger examines
the night motive in poetry and painting.
Nocturnes of Chopin, John Field, and night-
pieces of Schumann, as well as nocturnes of
later composers, are surveyed. A useful
historical examination of the nocturne.
Illustrations, musical examples, bibliography,
four indexes (abbreviations, nocturnes, cited
writings, persons).

321. Lubin, Ernest. *The Piano Duet: A Guide for*
      Pianists. New York: Grossman Publishers,
      1970. xii, 221 p. ISBN 0-6705-5307-7
      OCLC 138203   ML700 L82; Reprint. New
      York: Da Capo Press, 1976. ISBN 0-3068-
      8045-4   OCLC 2121690   ML 700 L82 1976

      An important contribution to the study of
      the piano duet. A survey of music composed
      for that medium, primarily by major composers
      from Mozart to Debussy. Arrangements of
      other works for duet and literature for two
      pianos are not considered here. Lubin ef-
      fectively describes major works by Mozart,
      Beethoven, Schubert, Schumann, Grieg, Dvořåk,
      et al, noting historical background and
      stylistic characteristics. The only facet
      missing, the inclusion of which would be most
      helpful, is interpretive commentary. Illus-
      trations, musical examples, appendixes (notes
      on two-piano literature; biographical and
      historical notes; duet material for beginning
      pianists), composition index and name index.

322. Moldenhauer, Hans. *Duo-Pianism.* Chicago:
      Chicago Musical College Press [thesis],
      1950. 400 p. OCLC 10972012   ML 700
      M717

      A survey of the history, literature, and
      performance of the art of duo-pianism.
      Though this volume deals primarily with the
      practical aspects of duo-piano performance
      i.e., program building, performance, mechan-

ics, partnership, practicing, techniques,
pedagogical applications, etc., there is
material on the history of the art and on
the literature of the genre. Moldenhauer
also surveys duo-piano teams of the time.
There are various lists: original two-piano
music, recorded two-piano music, standard
repertoire, etc.. Bibliography (annotated),
name index.

323. Müller-Blattau, Joseph. "Zur Geschichte und
      Stilistik des vierhändigen Klaviersatzes."
      [On the history and style of the four-hand
      piano piece] *Jahrbuch der Musikbibliothek
      Peters für 1940* 47 (1941): 40-58.

The author surveys the history of four-hand
piano compositions from the time that Wolfgang
and Nannerl Mozart performed at one keyboard
(c.1765) to the time of Schubert's *Fantasia*
Op.103 and the *Allegro* Op.posth. 144, written in 1828. Müller-Blattau offers a stylistic analysis of four-hand compositions by
Johann Christian Bach, Mozart, Beethoven,
and Schubert. He points out the decline of
Hausmusik since the turn of the century.

324. Powell, Linton. *A History of Spanish Piano
      Music.* Bloomington, Ind.: Indiana Univer-
      sity Press, 1980. viii, 213 p. ISBN 0-25-
      31-8114-3   OCLC 6278165   ML 738 P7

A survey of solo piano music in Spain, from
composers of the eighteenth century (Domenico
Scarlatti and Soler) to music of Suriñach,
Castillo, De Pablo, *et al.*. All too brief
are the descriptions of composers and some
of their works. Powell includes a short
chapter on the influence of the guitar on
Spanish keyboard music. Musical examples,
appendixes, glossary, bibliography (over 100
entries), index.

325. Puchelt, Gerhard. *Verlorene Klänge: Studien
      zur Deutschen Klaviermusik 1830-1880*. [Lost
      Sounds: Studies on German Piano Music 1830-
      1880] Berlin-Lichterfeld: Lienau, 1969.
      88 p. OCLC 229779 ML 726.4 P83

      A critical historical examination of Ger-
      man piano music (1830-80). It is the author's
      intent to focus on an ignored part of the Ro-
      mantic period: that of the *"Kleineren Geister
      von romantischer und Klassizistischer Haltung"*
      ["smaller spirits of the Romantic and Classic
      style"] and to present more clearly their con-
      tribution to the piano literature of the nine-
      teenth century. Puchelt examines worthwhile
      composers who were often overshadowed by more
      renowned contemporaries and offers a subjec-
      tive selection (with descriptions) of their
      piano works from the period 1830-1880. He
      reveals some of the riches that are available,
      but almost forgotten, from this epoch. Adolf
      Henselt, Sigismund Thalberg, Stephen Heller,
      Norbert Burgmüller, Ferdinand Hiller, Robert
      Volkmann, Carl Reinecke, Woldemar Bargiel,
      Friedrich Kiel, Theodore Kirchner, and Adolf
      Jensen are given proper relative historical
      placement as to innovations, influences,
      style, creativity, etc.. A valuable study.
      Portraits, musical examples, bibliography;
      lacks an index.

326. Schulz, Ferdinand F. *Pianographie: Klavier-
      bibliographie der lieferbaren Bücher und
      Periodica sowie der Dissertationen in
      deutscher, englischer, französischer und
      italienischer Sprache*. [Pianography: Key-
      board bibliography of available books,
      periodicals and dissertations in German,
      English, French and Italian languages]
      2d [ed.] verb. und erheblich erw. Aufl.
      Recklinghausen: Piano-Verlag, 1982. xvii,
      458 p. OCLC 8656546   ML 128 P3 S38 1982

      This is a greatly enlarged edition of the
      the work that was first published in 1978.

The first edition contained 800 entries; the
second edition adds 1600 more entries. The
introduction (by Paul Badura-Skoda) and preface to each edition are in German and English. The useful, but unannotated, bibliography lists books, articles, and dissertations written in German, English, French and
Italian, though the majority of the entries
are in German and English. Schulz has made
an effort to include numerous German and
American dissertations. Subject headings:
composers, piano music, piano playing, pianists, piano building (including tuning, repair, etc.) and miscellaneous items. The
work is divided into clearly defined subjects
and has several lists: periodicals, publishers, libraries, piano competitions, and music societies. Illustrations, indexes (composer and author).

327.   Sonnedecker, Donald I.   "Cultivation and Con-
       cepts of Duets for Four Hands, One Keyboard,
       In the Eighteenth Century." Ph.D. diss.,
       Indiana University, 1953. xvii, 320 p.
       Ann Arbor, Mich.: University Microfilms
       International, 1953. OCLC 8836397

       A historical study of the duet from its
       origin to c.1800. There is some analysis of
       works by Mozart as well as by other compos-
       ers. The author presents a critical survey
       of the history of the duet, viewing composers
       who wrote in that genre (in Austria, Germany,
       France, England, USA, and in other countries).
       Mozart is given a great deal of coverage.
       The importance of the duet in social gather-
       ings is stressed. Musical examples, bibliog-
       raphy (extensive).

328.   Tovey, Donald Francis. *Essays in Musical*
       Analysis: Volume III Concertos. London:
       Oxford University Press, 1936. [7 vols.]
       ix, 226 p. OCLC 930485   MT 90 T6 E8

Tovey analyzes piano concerti (in "classical" form) by: Mozart K.414, 450, 453, 488,
491, Beethoven Op. 15, 37, 58, 73, Chopin
Op.21, Brahms Op. 15, 83, Franck *Variations
symphoniques*, Arthur Somervell *"Normandy":
Symphonic Variations*, Dohnányi *Variations
on a Nursery Song*, Schumann Op. 54, Saint-
Saëns Op.44, Glazunov Op.92, Richard Strauss
*Parergon to the "Sinfonia Domestica" for Pi-
áno with Orchestra* Op.73, and Franz Schmidt
Variations on a Theme of Beethoven. Tovey
also notes derivations and influences in his
vivid critical analyses. Depth of coverage
is uneven, with some concerti receiving better analyses than others. The volume also
includes concerti for other solo instruments.
Musical examples; lacks an index.

329.   ------. *Essays in Musical Analysis: Vol-
          ume IV Illustrative Music.* London:
          Oxford University Press, 1936. [7 vols.]
          viii, 176 p.   OCLC 930485   MT 90 T6 E8

Tovey states, "This volume deals with
music which, being under no compulsion to
adapt its habit to words, actions, or cer-
emonies, confesses itself to be descriptive
independently of circumstances." The descriptive compositions for piano that Tovey
critically analyzes are: Weber *Conzertstück*
in F Minor Op.79, Schubert-Liszt *Fantasia
("The Wanderer")*, arranged for piano and
orchestra, and the Schumann *Carnaval* Op.9.
The majority of compositions surveyed are
non-piano works. As in the other analytical
volumes by Tovey, there are many colorful
impressions and commentaries. Musical examples; lacks an index.

330.   ------. *Essays in Musical Analysis: Chamber
          Music.* Edited by Hubert J. Foss. London:
          Oxford University Press, 1944. [7 vols.]
          viii, 217 p.   OCLC 2942967   MT 90 T6 E8

Published after the death of Tovey (1940).
Editor Hubert J. Foss collected these chamber
music analyses written by Tovey between the
years 1900 and 1936. In addition to chamber
music, the volume contains solo literature
which Tovey felt could easily fit into the
context of chamber music. He critically analyzes: Haydn's *Sonata in E-Flat Major*
H.XVI/52, Mozart's *Quintet in E-Flat Major*
K.452, Beethoven's *Thirty-Three Variations
on a Waltz by Diabelli* Op.120, and *Sonata
in A Major for Violin and Piano* Op.47,
Schumann's *Novelette in F-Sharp Minor* Op.21,
No.8, and *Quintet in E-Flat Major* Op.44,
Chopin's *Etudes* Op.25, Nos.7 and 12, *Trois
nouvelles études* Nos.1 and 3, Brahms'
Variations and Fugue on a Theme by Handel
Op.24, *Variations on a Theme by Paganini*
Op.35, *Quartet in G Minor* Op.25, *Quartet
in A Major* Op.26, and *Quartet in C Minor*
Op.60. Tovey's colorful, critical observa-
tions note influences and derivations. Mu-
sical examples, name-composition index.

331.   Townsend, Douglas. "The Piano-Duet." *Piano
       Quarterly* 61 (Fall 1967): 14-18.

A concise history of the piano duet, along
with recommended literature. Includes a list
of works for one piano—three hands; one piano—
four hands; one piano—six hands; one piano—
four hands and various instruments.

332.   Westrup. J.A. "Le mouvement pianistique en
       angleterre." *Revue internationale de mu-
       sique* 1 (Numéro spécial Avril 1939):
       863-70.

Westrup's short history of keyboard music
in England appears in English as well as in
French. The study commences with English
composers of virginal music i.e., William
Byrd, Giles Farnaby, John Bull, and Peter
Phillips, and moves on to Muzio Clementi,

John Field, etc.. Westrup concludes with
mention of keyboard works by Ralph Vaughan-
Williams, Arnold Bax, and William Walton.
A cursory account of England's contribution
to keyboard literature.

THE MUSIC

IX. Historical Studies

Repertoire

333. Bosquet, Emile. *La musique de clavier:*
      Manuel Encyclopédique Historique et
      Pratique. Bruxelles: Les amis de la
      musique, 1953. 670 p. OCLC 422240
      ML 700 B65 M8

      A chronological listing of keyboard (clav-
      ichord, harpsichord, piano) literature by
      century, beginning in Greek times B.C. to
      the twentieth century. Some early lute works
      are also listed. Works are described in
      terms of key, form, thematic analysis, and
      aesthetic qualities. Not all works are
      treated equally, some are just mentioned,
      others are examined in depth. Each unit/
      century, is given an introduction which de-
      scribes the period musically, the instruments
      of the time, interpretations of the current
      keyboardists. It also gives concise biogra-
      phies of major composers. Individual liter-
      ature coverage is not consistent in quantity
      or quality. Musical examples, bibliography
      (incomplete data), indexes (publishers, com-
      positions [by genre], names).

334. Brinkman, Joseph, and Benning Dexter. *Piano*
      Music. Ann Arbor, Mich.: University of
      Michigan Official Publication, 1956. 19 p.
      016.7864 P573 1955

      Listing of 27 major piano composers (Albeniz

to Scriabin) and available editions of their
music. A secondary list mentions contemporary composers (Antheil to Webern) and their
publishers. Useful in 1956, but in need of
revision and expansion for the 1980s.

335. Brown, Ernest James. "An Annotated Bibliog-
      raphy of Selected Solo Music Written for
      the Piano by Black Composers." DMA diss.,
      University of Maryland, 1976. Ann Arbor,
      Mich.: University Microfilms, 1976. 100 p.
      OCLC 8619148

      Surveys works of 27 black composers, noting
      particulars such as: biographical background,
      education, accomplishments, style of compo-
      sitions, etc.. Many of the compositions are
      described. Other lists include: selected
      black composers (seven) born after 1940 (list
      derived from the Afro-American Music Oppor-
      tunities Association, Inc.), chronological
      list of selected black composers and some
      of their contemporaries, and a select group
      of "classic" rag composers (10). Various
      compositions appearing in the lists are also
      described. Composers and their music are
      categorized according to how close they have
      been identified with black culture of the
      USA; if identification is strong, the com-
      poser is listed regardless of mixed racial
      background. A good survey of black compos-
      ers of piano music. The author would do
      well to amplify the work with additional
      composers and more data, as well as bring it
      up to date. Musical examples, list of pub-
      lishers, bibliography (nine entries).

336. Butler, Stanley. *Guide to the Best in Con-
      temporary Piano Music: An Annotated List
      of Graded Solo Piano Music Published Since
      1950*. Metuchen, N.J.: Scarecrow Press,
      1973. ISBN (vol.1) 0-8108-0628-2   OCLC 6-
      14182   ML 132 P3 B88; ISBN (vol.2) 0-81-
      08-0669-X   ML 132 P3 B88

A selection of 825 titles deemed worthy of
performance by the author, out of 3000 examined. Vol.1 covers levels of difficulty
from 1 through 5 and vol.2 covers levels 6
through 8. Contemporary piano compositions
by international composers are described.
Pertinent data includes: year of composition,
translation of title, publishers, performance
time, pedaling, fingering, etc.. The annotations are helpful. Glossary, index to musical and pianistic features, index to composers and compositions, publishers.

337. Chang, Frederic Ming, and Albert Faurot.
      *Team Piano Repertoire: A Manual of Music
      for Multiple Players at One or More Pian-
      os.* Metuchen, N.J.: Scarecrow Press,
      1976. 184 p. ISBN 0-8108-0937-0 OCLC 2-
      189314 ML 128 P3 C48

      Literature for multiple pianos is divided
      according to scoring: Two at One Piano, Two
      at Two Pianos, Three or Four at Two pianos,
      Three at Three Pianos, and Four at Four Pian-
      os. Only published works are reviewed. Pub-
      lishers of listed compositions are noted.
      Concerti with orchestral reductions for a
      second piano are not considered here, for
      they do not exemplify the genre covered by
      this volume. Concerti for two or more pian-
      os are included if the orchestral part can be
      incorporated into the piano parts. Each work
      is given a concise description, with the ex-
      ception of a few arrangements and transcrip-
      tions. No index.

338. Fallows-Hammond, Patricia. *Three Hundred
      Years at the Keyboard.* Berkeley, Cal.:
      Ross Books, 1984. x, 302 p. ISBN 89496-
      045-6 OCLC 10147092 MT 140 F2 1984

      Opening chapters deal with the evolution
      of the piano and changing styles in keyboard
      technique. The work's main portion describes

the different periods in music, represents
each period with single works of selected
major composers of that period, and lists
important keyboard compositions written by
each representative composer. A chapter
dealing with National Schools covers composers from specific countries. Fallows-Hammond presents a useful volume, effectively
combining historical data with choice representative literature. Music, illustrations,
appendixes, bibliography (28 entries), name
index.

339.   Faurot, Albert. *Concert Piano Repertoire, A
        Manual of Solo Literature for Artists and
        Performers.* Metuchen, N.J.: Scarecrow Press,
        1974. xiv, 338 p. ISBN 0-8108-0685-1   OCLC
        703192   ML 128 P3 F39

        Alphabetical listing by composer of major
        compositions for piano. Annotations offer
        informal descriptions of compositions, making
        note of: key, form, difficulty, and histori-
        cal background. Commentary at times reveals
        biased opinions, for which Faurot, as stated
        in his introduction, does not offer an apol-
        ogy-- "one man's cup of tea is another's vial
        of poison." Faurot reviews compositions of
        some 370 composers of all nationalities, in-
        cluding a few Japanese composers. One impor-
        tant drawback of this work is the lack of
        publisher data for the listed compositions.
        Chronology of composers, bibliography (90
        entries), no index.

340.   Friskin, James, and Irwin Freundlich. *Music
        for Piano. A Handbook of Concert and Teach-
        ing Material from 1580 to 1952.* New York:
        Holt, Rinehart and Winston, 1954. 432 p.
        OCLC 526075   ML 128 P3 F7; Reprint. New
        York: Dover Publications, 1973. 434 p. ISBN
        0-486-22918-1   OCLC 763470   ML 128 P3 F7
        1973

The Dover edition is an unabridged, slightly
corrected republication of the work orginally
published in 1954. A new preface by Freundlich
and a new biographical appendix have been added
to the Dover edition. The book was innovative
in its time and filled an informational void
which then existed. Descriptions of works
listed include characteristics and difficulty
of the composition as well as publisher information. Selected music of the *clavecinistes*
and virginalists are listed as well as works
for one/two pianos four hands, and works for
piano and orchestra. Chief drawback is the
format of the volume. It is not constructed
alphabetically, but instead is arranged by
country or period, which necessitates fre-
quent use of the index. Friskin and Freundlich's pioneer work in this field is largely
superseded by Maurice Hinson's current works
on the literature of the piano. Appendixes,
name (composer) index.

341.   Georgii, Walter. *Klaviermusik: mit 329
       Notenbeispielen und einer Zeittafel.*
       [Piano music: with 329 musical examples
       and a chronology] 5d ed. Zurich: Atlan-
       tis, 1976. xii, 652 p. ISBN 3-7611-
       0222-4   OCLC 2858272   ML 700 G4 1976

The first edition of Georgii's informative
and useful compilation appeared in 1941 and
was solely a survey of piano literature for
two hands; subsequent editions contained sup-
plements, including literature and material
on piano music for multiple performers. The
use of many musical examples facilitates the
author's explanation of style. Georgii offers a historical approach to the literature
of the piano, commencing with early times (up
to 1600), the period of the virginalists and
the *clavecinistes*, through to contemporary
times. A great deal of background data is
given on the compositions, as well as notes
on style and form of same. The author should
be commended for the attention given to minor

composers and those composers who are often
slighted in works such as this. How often
are composers of Greece, Finland, Yugoslavia,
Switzerland, etc. included in overviews of
literature? Georgii does favor the German-
ic composers, with which the repertoire is
richly endowed. The work effectively cap-
tures the total output of the major composers and notes their importance in the larger
realm of the history of piano literature. A
significant study of piano literature. Musical examples, chronology (to 1800), name index, composer-editions index, other arts and
philosophers index, author-editor-publisher
index.

342.   Gillespie, John, and Anna Gillespie. *A Bib-*
       liography of Nineteenth-Century American
       Piano Music. Westport, Conn.: Greenwood
       Press, 1984. xii, 359 p. ISBN 0-313-240-
       97-3   OCLC 10753997   ML 128 P3 G54 1984

       A select bibliography of available published
American piano music dating from the close of
the eighteenth century to the first few dec-
ades of the twentieth century. The authors
include pertinent information such as: biographical sketch of the composer, composition's publisher and date of publication,
library data, and an occasional comment about
the composition. The authors have selected
music that typifies American piano music of
that period, i.e., compositions conservative
in nature, salon style as well as serious music, highly descriptive works, and music for
amusement. Unfortunately, date of composition is not included in the data, and there
are too few pieces that receive descriptive
comments. Since most of the works regarded
in this bibliography are not well known, it
would be ideal if all the compositions had
some basic description. The bibliography
provides information for musicians and those
interested in the cultural aspect of the period. Biographies, list of publishers, li-

brary sources, reference sources, no index.

343. Hinson, Maurice. *Guide to the Pianist's
     Repertoire.* Edited (with preface) by
     Irwin Freundlich. Bloomington, Ind.: In-
     diana University Press, 1973. xiv, 831 p.
     ISBN 0-2533-2700-8   OCLC 599530   ML 128
     P3 H5; Also, 2d ed., rev. and enl. Bloom-
     ington, Ind.: Indiana University Press,
     1987. xxxiii, 856 p. ISBN 0-2533-2656-7
     OCLC 13217904   ML 128 P3 H5 1987

344. ------. *The Piano in Chamber Ensemble: An
     Annotated Guide.* Bloomington, Ind.: In-
     diana University Press, 1978. xxxiii,
     570 p. ISBN 0-253-34493-X   OCLC 3204913
     ML 128 C4 H5; Also, Hassocks, Sussex: Har-
     vester Press, 1978. ISBN 0-855-27634-7
     OCLC 7311493   ML 128 C4 H5 1978a

345. ------. *Guide to the Pianist's Repertoire.
     Supplement.* Bloomington, Ind.: Indiana Uni-
     versity Press, 1979. xxxiii, 413 p. ISBN 0-
     253-32701-6   OCLC 10830682   ML 128 P3 H5
     Suppl.

346. ------. *Music for Piano and Orchestra: An
     Annotated Guide.* Bloomington, Ind.: Indiana
     University Press, 1981. xxiii, 327 p. ISBN
     0-253-12435-2   OCLC 6863119   ML 128 P3 H53

347. ------. *Music for More Than One Piano: An An-
     notated Guide.* Bloomington, Ind.: Indiana
     University Press, 1983. xxvii, 218 p. ISBN
     0-253-33952-9   OCLC 9371185   ML 128 P3 H52
     1983.

Hinson's extensive compilation of piano literature represents a comprehensive survey of
that genre. The five volumes, hereafter referred to as: *Guide, Guide-Supplement, Piano
and Orchestra, Piano Chamber Ensemble,* and
More Than One Piano, have similar formats.
Each volume contains: literature listed under
composer's name filed alphabetically, key,

duration, composer's dates, date of composition, publishers (some with copyright dates),
annotations, level of difficulty, bibliogra-
phies (annotated), biographical sketches,
and cross indexing. Annotations contain information as to style, form, interpretation,
etc.. Generally, works listed are from 1700
on, although *Guide* includes works prior to
that when suitable for performance on the
modern piano. *Guide* and *Guide-Supplement*
list solo literature; *Guide-Supplement*
brings *Guide* up-to-date (to 1979) with new
literature not listed in *Guide* (except in
qualified instances); *Guide* contains historical recital programs of Busoni and Anton
Rubinstein. In all five volumes, transcriptions are generally excluded (except in qualified instances). *Piano Chamber Ensemble*
lists works for no more than eight instruments
including piano. *Piano and Orchestra* lists
compositions for more than eight instruments
including piano, to delineate these from chamber music; it also lists various concerto ca-
denze. *More Than One Piano* lists music for
two or more keyboard instruments, alone or
with other parts. All five volumes cover
standard composers and introduce many contemporary composers of merit. An indispensable
collection which supersedes many outdated and
incomplete catalogues of piano literature.
Recommended.

The second edition (1987) of *Guide to the
Pianist's Repertoire* (solo literature) represents a major reorganization of the first
edition (1973), principally by incorporating
a large part of the *Supplement* (1979) volume. Both the first edition (1973) and the
Supplement (1979) have been entirely revised, corrected, enlarged and combined into
one large volume. The second edition appears
more confident in thrust; there are more descriptive annotations about the music (e.g.,
each Prelude and Fugue of Bach's WTC, each
Beethoven sonata, etc.); and generally there
is much more information in the new edition.
The second edition of *Guide to the Pianist's*

Repertoire is a major improvement on the
preceding edition in that it ties loose ends
together, eliminating a few sketchy inclusions
as well as incorporating the major part of the
separate *Supplement* volume. Some composers
listed in first edition of *Guide* (1973) and
Supplement (1979) have been dropped from the
new second edition, although many more new
composers' names appear in the revised edition.
The area of contemporary music is addressed
with the inclusion of many new works. This
new edition is highly recommended. Material
on anthologies and collections, bibliography
(extensive), appendix (historical recital programs), indexes (list of composers under na-
tionality, and list of anthologies/collections).

348. Hutcheson, Ernest. *The Literature of the*
      Piano: A Guide for Amateur and Student.
      New York: Knopf, 1948. viii, 374 p.
      OCLC 1200518   MT 140 H95; Also, 3d ed.,
      rev. and enl. New York: Knopf, 1964, 1968,
      1975. xvi, 436 p. OCLC 9480215   MT 140
      H95 1968

Hutcheson's volume is labeled, "a guide for
amateur and student," but woe to the amateur
or student who is not well versed in music
history or theory, for the author's musical
descriptions assume that the reader has this
knowledge. The volume describes the major
piano (keyboard, in Bach's case) compositions
of composers from J.S. Bach to Aaron Copland.
Works surveyed include solo compositions,
concerti, and chamber music. Data on editions is inconsistent, since only editions
of major composers are compared. Subsequent
editions include errata.
      Third edition has been revised and brought
up to more recent date by Rudolph Ganz. Material added by Ganz in the text is bracketed.
He also includes a new chapter titled "Living
Composers and the State of Music since Hutcheson" and units on technique and fingerings.
Musical examples, appendixes, bibliography

(190 entries covering dictionaries, piano and
its predecessors, piano music, acoustics, and
biographies [the Ganz edition contains a revised bibliography]), name-composition index.

349. Lockwood, Albert Lewis. *Notes on the Liter-
      ature of the Piano.* Ann Arbor, Mich.: Uni-
      versity of Michigan Press; London: Oxford
      University Press, 1940. xx, 235 p. OCLC
      412396   ML 128 P3 L3; Reprint. (with new
      preface by Frederick Freedman) New York:
      Da Capo Press, 1968. OCLC 654675   ML 128
      P3 L38 1968

      Frederick Freedman, in his preface to this
      volume, attempts to justify Lockwood's unmusi-
      cological approach as well as Lockwood's high-
      ly opinionated observations. Both aspects
      are apparent in *Notes on the Literature of
      the Piano.* The work is quite selective,
      whimsically opinionated, and lacking in con-
      sistency. Lockwood's work lists piano compo-
      sitions under composer's name, filed alpha-
      betically; some compositions are commented
      on. Includes various lists: works for piano
      and orchestra, sonatas, works for two pianos,
      concert études, pieces for young people,
      Anton Rubinstein's historical recital series,
      and more. Bibliography, name index.

350. McGraw, Cameron. *Piano Duet Repertoire: Mu-
      sic Originally Written for One Piano, Four
      Hands.* Bloomington, Ind.: Indiana Univer-
      sity Press, 1981. xxxix, 334 p. ISBN 0-
      253-14766-2   OCLC 6735069   ML 128 P3 M2

      A comprehensive listing of piano duet liter-
      ature. This is a scholarly work that offers
      the reader a great deal of information. Mc-
      Graw's work only deals with original works for
      one piano, four hands. Complete data is indi-
      cated: composer's dates, original foreign ti-
      tles, key, place and date of publication,
      publisher, location (if in manuscript), de-

scriptive comments, and grade of difficulty.
A very useful volume for the pianist and
teacher who is interested in this genre, or
for one who would like to study the sociolog-
ical history of the piano duet. Indexes, appendixes, bibliograpy (15 annotated entries).

351. Rezits, Joseph, and Gerald Deatsman. *The*
Pianist's Resource Guide: Piano Music in
Print and Literature on the Pianistic Art.
San Diego, Cal.: Pallma Music Co./Neil A.
Kjos Jr., 1978. x, 1491 p. ISBN 0-8497-
7800-X OCLC 4456053 ML 128 P3 R5 1978

Cross-referenced guide to published piano
music currently available, divided into two
main sections: composer index and title index. Composer index lists works under composer, with data as to editor, grade level,
title, and publisher. Title index lists
works under title, with information on title,
compiler/arranger, and composer. Sub-clas-
sifications place works according to genre
e.g., concerti, popular music, études, left-
hand alone works, preludes, sonatas/sona-
tinas, variations, technical material. Supplementary units include: "Literature on the
Pianistic Art," which lists 2300 English language books under several indexes (author,
title, classification, etc.). "Piano Reader's
Guide," which offers critical evaluations (by
Rezits) of 118 books, and an Index to Publishers, giving names and addresses of publishing firms. The work is well indexed.
Especially useful for noting and comparing
various editions of a common work, as well
as for tracking down an elusive composition.

352. Rowley, Alec. *Four Hands-One Piano; A List*
of Works for Duet Players. London, New
York, Toronto: Oxford University Press,
1940. 38 p. OCLC 3365341 786.49 R88F

Lists of duet literature arranged by var-

ious categories e.g., classics, French and
English compositions, educational works,
études, general works. Contains a list
of publishers (no addresses) and an alphabetical list of composers. This was one of
the first English-language guides to four-
hand duet literature. Rowley, a pianist and
composer, contributed to the literature with
several duets. The list contains no descriptive annotations. The work is now outdated
and superseded by Cameron McGraw's work, *Piano Duet Repertoire* (1981).

353. Rüger, Christof. *Konzertbuch: Klaviermusik
      A-Z.* Leipzig: VEB Deutscher Verlag für
      Musik, 1982. 784 p.   OCLC 10273383
      MT 140 K6 1982

      Repertoire of solo music for one or more
      pianos and performers, listed alphabetically
      by composer's name. A short biography of
      each composer, noting dates, musical educa-
      tion, and musical life, etc., is followed by
      a directory of piano works (published original
      works and essential adaptions), offering in-
      formation such as: key, titles of cyclic
      movements, date of completion, points on
      style. This in turn is followed by a criti-
      cal discussion of the major piano works.
      Directory of works under each composer is
      arranged by genre. Rüger states that he
      presents a broader view of Russian/Soviet
      and East German piano literature, since both
      areas are generally insufficiently covered
      in earlier repertoire guides. He does in-
      clude the notable Russian and Soviet compos-
      ers and several contemporary German compos-
      ers. However, he slights important keyboard
      composers of other nations (Ives is the only
      American included). There are pre-piano
      composers present i.e., J.S. Bach, François
      Couperin, J.J. Froberger, Händel, Rameau.
      Rüger's compilation is well laid-out, with
      informative commentary on the major works and
      pertinent data on the composers and their

works. Especially useful for its coverage of German and Russian composers. Musical examples, name-composition index.

354. Schumann, Otto. *Handbuch der Klaviermusik*. 2. Auflage, Wilhelmshaven: Heinrichshofen's Verlag, 1969. 709 p. OCLC 6795781 MT 140 S33 H3 1969

Previously published in 1952 under the title *Klaviermusikbuch*. Directed toward the German friend of music (the amateur), the work offers an overview of selected concert music as well as "*Hausmusik*." Schumann does not attempt to be comprehensive in his coverage, but rather concentrates on surveying the works of the major composers e.g., Händel, J.S. Bach, Mozart, Beethoven, Schubert, Chopin, Schumann, *et al*. Unfortunately, many other important composers are slighted. Domenico Scarlatti receives only two pages of coverage, Debussy three pages, Ravel two pages, and Prokofiev three pages of attention. Many contemporary composers are grouped in a separate chapter ("Ergänzende übersicht") [Supplementary survey], receiving only cursory coverage. Attention given to J.S. Bach, Mozart, Beethoven, and other major composers includes viewing each fugue, sonata, variation, etc.. Biographical sketches of the composers are included in the coverage. One chapter addresses "new music": the compositional trends from Schönberg to Stockhausen. Musical examples, glossary, name/work index.

355. Wolters, Klaus, and Franzpeter Goebels. *Handbuch der Klavierliteratur. 1. Klaviermusik zu zwei Hände, von Klaus Wolters*. Zürich: Atlantis Verlag, 1967. 650 p. OCLC 3116097 ML 128 P3 W647; Also 2d ed., rev. and enl. Zürich: Atlantis Verlag, 1977. 660 p. OCLC 3654396 ML 128 P3 W647.

Wolters' volume on piano music for two hands
is of value to the piano pedagogue, student,
and accomplished musician. Wolters' format
is unusual; avoiding the alphabetical name
sequence, he groups his composers into periods, beginning with the Renaissance and Baroque on through our Contemporary period.
Included are chapters on Piano Schools, Technical Works (Etudes), Methods and Pedagogical
Writings, Anthologies, and National Schools
of the nineteenth Century. The greatest depth
of investigation is given to Bach, Haydn,
Mozart, Beethoven, Schubert, and Chopin. As
the author states, there are more minor composers of Germany, Austria and Switzerland
included than of other countries, where only
the most important composers are observed.
German editions are also relied on heavily
in the work. American composers contained
herein are: MacDowell, Ives, Bloch, Antheil,
Copland, Barber, Hovhaness, Rorem, Cage,
Feldman, and Donald Lybbert, all given brief
consideration. Despite these necessary limitations in scope, Wolters' work is significant,
especially for his review of technical and
pedagogical works, his inclusion of pertinent
data regarding the compositions, and the critical appraisal of different editions. Musical examples, errata, name index.

THE MUSIC

X. Music of Specific Composers

Charles Valentin Alkan
(1813-1888)

356. Schilling, Britta. *Virtuose Klaviermusik
des 19. Jahrhunderts am Beispiel von
Charles Valentin Alkan (1813-1888).*
[Virtuoso piano music of the 19th century
in the example of Charles Valentin Alkan
(1813-1888)] Regensburg: Gustav Bosse,
1986. 420 p. ISBN 3-7649-2317-2 OCLC 1-
5859312 ML 410 A5 S35 1986

An analytical study of Charles Valentin
Alkan's piano music in reference to the history of virtuoso piano literature. There is
biographical material on Alkan and a brief
historical survey of virtuoso piano literature and style. The analytical material examines melody, rhythm, harmony, forms, poly-
phony in the virtuoso piece, as well as techniques and characteristic styles. Useful in
the study and understanding of Alkan's piano
compositions. Illustrations, musical examples, bibliography (subject-related articles
and books, practical editions, Alkan's letters, general and specialized literature on
Alkan and piano music of the nineteenth century and French Romanticism), no index.

Carl Philipp Emanuel Bach
(1714-1788)

357. Barford, Philip. *The Keyboard Music of C.
      P.E. Bach, considered in relation to his
      musical aesthetic and the rise of the so-
      nata principle.* London: Barrie and
      Rockliff, 1965. xv, 186 p. OCLC 2097393
      MT 145 B12 B4; Also, New York: October
      House, 1966. OCLC 615833   MT 145 B12
      B4 1966

      A theoretical, historical, and descriptive
      analysis of Carl Philipp Emanuel Bach's key-
      board compositions. Although, states Barford,
      "the *Sonatas, Fantasias, and Rondos for Con-
      noisseurs and Amateurs*' are styled 'for for-
      tepiano'," he believes the works sound best
      on the clavichord and that the designation
      "for fortepiano" should not be taken too
      seriously. An in-depth study of the key-
      board works and style of C.P.E. Bach. Musi-
      cal examples, bibliography, discography,
      modern editions, name index.

Samuel Barber
(1910-1981)

358. Carter, Susan Blinderman. "The Piano Music
      of Samuel Barber." Ph.D. diss., Texas
      Tech University, 1980. Ann Arbor, Mich.:
      University Microfilms International, 1980.
      193 p. UM 80-22, 610 DA XLI 4, p.1270-A
      ML 417 B22 C3

      The author offers a concise biography of
      Samuel Barber and stylistic analyses (e.g.,
      form, line, rhythm) of his piano music; she
      also comments on interpretation and perform-
      ance problems and notes characteristic qual-
      ities apparent in the compositions. Each
      piano composition (including the *Piano Con-
      certo*) is analytically observed. Carter
      includes a summation statement, where, among
      other qualities noted, she writes that Barber's

music is basically neo-Romantic, conservative,
and lyric. Musical examples, appendixes (lec-
ture-recital text, discography [10 items]),
bibliography (sources), no index.

359. Miller, Elaine K. "A Study of Samuel Barber's
      Piano Music." Master's thesis, Kent State
      University, 1960. iii, 67 p. OCLC 2011711
      MT 145 B29 M5x

      An analytical survey of Barber's piano music.
      A short biographical sketch is followed by de-
      scriptive commentary and a formal analysis of
      the piano works (to 1960). The *Sonata* Op.26
      is given an in-depth examination. Musical ex-
      amples, bibliography (18 entries), no index.

                    Béla Bartók
                    (1881-1945)

360. Stevens, Halsey. *The Life and Music of Béla
      Bartók*. rev. ed. New York: Oxford Univer-
      sity Press, 1964. xvi, 364 p. OCLC 711288
      ML 410 B26 S8 1967; Reprint. London/New
      York: Oxford University Press, 1968. OCLC 4-
      68044 ML 410 B26 S8 1968

      Stevens' work is concerned primarily with
      Bartok's music, approached from both analyti-
      cal and critical points of view. The piano
      works are examined in terms of derivation,
      folk influence, harmonic scheme, mood, etc..
      The descriptions are helpful in regard to
      background information and viewpoints of in-
      terpretation. Illustrations, musical ex-
      amples, chronological list of works, bibli-
      ography (extensive; includes literature by
      Bartók and works that make reference to
      Bartók), name-composition index.

361. Suchoff, Benjamin. *Guide to Bartok's Mikro-
      kosmos*. rev. ed. London: Boosey and Hawkes,
      1971. vii, 152 p. OCLC 153676   MT 145 B25

S89; Reprint. rev. ed., new introduction by
György Sandor. New York: Da Capo Press, 1983.
ISBN 0-3067-6159-9   OCLC 8382107   MT 145
B25 S89 1983.

A handy guide for pianists and teachers;
the volume illustrates various musical aspects
of the *Mikrokosmos*. Preliminary sections
offer a biographical sketch of Bartók and
units on tonality, rhythm, harmony, form, and
pedagogical principles. The main portion of
the book consists of analytical commentary on
each piece of the *Mikrokosmos*. Aspects covered are: technique, musicianship, Bartók's
comments; in addition, the author's suggestions for interpretation are offered for each
composition. Commentary on the pieces is
succinct, describing technique and interpretation with one or two words. It would be
most helpful if there were more musical examples to illustrate stylistic characteristics of the pieces, and an expanded text describing aspects mentioned. Musical examples, bibliography (100 entries), index.

Ludwig van Beethoven
(1770-1827)

362. Badura-Skoda, Paul, and Jörg Demus. *Die
      Klaviersonaten von Ludwig van Beethoven.*
      Wiesbaden: F.A. Brockhaus, 1970. 223 p.
      ISBN 3-7653-0118-3   OCLC 764569   MT 145
      B42 B2

      Descriptive analysis of the Beethoven so-
      natas for piano. The authors' plan of anal-
      ysis includes attention to: individuality of
      each sonata, brief historical background,
      interpretative considerations, and comparison
      with other composers' works. The volume al-
      so contains units: *"Zum Beethovenspiel"*
      [on playing Beethoven] and *"Zur Beethoven-
      Interpretation"* [on interpretation of
      Beethoven]. A useful work for pianists inter-
      ested in performance practices and interpre-

tation. Musical examples, name index, biographical sketches of Badura-Skoda and Demus.

363. Barford, Philip. "The Piano Music - II." in
      The Beethoven Companion. edited by Denis
      Arnold and Nigel Fortune. London: Faber &
      Faber, 1971. 542 p. ISBN 0-5710-9003-6
      OCLC 154784   ML 410 B4 A75

      An analysis of the Beethoven piano composi-
      tions written in the last 18 years of the
      composer's life (from Op.78). Barford ex-
      amines thematic construction and form in the
      compositions. He compares some of Beethoven's
      piano music with that of C.P.E. Bach. Barford
      gives the "*Hammerklavier*" sonata special
      attention, offering a thematic layout of the
      fugue. Musical examples. "Piano Music - I,"
      also in *The Beethoven Companion* is written
      by Harold Truscott.

364. Burk, John Naglee. *The Life and Works of
      Beethoven.* New York: Modern Library, 1946.
      viii, 483 p. OCLC 404438   ML 410 B4 B875x

      Concise information on the piano composi-
      tions of Beethoven, cross-referenced with
      material in the biographical section of the
      volume. Burk gives a descriptive analysis
      of the compositions, observing dates of com-
      position, first performance dates (of the
      concerti), historical background, and dedi-
      cations. Musical examples, discography,
      name index.

365. Deane, Basil. "The Concertos." in *The
      Beethoven Companion.* edited by Denis
      Arnold and Nigel Fortune. London: Faber
      & Faber, 1971.   ISBN 0-5710-9003-6
      OCLC 154784   ML 410 B4 A75

      Descriptive analyses of the Beethoven con-
      certi. Basil notes early influences and the-

matic form. Coverage lacks depth of treatment.
Musical examples.

366. Elterlein, Ernst von. *Beethoven's Pianoforte
Sonatas: Explained for the Lovers of the
Musical Art.* (Original title *Beethovens
Clavier-Sonaten für Freunde der Tonkunst*
published in Leipzig by Heinrich Matthes,
1856) Trans. by Emily Hill. London: William
Reeves, 1898. 141 p. OCLC 10182330 MT 145
B42 E42

The Beethoven sonatas are regarded aesthet-
ically as well as formally and harmonically,
with the flowery descriptions that were typical of the writing of the time. Elterlein
often refers to three other studies in his
colorful observations: two works by Adolf
Bernhard Marx (*Anleitung zum Vortrag Beetho-
venischer Klavierwerke.* Berlin: Janke, 1863,
4th ed. 1912; and *Ludwig van Beethoven: Leben und Schaffen.* Berlin, 1859) and one by
Wilhelm von Lenz (*Beethoven: eine Kunststudie.*
Hamburg: Hoffmann & Campe, 1855-60). The
early Elterlein German edition contains material on the sonata after Beethoven i.e.,
Schubert, Schumann, Chopin, Liszt, etc.. Illustrations, no index.

367. Fischer, Edwin. *Beethoven's Pianoforte Sonatas: A Guide for Students & Amateurs.* [Orig-
inal title *Ludwig van Beethovens Klaviersonaten* published in Wiesbaden by Insel-Verlag,
1956] Translated by Stanley Godman with the
collaboration of Paul Hamburger. London:
Faber and Faber, 1959. 118 p. OCLC 2111646
MT 145 B42 F61

Fischer's analysis of the Beethoven sonatas
is based on lecture notes for a course he
taught in 1945. He observes compositional
techniques, form, harmony, interpretation,
and also includes short units on Beethoven's
piano playing, his personality, his instru-

ments, his friends, practicing in general,
tempi, and various interpreters. Information
is inconsistent; some sonatas receive close
examination, others are briefly mentioned, and
dates of composition are not always present.
Illustrations, musical examples, no index.

368. Fortune, Nigel. "The Chamber Music With Piano." in *The Beethoven Companion.* edited
by Denis Arnold and Nigel Fortune. London:
Faber & Faber, 1971. 542 p. ISBN 0-5710-
9003-6   OCLC 154784   ML 410 B4 A75

Chronological survey of Beethoven's development and treatment of the genre of piano chamber music. Descriptive analyses, comparisons,
influences, and attention to style are included
in Fortune's survey. Musical examples.

369. Kaiser, Joachim. *Beethovens 32 Klaviersonaten
und ihre Interpreten.* Frankfurt am Main:
S. Fischer, 1975. 661 p. ISBN 3-1003-8601-9
OCLC 2061327   MT 145 B42 K27

An interpretative survey of the Beethoven
sonatas, critically comparing performances of
diverse pianists, i.e., Claudio Arrau, Wilhelm
Backhaus, Paul Badura-Skoda, Daniel Barenboim,
Alfred Brendel, Friedrich Gulda, Wilhelm Kempff,
Yves Nat, Artur Schnabel, Dieter Zechlin, and
others. Analytical observations are in non-
technical language so that the lay person can
also benefit from the work. The author employs
the Urtext Henle edition (B.A. Wallner) for his
illustrated examples. An interesting and useful overview of interpretative possibilities
in the Beethoven sonatas. Also useful for
its insight into influences (similarities
to other works by Beethoven and to works by
other composers are noted). Musical examples,
discography (compiled by Claus-Dieter Schaum-
kell), bibliography (29 entries), index (compiled by Claudia Pabel).

370. Mellers, Wilfrid Howard. *Beethoven and the
     Voice of God.* London: Faber and Faber, 1983.
     vii, 453 p. ISBN 0-571-11718-X OCLC 9340-
     434 ML 410 B42 M33 1983; New York: Oxford
     University Press, 1983. ISBN 0-195-20402-6
     OCLC 9347483 ML 410 B4 M47 1983

     Critical analysis of selected Beethoven pi-
     ano sonatas, *Diabelli Variations*, and the
     Bagatelles, as well as analyses of several
     non-piano works. Mellers imbues his analyses
     with physiological, literary, theological,
     and psychological connotations. Included is
     a unit that observes Beethoven's piano (Graf)
     and refers often to Badura-Skoda and Demus'
     interpretive concepts. Mellers writes color-
     ful, descriptive analyses of the major piano
     sonatas. Worth investigating. Musical exam-
     ples, appendixes, bibliography, name-composi-
     tion index.

371. Tovey, Donald Francis. *A Companion to
     Beethoven's Pianoforte Sonatas.* Lon-
     don: The Associated Board of the Royal
     Schools of Music, 1931. xiv, 284 p.
     OCLC 2749943   MT 145.B42 T6 1931;
     New York: Mills Music Co., 1931. OCLC
     3867027; Also, London: Associated Board
     of the Royal Schools of Music, 1945. xiv,
     301 p. OCLC 2041613   MT 145.B42 T6 1945

     A bar-to-bar, phrase-to-phrase harmonic
     analysis, with attention to key relationship
     and form. Each sonata is prefaced by histo-
     rical data. A theoretical aid to understand-
     ing the Beethoven sonatas. Portrait, musical
     examples, lacks an index.

372. Truscott, Harold. "The Piano Music-I." in
     The Beethoven Companion. edited by Denis
     Arnold and Nigel Fortune. London: Faber &
     Faber, 1971. 542 p. ISBN 0-5710-9003-6
     OCLC 154784   ML 410 B4 A75

An effective study of the piano works of
Beethoven up to *Sonata* Op.57. Truscott
examines the works in regard to influences
of Clementi and Dussek. The influence of
Clementi on Beethoven's style is readily
apparent through the author's comparisons
both in text and in musical examples. He
traces the creative process in Beethoven's
piano literature. Truscott states, "[Beetho-
vens' piano writing] was the writing of a
virtuoso, using the basic techniques of
Clementi and Dussek, but gradually developing their potential in his own way...."
The author presents a useful study of influences and the growth of Beethoven's compositional style. Musical examples. "Piano
Music - II," also in *The Beethoven Companion*, is written by Philip Barford.

373. Uhde, Jürgen. *Beethovens Klaviermusik I:
Klavierstücke und Variationen.* Stuttgart:
Philipp Reclam jun., [1968], 1980. 568 p.
ISBN 3-1501-0139-5 OCLC 1208860 MT 145
B4 U4 1980; v.1 *Beethovens Klaviermusik II:
Sonaten 1-15.* Stuttgart: Reclam, [1970],
1980. 415 p. ISBN 3-1501-0147-6 MT 145
B4 U4 1980; v.2 *Beethovens Klaviermusik III:
Sonaten 16-32.* Stuttgart: Reclam, [1974],
1980. 632 p. ISBN 3-1501-0151-4 OCLC
10273073 MT 145 B4 U4 1980 v.3

The second edition of Uhde's three-volume
set is revised. The author presents a critical analysis of Beethoven's piano works, noting form, melodic structure, prior influences,
and harmonic scheme. The melodic structure
is stressed, noting skeletal structure, development, and derivative influences. The first
volume regards the piano pieces e.g., *Rondos,
Bagatelles, Waltzes, "Für Elise", Variations.*
Volume Two examines *Sonatas* (Nos.1-15) and
Volume Three the *Sonatas* (16-32). Uhde's
foreword to the set is quite philosophical,
concerned with the actuality of Beethoven's
music in the past in contrast with the music

of today. An informative work which helps in
the understanding of Beethoven's process of
creativity. Musical examples. Volume Three
contains a bibliography (20 entries), index
of works and related works, and name index.

374. Westerby, Herbert. *Beethoven and His Piano*
      Works. London: William Reeves, [1931].
      xii, 114 p. OCLC 1563044   MT 145 B42 W5

      This is a slightly revised version of the
      section on Beethoven originally contained
      in the author's larger volume titled *The*
      Piano Works of the Great Composers. Wes-
      terby attempts to draw a middle line between
      Elterlein's flowery interpretations and the
      more formal analytical texts of the time.
      The descriptions are vivid, brief, and rather
      shallow. Works are viewed according to Bee-
      thoven's three compositional periods, which
      Westerby places as: "First Period (1781-1800),"
      "Mature Period (1800-14)," and "Third Period
      (1816-23)." Illustrations, musical examples,
      list of principal editions, no index.

                      Johannes Brahms
                       (1833-1897)

375. Evans, Edwin. *Handbook to the Pianoforte*
      Works of Johannes Brahms: Comprising the
      Complete Solo Works; Works for Piano and
      Orchestra, also Works for Piano Duet and
      Organ Works as Applicable to Pianoforte
      Solo. New York: Scribner's; London:
      Reeves, 1936. xv, 327 p. OCLC 14523309
      ML 410 B8 E84 1936; Reprint. New York:
      B. Franklin, 1970. OCLC 108336   ML 410
      B8 E84 1970

      Historical, descriptive and analytical
      account of the Brahms piano works. Exam-
      ination of works includes attention to form,
      thematic development, rhythm, harmony, etc..
      Compositions are arranged according to opus

number, not by genre. Introductory material
focuses on Brahms as composer, on the character of the compositions, on technical points
and classification. Evans classifies the piano compositions into three categories: symphonic, technical, and contemplative. The
author often quotes descriptions and opinions
of James Huneker and J.A. Fuller Maitland.
Musical examples, bibliography (works from
1876 to 1936), indexes (name, composition,
analytical).

376. Geiringer, Karl. *Brahms: His Life and Work.*
      Translated by H.B. Weiner and Bernard Miall.
      2d ed., rev. and enl. Garden City, N.Y.:
      Anchor Books (Doubleday), 1961. xi, 344 p.
      OCLC 3313859   ML 410 B8 G42 1961; 3rd
      ed., rev. and enl., with a new appendix
      ("Brahms as a Reader and Collector").
      London: G. Allen & Unwin, 1982. XV, 397 p.
      ISBN 0-0478-0027-5   OCLC 13550056   ML
      410 B8 G42 1982; Reprint of 3rd ed. New
      York: Da Capo Press, 1982. ISBN 0-3067-
      6093-2; 0-3068-0223-6 (pbk.)   OCLC 77740-
      71   ML 410 B8 G42 1982

      Descriptions of works are based on back-
      ground information which is partly derived
      from the Brahms letters (to which Geiringer
      had access). In addition to regarding the
      solo piano compositions, Geiringer also dis-
      cusses the chamber music works. There is
      less attention paid to the piano concerti.
      Musical examples, appendix (40 Brahms let-
      ters), name-composition index.

                   Ferruccio Busoni
                     (1866-1924)

377. Beaumont, Antony. *Busoni the Composer.*
      Bloomington, Ind.: Indiana University
      Press, 1985. 408 p. ISBN 0-2533-1270-1
      OCLC 10506944   ML 410 B98 B4 1985; Also,
      London: Faber, 1985. ISBN 0-5711-3149-2

OCLC 12514345   ML 410 B98

Beaumont examines and describes the last
58 compositions and transcriptions of Fer-
ruccio Busoni, beginning with the *Konzert-
stück* Op. 31a (1890) and ending with *Doktor
Faust* (1923, unfinished). Descriptions in-
corporate historical data, literary influence,
derivations, style, etc.. Data regarding
compositions includes date completed, first
performance, dedication, publisher, scoring,
etc.. There are many piano works discussed.
An aid to understanding the compositions of
Busoni. Illustrations, musical examples,
appendixes (chronological catalogue of Busoni's
works, catalogue of transcriptions and caden-
zas), bibliography (general, writings by Busoni, letters, articles, special Busoni is-
sues), general index, composition index.

378. Sitsky, Larry. *Busoni and the Piano: The
      Works, the Writings, and the Recordings.*
      Westport, Conn.: Greenwood Press, 1986.
      xiv, 409 p. ISBN 0-3132-3671-2   OCLC 10-
      457728   ML 410 B98 S57 1986

      Survey of Busoni's piano music (solo, four-
      hands, two piano, piano and orchestra, ar-
      rangements, transcriptions, etc.). Unpub-
      lished works are identified. Works are de-
      scribed with some analysis, along with perti-
      nent data (e.g., dates, publishers). The
      large compositions, i.e., concerto, *Fan-
      tasia Contrappuntistica, Klavierübung* are
      given in-depth coverage, including historical
      information and influences. Sitsky's chapter
      on Busoni and Bach points out Busoni's admira-
      tion of the earlier composer and also adds
      a rationale for Busoni's many arrangements
      of other composers' music. Of special inter-
      est is Sitsky's discussion of Busoni's char-
      acteristic notation in the piano scores. A
      useful study. Illustrations, musical exam-
      ples, list of works, bibliography (including

articles and books by Busoni and about Busoni, and about his performance style), composition index, general index.

Frédéric François Chopin
(1810-1849)

379. Jonson, George Charles Ashton. *A Handbook to Chopin's Works, for the Use of Concert-Goers, Pianists, and Pianola-Players.* New York: Doubleday; London: Heinemann, 1905. 200 p. OCLC 16453136 ML 410 C54 J8; Also, 2d ed., rev. London: Reeves, 1908. 287 p. OCLC 1278320; Also, Reprint of the 1905 ed. Freeport, N.Y.: Books for Libraries Press, 1972. 200 p. ISBN 0-8369-6916-2 OCLC 0354211 ML 410 C54 J8 1972; Also, Reprint of the 2d ed., rev. Boston: Longwood Press, 1978. ISBN 0-8934-1078-0 OCLC 4516168 ML 410 C54 J8 1978

Descriptive annotations regarding Chopin's piano music. A collection of colorful remarks culled from the writings of various pianists, critics, and authors. As might be expected, the descriptions reflect the language of the time (1905); that is, they are inclined toward sentimentalism. Jonson refers to remarks by: Frederick Niecks, Franz Liszt, James Huneker, Moritz Karasowski, Jean Kleczynski, Anton Rubinstein, etc. in his brief descriptions of the compositions. Arrangement of the volume is based on opus numbers, not genre, which causes difficulty in tracing works (i.e., Mazurkas are interspersed in the volume because of the wide range of opus numbers). Lacks an index.

380. Landowski, W[anda]. [Alice] L. *Frederic Chopin et Gabriel Fauré.* Paris: Richard-Masse, 1946. 222 p. OCLC 4914598 ML 390 L24

An interesting comparison of the music of
Chopin and Fauré, especially as to their
solo piano compositions. Influences on both
composers are noted. Includes separate chapters on their lives, observes parallels between the two composers in nocturnes, preludes, barcarolles, trios, ballades, and
fantasies. Landowski surveys the origin,
development and position of these works in
the history of music. Illustrations, list
of works of both Chopin and Fauré (with
dedications and date of publication); lacks
an index.

381. Samson, Jim. *The Music of Chopin.* London;
     Boston: Routledge and Kegan Paul, 1985.
     262 p. ISBN 0-7100-9688-7 OCLC 11089911
     ML 410 C54 S188 1985

An analytical examination of Chopin's works.
Samson presents a scholarly and useful source
of information regarding the complexities of
Chopin's piano music. Samson's work is a wel-
come study in straightforward style, in contrast to the colorful prose of older descriptive accounts of the composer's music (e.g.,
James Huneker's *Chopin, The Man and His Music* [1900]). Samson points out works and
composers that influenced Chopin, and also
stresses Chopin's harmonic, melodic, and
structural style. Includes biographical
material and summation ("Epilogue"). Illustrations, musical examples, bibliography (extensive), list of works (largely chronological), name-composition index.

382. Walker, Alan, ed. *The Chopin Companion;
     Profiles of the Man and the Musician.*
     New York: Norton, 1966. 312 p. ISBN 0-
     3930-0668-9   OCLC 514592   ML 410 C54
     W16 1973

The result of a collaboration by several
musicians: Alan Rawsthorne covers the "*Bal-*

lades, Fantasy, and *Scherzos,*" offering an
effective, picturesque, and often literary-
based account of these forms; Paul Hamburger
reviews the "*Mazurkas, Waltzes, Polonaises,*"
with attention to structure and form; Robert
Collet covers the "*Studies, Preludes* and
Impromptus," with historical background regarding the étude and the prélude; Peter
Gould writes on the "*Sonatas* and *Concertos,*"
presenting historical comparisons with other
composers who wrote concerti and a descriptive commentary on the sonatas; and Lennox
Berkeley regards the "*Nocturnes, Berceuse,*
Barcarolle" in a descriptive style. Illustrations, musical examples, biographical summary (chronology), catalogue of Chopin's works
(with data), chronology of works, bibliography
(extensive), index of musical examples, general index.

383. Weinstock, Herbert. *Chopin: The Man and*
His Music. New York: Knopf, 1969.
xiii, 336, xxii p. OCLC 855098 ML 410
C54 W26

An analytical examination of Chopin's piano works. Form, harmonic structure, and
characteristic features are noted. Background data is also included. Not all works
receive the same attention e.g., not every
Etude and *Prelude* is analyzed. Coverage
is not consistent e.g., the short *Fantaisie-*
Impromptu Op.66 receives as much attention
as the *Sonata in B Minor* Op.58. Illustrations, musical examples, appendixes (works
without opus numbers, Chopin's birth registry and baptismal certificate, genealogy),
bibliography, name-subject index, composition index.

Muzio Clementi
(1752-1832)

384. Dale, Kathleen. "The Three C's: Pioneers of
Pianoforte Playing." *Music Review* 6 (Au-

gust 1945): 138-48.

Comparative critical commentary on Muzio
Clementi, Carl Czerny, and Johann Baptist
Cramer. Dale effectively surveys and compares the lives and works of the three fore-
most composers of technical material. She
notes the association of the three with prominent composers of their time.

385. Plantinga, Leon. *Clementi: His Life and
      Music.* London/New York: Oxford University
      Press, 1977. xiii, 346 p. ISBN 0-1931-
      5227-4   OCLC 2891450   ML 410 C64 P5;
      Reprint. New York: Da Capo Press, 1985.
      ISBN 0-3067-6198-X   OCLC 10375179   ML 410
      C64 P5 1985

A comprehensive examination and assessment
of Muzio Clementi's music. Plantinga provides:
historical background on Clementi's piano
works and also points out stylistic similarities to his contemporaries (e.g., Mozart,
Haydn, Beethoven), descriptive commentary
(form, style, etc.) regarding the compositions, manuscript and publisher data, Clementi's performance style, his relationship with
his contemporaries, biographical material,
etc.. The author's text includes a great
deal of information about Clementi and his
music. Plantinga divides Clementi's life
and works into seven periods: "Rome and Dor-
set" (1752-1774), "London" (1774-1780), "Ad-
ventures Abroad" (1780-1785), "Middle London
Years [I]" (1785-1790), "Middle London Years
[II]" (1791-1802), "Years of Travel" (1802-
1810), and "Late Years" (1810-1832). One of
the chapters, "Clementi and the Pianoforte,"
examines the composer's choice of instruments
(his conversion from harpsichord to pianoforte
was complete by the mid-1780s), and his performance style. An excellent volume, fully
documented. Illustrations, musical examples,
appendixes (*Sonata* WO 14, first movement;
index of Clementi editions), bibliography

(extensive), name index.

Aaron Copland
(b. 1900)

386. Butterworth, Neil. *The Music of Aaron Copland.* London: Toccata Press, 1985; New York: Universe Books, 1986. 262 p. ISBN 0-8766-3495-1 (USA), 0-9076-8907-8 (UK) OCLC 12974711 ML 410 C756 1986

Butterworth concentrates on Copland the composer, noting backgrounds of the works and adding descriptive commentary for each composition. He does not explore the works in detailed analysis but rather regards influences and examples of Copland's unique musical style. The volume includes an intriguing conversation (1977) between Copland and Leo Smit in which the composer explains his method of writing (e.g., *Piano Variations* and *Piano Fantasy*). Illustrations, musical examples, list of works (including pertinent data) arranged chronologically and by genre, bibliography (extensive), name-composition index.

Claude Debussy
(1862-1918)

387. Cortot, Alfred. *The Piano Music of Claude Debussy.* Translated from the French by Violet Edgell. London: Chester, 1922. 24 p. OCLC 8348515 ML 410 D28 C5

In an awkward translation by Edgell, Cortot marvels at Debussy's style, noting the literary inspiration, sensuality, exotic sonorities, and descriptive sensations that permeate his piano music. Cortot offers a vivid, often picturesque, descriptive analysis of Debussy's piano works. He also compares Debussy's piano performance style with that of Chopin, in that both composers employed

a delicate, intimate touch and both treated
the pedals with artistic refinement. No index.

388. Dawes, Frank. *Debussy Piano Music.* Seattle,
      Wash.: University of Washington Press, 1971.
      64 p.   MT 145 D4 D4

      Concise survey of Debussy's piano composi-
      tions. The author notes characteristic
      style, background information, influences,
      relation to painting (Impressionism), and,
      when appropriate, items relating to form.
      Musical examples; lacks an index and bib-
      liography.

389. Schmitz, E[lie] Robert. *The Piano Works of
      Claude Debussy.* Foreword by Virgil Thom-
      son. New York: Duell, Sloan & Pearce, 1950.
      xix, 236 p.   OCLC 918586   MT 145 D4 S3;
      Reprint. (unabridged and corrected) New
      York: Dover, 1966. ISBN 0-4862-1567-9
      OCLC 615631; Reprint. Westport, Conn.:
      Greenwood Press, 1970.   ISBN 0-8371-3822-1
      OCLC 128972; Reprint. New York: Da Capo
      Press, 1984. ISBN 0-3067-6199-8   OCLC 9-
      132084

      An analytical and descriptive examination
      of Debussy's piano works. Contains biograph-
      ical, interpretative, structural, stylistic,
      and background information regarding the pi-
      ano works.   An aid to understanding the
      aesthetics of Debussy's piano compositions.
      Illustrations, appendixes (list of piano
      works, bibliography [17 items]), index.

                        Manuel de Falla
                         (1876-1946)

390. Demarquez, Suzanne. *Manuel de Falla.*
      Translated from the French by Salvator
      Attanasio. Philadelphia: Chilton, 1968.

viii, 253 p. OCLC 171743   ML 410 F215
D43

Descriptions of De Falla's major piano
works. Especially useful are the examinations of *Nights in the Gardens of Spain,*
and *Fantasia Baetica.* Besides descriptive
material there is some musical analysis and
informative data. Musical examples, bibliography, list of works (chronological), name
index, lacks a composition index.

Gabriel Fauré
(1845-1924)

391. Landowski, W[anda]. [Alice] L. *Frederic
Chopin et Gabriel Fauré.* Paris: Rich-
ard-Masse, 1946. 222 p.   OCLC 4914598
ML 390 L24

An interesting comparison of the music of
Fauré and Chopin, especially as to their solo
piano compositions. Influences on both composers are noted. Includes separate chapters
on their lives, observes parallels between
the two composers in nocturnes, preludes,
barcarolles, trios, ballades, and fantasies.
Landowski surveys the origin, development
and position of these works in the history of
music. Illustrations, list of works of both
Fauré and Chopin (with dedications and date
of publication), no index.

392. Suckling, Norman. *Fauré.* London: Dent,
1946. vii, 229 p. OCLC 1839435   ML 410
F27 S8 1951; Reprint. Westport, Conn.:
Greenwood Press, 1979. ISBN 0-3132-0667-
8   OCLC 4493167   ML 410 F27 S8 1979
A relatively early, full-length English-
language study of Fauré's music. The
author compares the music of Fauré with
that of his contemporaries and predecessors,
offers some analysis, and discusses his compositional style. Illustrations, musical

examples, chronology, list of works (by
genre; lacks complete data), personalia,
bibliography (20 items), name-composition
index.

393. Vuillermoz, Emile. *Gabriel Fauré.* Paris:
      Flammarion, 1960. 206 p. OCLC 1-282582
      ML 410 F27 V93; In English, translated by
      Kenneth Schapin. Philadelphia: Chilton
      Book Co., 1960. xiv, 265 p. OCLC 36252
      ML 410 F27 V93 1969; Reprint of English
      translation edition. New York: Da Capo
      Press, 1983. ISBN 0-3067-6203-X   OCLC 9-
      132081   ML 410 F27 V93 1983

      Vuillermoz was a student of Fauré's but
      his descriptive commentary regarding the pi-
      ano compositions is broad rather than detailed.
      In-depth coverage is given only a few compo-
      sitions e.g., *Dolly Op.56*, *Thème et varia-
      tions Op.73*. The piano chamber music is al-
      so reviewed. Chronology, list of works, dis-
      cography (by Steven Smolian), name-composition
      index.

                        César Franck
                        (1822-1890)

394. Indy, Vincent d'. *César Franck.* Transla-
      tion from the French. London: John Lane
      Bodley Head, Ltd., 1910. 286 p. OCLC 987-
      928   ML 410 F82 I63; Reprint. New York:
      Dover, 1965. OCLC 617767   ML 410 F82 I63
      1965

      Of historical interest. D'Indy was a pu-
      pil of César Franck. He divides Franck's
      compositions into three periods: 1841-1858,
      1858-1872, and 1872-1890. The text is not
      dated in language, as one might suspect for
      a work of this vintage. D'Indy offers a ra-
      ther direct description and analysis of the
      piano works, including chamber music. Illus-
      trations, musical examples, list of works

(chronological), bibliography (34 entries),
name-composition index.

George Gershwin
(1898-1937)

395. Goldberg, Isaac. *George Gershwin: A Study
     in American Music.* [New ed.] New York:
     Frederick Ungar Pub., 1958. xviii, 387 p.
     OCLC 602214   ML 410 G288 G7 1958

     First published in 1931, six years before
     Gershwin's death. A supplement to the 1958
     edition is written by Edith Garson and covers
     the works written by Gershwin during his last
     six years (1931-1937). Of interest in this
     volume is the background data concerning the
     Gershwin piano works. There is some analysis
     but not in great depth. Instead, Goldberg of-
     fers practical critical observations of the
     compositions. Illustrations, musical exam-
     ples, discography (compiled by Alan Dashiell),
     name-composition index to first edition (1931),
     name-composition index to supplement (1958).

Lodovico Giustini
(1685-1743)

396. Bloch, Joseph. "Lodovico Giustini and the
     First Published Piano Sonatas." *Piano
     Quarterly* 86 (Summer 1974): 20-24.

     Bloch examines the historical background
     of Giustini's 12 *Sonate da cimbalo di piano
     e forte, detto volgarmente di martelletti.*
     The sonatas, printed in 1732, are historical-
     ly reputed to be the first compositions writ-
     ten for the pianoforte. The author describes
     the sonatas and includes the score of the com-
     plete *Sonata No. IV* in E Minor.

Edvard Grieg
(1843-1907)

397. Dale, Kathleen. "The Piano Music." in *Grieg:
      A Symposium.* edited by Gerald Abraham.
      London: L. Drummond, 1948. 144 p. OCLC 1-
      045277   ML 410 G9 A47; Reprint. London;
      New York: Oxford University Press, 1952.
      OCLC 2452867; Reprint. Westport, Conn.:
      Greenwood Press, 1971. ISBN 0-8371-5549-5
      OCLC 251346

      Descriptive analysis of Grieg's piano com-
      positions. Dale notes the influence of
      Schumann. This work lacks the detail of his-
      torical background which Dale so effectively
      covered in her Schumann piano survey. In the
      remainder of the book, Gerald Abraham covers
      "The Piano Concerto" (with revisions to the
      original score) and Alan Frank surveys "The
      Chamber Music." Chronology, bibliography,
      list of compositions, musical examples; lacks
      an index.

Roy Harris
(1898-1979)

398. Stehman, Dan. *Roy Harris: An American
      Musical Pioneer.* Boston: Twayne Pub.,
      1984. 296 p. ISBN 0-8057-9461-1
      OCLC 10558189   ML 410 H2055 S7 1984

      Stehman examines Harris' solo piano works
      as well as the piano in chamber music and
      the concerti. Various musical aspects are
      observed. Roy Harris' piano works are not
      in the mainstream of today's musical taste,
      but though their number is comparatively
      small, his works should be inspected. Steh-
      man offers the first complete examination of
      Harris' life and works. Musical examples,
      bibliography (divided into categories: books,
      articles, encyclopedias, program notes,
      theses, documents), list of works (chron-
      ological), discography (only 33 1/3 discs),

name-composition index.

Franz Joseph Haydn
(1732-1809)

399. Abert, Hermann. "Joseph Haydns Klavier-
     werke: Band I (Sonaten Nr.1-22)."
     Zeitschrift für Musikwissenschaft
     2 (July 1920): 253-73; and continued
     as "Joseph Haydns Klaviersonaten: II
     und III Band." *Zeitschrift für Musik-
     wissenschaft* 3 (June-July 1921): 535-
     52.

     A critical examination of the piano sona-
     tas of Haydn. Abert notes form, derivations
     and influences. He is especially aware of
     the influence of Georg Christoph Wagenseil
     in the sonatas of Haydn. Abert uses the
     Breitkopf & Härtel edition in his survey
     of the sonatas. First installment of the
     examination of the sonatas (nos.1-22) was
     published in *Zeitschrift für Musikwissen-
     schaft* in 1920. The remaining sonatas
     (nos. 23-52) were covered in the June-July
     1921 issue. Musical examples.

400. Brown, A. Peter. *Joseph Haydn's Piano Music:
     Sources and Style.* Bloomington, Ind.:
     Indiana University Press, 1986. xxiv, 450 p.
     ISBN 0-2533-3182-X   OCLC 12421123   ML 410
     H4 B86 1986

     Historical and critical examination of
     Haydn's keyboard music. A scholarly approach
     to the study of the composer's keyboard works.
     Brown's fine work is arranged topically rath-
     er than chronologically and is divided into
     two parts: sources and style. Chronology
     and authenticity of the keyboard works are
     of prime concern to Brown. Haydn's stylistic
     heritage is well traced. A chapter on the
     question of Haydn's keyboard idioms includes
     material (documented) on the composer's key-

board instruments, the fortepiano in Vienna,
and Haydn's keyboard terminology (i.e., for
what instrument the work was written). The
influence relationship between Haydn and
C.P.E. Bach is inspected in detail. Major
portion of the volume deals with the composer's style (structure and genre), noting
among other things his contribution to the
development of the sonata. An excellent
in-depth study/survey of Haydn's keyboard
works. Well documented. Illustrations,
musical examples, bibliography (extensive),
general index, index of works.

Paul Hindemith
(1895-1963)

401.   Neumeyer, David.   *The Music of Paul Hindemith.*
       New Haven, Conn. and London: Yale Universi-
       ty Press, 1986.   294 p.   ISBN 0-3000-3287-0
       OCLC 14134515   ML 410 H685 N5 1986

       A formal analytical-theoretical examina-
       tion of the works of Hindemith. The author
       divides the volume into four parts, I - the-
       ory, composition and analysis, II - *Mathis
       der Maler,* III - music before *Mathis,*
       and IV - music after *Mathis.* A detailed
       structural view of the piano works. Neu-
       meyer's early chapters outline his analyti-
       cal approach and explore Hindemith's com-
       positional style. The author offers inter-
       pratative suggestions to performers. A use-
       ful study for understanding the music of Paul
       Hindemith. List of works (with pertinent
       data compiled by Luther Noss, curator,
       Hindemith Collection, Yale University), musi-
       cal examples, bibliography (extensive), name-
       composition index.

Charles Edward Ives
(1874-1954)

402.   Cowell, Henry, and Sidney Cowell.   *Charles*

Ives and His Music. New York: Oxford University Press, 1955. x, 245 p. OCLC 3369-70   ML 410 I94 C6

A good study of Ives' style. The authors examine three works in detail: *Paracelsus* (song written in 1921), *Sonata No.2 for Piano "Concord, Mass., 1840-1860"* , and the *Universe Symphony.* These works are fully analyzed. The other piano compositions are described in terms of background. A useful study of Ives' highly individual musical style. Illustrations, musical examples, list of works (chronological; with data), bibliography, name-composition index.

Leoš Janáček
(1854-1928)

403.   Hollander, Hans. *Leoš Janáček: His Life and Work.* Translated by Paul Hamburger. London: John Calder, 1963. 222 p. OCLC 5-93443   ML 410 J18 H638; Also, New York: St. Martin's Press, 1963. OCLC 376695 ML 410 J18 H64; In German. *Leoš Janáček: Leben und werk.* Zurich: Atlantis, 1964. OCLC 10734837   ML 410 J35 H65

An examination of Janáček's life and musical style. The author clearly sees the Romantic lines of Schumann and Mussorgsky in Janáček's piano compositions. The chamber music and piano works are described as to mood and style, and background information is included. The chapter dealing with Janáček's style is helpful in understanding the works of the composer. Illustrations, musical examples, list of works (with dates of completion), bibliography (many Czech items), name-composition index.

Aram Ilich Khachatur\u0302ian
(1903-1978)

404.   Yuzefovich, Victor [Arnovich].   *Aram*
       Khachaturyan.   Translated by Nicholas
       Kournokoff and Vladimir Bobrov.   New
       York: Sphinx Press, 1985.   ix, 286 p.
       ISBN 0-8236-8658-2   OCLC 12343640
       ML 410 K39 I95 1985

       Despite its heavy Soviet politicism, the
       volume fills in background data on the *Con-*
       certo for Piano and Orchestra and the *Toc-*
       cata.   Yuzefovich does not delve into de-
       tailed descriptions, but rather discusses
       the musical climate surrounding the composer
       at the time, and his relationship with his
       Soviet colleagues.   Illustrations, bibliogra-
       phy (extensive); unfortunately, lacks a list
       of works and an index.

Franz Liszt
(1811-1886)

405.   Beckett, Walter.   *Liszt.*   rev. ed.   London:
       Dent; New York: Farrar, Strauss, and Cudahy,
       1963.   ix, 185 p.   OCLC 601646   ML 410 L7
       B295 1963

       Sketchy commentary on the piano works
       of Liszt, including the concerti.   A con-
       cise volume that fails to delve into its sub-
       ject in depth, although it does present var-
       ious musical aspects of the multi-talented
       composer.   Illustrations, musical examples,
       appendixes (chronology, list of works [by
       genre], personalia, bibliography, inaccura-
       cies in the biographies of Liszt, the Liszt
       Society), name-composition index.

406.   Saffle, Michael.   "Liszt Research Since 1936:
       A Bibliographic Survey."   *Acta Musicologica*
       58 (December 1986): 231-81.

A good bibliographic source for recent research studies on Liszt. Saffle's useful
survey is broken down into various categories.
Major units are: 1. General Studies, 2. Biographical Studies, 3. Musical Studies. Sub-
classifications of each unit are: 1. Interpretative Studies, Research Reports, Bibliog-
raphies, 2. Biographies, Documentary and
Source Studies, etc; 3. Musical Survey Studies, Compositional Techniques, Stylistic Influences, Compositional Genres, Pedagogy and
Performance Studies, etc.. Keyboard research
studies are found under the following headings:
"Original Compositions for Keyboard," "*Sonata
in B Minor*," "Other Works for Piano Solo,"
"Works for organ," "Paraphrases/Arrangements/
Transcriptions." Each unit is summarized.

407. Searle, Humphrey. *The Music of Liszt.*
London: Williams & Norgate, 1954. xi,
207 p. OCLC 382889 ML 410 L7 S395;
Reprint. 2nd rev. ed. New York: Dover,
1966. xi, 207 p. ISBN 0-4862-1700-0
OCLC 299947 ML 410 L7 S395 1966

General survey of Liszt's compositions.
Works are regarded in chronological order,
according to specific periods i.e., early
years (1822-1839), virtuoso period (1839-
1847), Weimar years (1848-1861), and final
period (1861-1886). Searle describes the
piano works in terms of background information and style while noting unique characteristics. Musical examples, chronology,
list of works (based on the author's list
prepared for the Grove *Dictionary of Music
and Musicians* 5th ed. [1954]), bibliography, name index, composition index.

408. Walker, Alan, ed. *Franz Liszt: The Man
and His Music.* London: Barrie & Jen-
kins, 1970. xiv, 471 p. ISBN 0-2146-
6688-3 OCLC 100660 ML 410 L7 W28 1970;
Also, New York: Taplinger, 1970. ISBN 0-

8008-2990-5   OCLC 88646   ML 410 L7 W28

A collection of essays written by various
authors and musicians. Louis Kentner writes
on the "Solo Piano Works of Liszt (1827-
1861)," including the *Sonata* and the *Tran-
scendental Etudes*; John Ogdon continues the
"Solo Piano Works (1861-1886)," covering the
late works; David Wilde observes the "Transcriptions" and Robert Collet discusses the
"Works for Piano and Orchestra." Other related subjects include "Liszt the Teacher
and Pianist" by Arthur Hedley, "Interpretation of Liszt's Piano Music" by Louis Kentner, "Liszt and the Twentieth Century" by
Alan Walker. A useful compendium of studies
on the art of Franz Liszt. Illustrations,
musical examples, chronology, personalia,
bibliography, list of works (based on Peter
Raabe and Humphrey Searle), general index,
composition index.

409.   Westerby, Herbert. *Liszt, Composer, and His
       Piano Works. Descriptive Guide and Criti-
       cal Analysis, Written in a Popular and
       Concise Style.* London: William Reeves,
       [1936]. xxii, 336 p. OCLC 647889 MT 145
       L51 W4; Reprint. Westport, Conn.: Green-
       wood Press, 1970. ISBN 0-8371-4365-9
       OCLC 128835   MT 145 L51 W4 1970

Westerby presents an overview and critical
analysis of Liszt's piano compositions in a
concise manner, not dwelling on any work in
great depth. He seeks programmatic narrative
in his annotative accounts of the compositions. There is some historical background
in the descriptive analyses. Westerby intended that his volume on Liszt be used primarily as a guide for the student who is ex-
ploring Liszt's piano compositions. Illustrations, musical examples, bibliography (includes books and articles [incomplete data]),
index of principal works, no general index.

Nikolai Karlovich Medtner
(1880-1951)

410. Surace, Ronald D. "The Solo Piano Music of
Nicolas Medtner." DMA diss., University
of Cincinnati, 1973. 76 p.

Surace was fortunate in having input from
Olga Conus [Konîus] regarding the piano
music of Nicolas Medtner. She and her
husband, Lev Eduardovich Konîus, were close
friends of Medtner. The study includes a
biographical sketch, statement on style,
composers' influences on Medtner (e.g.,
Beethoven, Schubert, Schumann, Chopin,
Brahms), Medtner's view of "modern music,"
and stylistic analyses of the sonatas and
character pieces. Surace concludes his effective survey of Medtner's solo piano compositions with a critical summation. Musical examples.

Felix Mendelssohn (Bartholdy)
(1809-1847)

411. Radcliffe, Philip. *Mendelssohn.* rev. ed.
London: Dent; New York: Farrar, Straus and
Giroux, 1967. xi, 210 p. OCLC 457447
ML 410 M5 R25 1967; Also, London: Dent,
1976. ISBN 0-4600-3123-6   OCLC 3066733
ML 410 M5 R25 1976

The author discusses the solo piano works
and the concerti in terms of personal criticism, which includes references to derivative influences and the influence which Mendelssohn had on later composers. There is
excessive comparison with other composers,
and many descriptions lack detail and depth.
Appendixes (chronology, list of works, personalia, bibliography), name-composition
index.

Wolfgang Amadeus Mozart
(1756-1791)

412. Biancolli, Louis [Leopold]. ed. and comp.
      *The Mozart Handbook: A Guide to the Man
      and His Music.* [1st ed.] Cleveland and
      New York: World Publishing Co., 1954.
      xxi, 628 p. OCLC 223911   ML 410 M9 B38;
      Reprint. Westport, Conn.: Greenwood Press,
      1975. ISBN 0-8371-8496-7   OCLC 2187223
      ML 410 M9 B38 1975

      A compendium of previously published mate-
      rial on Mozart. Fragments of works by var-
      ious authors are utilized in examining com-
      positions of Mozart. The introductory unit,
      describing Mozart's piano concerti, is shared
      by five authors, each offering their view of
      the genre. The authors represented in this
      unit are: Alfred Einstein, Otto Jahn, Sach-
      everell Sitwell, A. Hyatt King, and Louis
      Biancolli. 13 piano concerti are given brief
      descriptions regarding form, background and
      construction. Coverage of the solo piano
      music largely uses material by Ernest Hutch-
      eson. Descriptions vary, depending on which
      author is speaking i.e., material by Ernest
      Hutcheson is very different from that by
      Alfred Einstein. The reader must adjust to
      changes of view in the description of a work,
      since an opinion expressed in one paragraph
      may be very different from the opinion re-
      vealed in the next. Portrait, appendixes
      (list of works by genre, using Köchel nos.
      [Alfred Einstein's 1937 list], chronology,
      bibliography), name-subject-composition index.

413. Blom, Eric. *Mozart.* London: Dent; New
      York: Dutton, 1935. xi, 388 p. OCLC 64-
      60614   ML 410 M9 B65; Reprint. New York:
      Pellegrini and Cudahy, 1949. OCLC 1298-
      770; In German. *Mozart.* Zürich:
      Büchergilde Gutenberg, 1954. OCLC 33-
      52449; Reprint. New York: Collier Books,
      1962. OCLC 3632553; Reprint. London:

Dent, 1974.   ISBN 0-4600-3157-0   OCLC
1385184

Survey of Mozart's life and works.   The
concerti, solo piano works, and chamber music are briefly described.   Illustrations,
musical examples, chronology, list of works
(by genre), personalia, bibliography, name-
composition index.

414.   Broder, Nathan.   "Mozart and the'Clavier'."
       Musical Quarterly 27 (October 1941):
       422-32.

       A study of Mozart's use, both as perform-
       er and composer, of the clavichord, harpsi-
       chord and pianoforte.   Broder examines var-
       ious sources to determine that keyboard works
       of Mozart written before 1773 were designed
       for the harpsichord, and those written after
       1777 were intended for the pianoforte.   Es-
       pecially interesting for the view of the
       keyboard instruments in the composer's home
       at different periods in Wolfgang's life.   A
       reprint of this article appears in *The
       Creative World of Mozart,* edited by Paul
       Henry Lang (New York: Norton, 1963).

415.   Burk, John Naglee.   *Mozart and His Music.*
       New York: Random House, 1959.   x, 453 p.
       OCLC 602192   ML 410 M9 B97

       Short descriptions of the concerti (with
       more attention to background than to form),
       the sonatas, the variations, the four-hand
       pieces, and the piano chamber works.   Musi-
       cal examples, appendixes (eighteenth-century
       money values, cadenzas, Köchel-Einstein
       list of compositions indexed to the volume),
       name index.

416.   Einstein, Alfred.   *Mozart; His Character,
       His Work.* Original title: *Mozart, sein*

Charakter, sein Werk. Translated by
Arthur Mendel and Nathan Broder. New York;
London: Oxford University Press, 1945.
xi, 492 p. OCLC 608175   ML 410 M9 E4;
Also, pbk. New York: Oxford University
Press, 1962. OCLC 7262893   ML 410 M9
E4 1962

Einstein's classic volume on Mozart was
the standard in-depth Mozart study of its
time and still retains its effectiveness.
The background information on the piano compositions is quite helpful. Einstein includes chapters on works for clavier, chamber
music (with clavier), and the concerti. His
descriptive survey of the keyboard literature
is worth investigating. Illustrations, list
of works (by Köchel-Einstein numbers, indexed to volume), name index.

417. Hutchings, Arthur. *A Companion to Mozart's
      Piano Concertos.* 2d ed. London: Oxford
      University Press, 1950. xiv, 211 p. OCLC
      593729   MT 130 M8 H8 1950

Hutchings offers a critical study of the
piano concerti. The flowery narrative style
of the author tends to deter him from getting
to the point. Thematic development, form,
historical background, and past and future
influences are observed. There is a thematic
guide; descriptions of first movement, slow
movement, and finale forms (using *Concerto*
K.466 as a "typical" Mozart concerto), as well
as movements employing the variation form.
A unit deals with concerti written before
Mozart's time, notably works of C.P.E. Bach
and J.C. Bach. The heart of the volume is
the examination of individual Mozart concerti.
The question of the performance of continuo
parts by the soloist is addressed. One unit
is dedicated to stylistic performance of the
concerti. Musical examples, bibliography
(14 entries), name-composition index.

418. Landon, H[oward].C[handler]. Robbins, and
     Donald Mitchell, eds. *The Mozart Com-
     panion.* xv, 397 p. London: Rockliff;
     New York: Oxford University Press, 1956.
     OCLC 885018 (UK), OCLC 602547 (USA)
     ML 410 M9 L24 1956; Reprint. Westport,
     Conn.: Greenwood Press, 1981. ISBN 0-3132-
     3084-6 OCLC 7459650 ML 410 M9 M63 1981

     A collection of studies on Mozart. Arthur
     Hutchings writes on the keyboard music, dis-
     cussing the background and style of the so-
     natas, variations, etc.. Friedrich Blume ex-
     amines the concerti, with attention to their
     sources, and editor H.C. Robbins Landon con-
     centrates on the musical origin and develop-
     ment of Mozart's concerti, noting background,
     derivations and structural form. A useful
     compilation of studies on Mozart's works,
     especially the studies on the concerti. Il-
     lustrations, musical examples, list of works
     (taken from Alfred Einstein's Köchel list-
     ing [1946]), index to musical examples, name-
     subject index.

419. Russell, John F. "Mozart and the Pianofor-
     te: A Prelude to the Study of the Concer-
     tos." *Music Review* 1 (August 1940): 226-
     44.

     Russell investigates Mozart's writings,
     letters, and criticisms and from these de-
     rives ideas on the composer's musical and
     performance style. Excerpts from letters
     throw light on Mozart's feelings for correct
     tempi, expression, technique, etc.. The au-
     thor comments on Mozart's harpsichord period,
     the influence of Johann Christian Bach, the
     four early piano concerti (which were arrange-
     ments of sonata movements by other composers),
     the Clementi-Mozart relationship, Viennese
     action, etc.. An effective study of Mozart's
     keyboard style. Sources are not documented.

420. Sadie, Stanley. *Mozart.* London: Calder
      and Boyers; New York: Vienna House, 1965.
      192 p. OCLC 11049480 (UK), OCLC 73980-
      69 (USA) ML 410 M9 S12 1965; New York:
      Grossman Publishers, 1970. OCLC 185118
      ML 410 M9 S15 1970

      An effective general survey of Mozart's life
      and works. The volume is heavily illustrated.
      The concerti, piano works and piano chamber
      music are given brief observations, with at-
      tention to form and style. Illustrations,
      musical examples, chronology, list of works
      (by genre), bibliography (15 items), compo-
      sition index, name index.

                  Modest Petrovich Mussorgsky
                          (1839-1881)

421. Calvocoressi, M[ichael].D[imitri].
      Mussorgsky London: Dent; New York:
      Dutton, 1946. viii, 216 p. OCLC 155-
      9285   ML 410 M97 C3; Also, rev. ed.
      London: Dent, 1974. ISBN 0-4600-3152-X
      OCLC 975283   ML 410 M97 C3 1974

      The author died (1944) before completing
      his volume on Mussorgsky. Gerald Abraham
      completed the work and prepared it for pub-
      lication. The chapter on instrumental and
      choral works was done entirely by Abraham.
      The few piano compositions written by Mus-
      sorgsky are examined by Abraham. He in-
      cludes background information and also of-
      fers a critical summary of Mussorgsky's pi-
      ano writing style. Illustrations, musical
      examples, chronology, list of works (by
      genre), personalia, bibliography (including
      Russian items), name-composition index.

                     Conlon Nancarrow
                          (b. 1912)

422. Doerschuk, Bob. "Conlon Nancarrow: The Un-

suspected Universe of the Player Piano."
Keyboard 13 (January 1987): 56-57,82,142.

Composer Nancarrow's performance medium
for his compositions is the player piano.
He punches his own rolls in a unique fashion, creating new sounds that the old player
piano could never attempt. His *Studies For
Player Piano* stand as a milestone in experimental music. Doerschuk narrates an interview with Nancarrow and surveys the composer's
activity. An example of new sounds from an
old-fashioned instrument. Interesting side-
light: Nancarrow does not play the piano.
Illustrations.

Francis Poulenc
(1899-1963)

423. Daniel, Keith W. *Francis Poulenc: His
Artistic Development and Musical Style.*
Ann Arbor, Mich.: UMI Research Press,
1982. 390 p. ISBN 0-8357-1284-2
OCLC 7998259 ML 410 P787 D3 1982

Among other works, the author examines
Poulenc's chamber music, concerti, and piano music. A comprehensive and informative study. Daniel examines the compositions as to form and melodic and harmonic structure. He compares the works
for piano with other Poulenc compositions
and with those of his contemporaries. Musical examples, list of works (chronological, with data), bibliography (extensive;
arranged by category [general works, French
music, writings by Poulenc, etc.]), composition index, general index.

Sergei Vasil'evich Rachmaninoff
(1873-1943)

424. Culshaw, John. *Rachmaninov: The Man and His
Music.* New York: Oxford University Press,

1950.   174 p.   OCLC 1205254   ML 410 R12
C82

The bulk of Culshaw's volume comprises a
critical examination of the piano works
of Rachamninoff. Culshaw chooses to be im-
partial in discussing strengths and weaknesses in Rachmaninoff's works, a stance
with which Natalîa Rachmaninoff (the composer's wife) was unhappy. The examination
of the piano compositions is largely descriptive, with some attention to form, though
the coverage is uneven. Illustrations, list
of works (by opus), bibliography (only four
entries), discography, name-composition index.

425.   Norris, Geoffrey. *Rakhmaninov.* London:
       Dent, 1976. xi, 211 p. ISBN 0-4600-
       3145-7; 0-4600-2175-3 (pbk)   OCLC 25-
       25693   ML 410 R12 N67; Also, Totowa,
       N.J.: Littlefield, 1978. ISBN 0-8226-
       0701-8

       The author surveys the piano works and
       concerti of Rachmaninoff. Chiefly consists
       of critical descriptions of the works, with
       little analytical examination. Includes in-
       formation on the revision (1917) of the *Con-
       certo for Piano and Orchestra No.1 in F-Sharp
       Minor* Op.1. Illustrations, musical exam-
       ples, appendixes (chronology, list of works
       [by genre, with pertinent data]), personalia,
       bibliography, name-composition index.

                    Maurice Ravel
                    (1875-1937)

426.   Demuth, Norman. *Ravel.* New York:
       Collier Books [Crowell-Collier Pub.],
       1947. 253 p. OCLC 13076857   ML 410
       R23 D4 1947; London: Dent, 1947. OCLC
       405615 ML 410 R23 D4; Reprint of 1947
       ed. pub. by Dent. Westport, Conn.:

Hyperion Press, 1979. ix, 214 p. ISBN
0-8835-5690-1   OCLC 4210996   ML 410
R23 D4 1979

Demuth conveys his perceptions of Ravel's
piano music in frank terms. The piano works
are divided into four chapters: Early Piano
Works, Later Piano Works, The Concertos, and
Chamber Music. He offers a concise overview
of the piano compositions. Musical examples,
appendixes (chronology, list of works [by gen-
re], personalia, bibliography [11 items], programs of London visits in 1928 and 1929, ora-
tion delivered at Oxford on 23 October 1928),
name-composition index.

427.   Myers, Rollo H. *Ravel: Life and Works.*
       London: Gerald Duckworth, 1960. 239 p.
       OCLC 926775   ML 410 R23 M9; Also, New
       York: Thomas Yoseloff, 1960   OCLC 602561
       ML 410 R23 M9 1960; Reprint of the Yose-
       loff ed. Westport, Conn.: Greenwood
       Press, 1973. ISBN 0-8371-6841-4   OCLC
       605696   ML 410 R23 M9 1973

       Piano works of Ravel are described in
       terms of background information and pianis-
       tic characteristics. For those interested
       in knowing what Ravel's hands looked like,
       Myers includes a photograph of his hands.
       Illustrations, musical examples, appendixes
       (biographical sketch [by Ravel], Ravel's let-
       ter to the *Ligue Nationale pour la défense
       de la musique française* [1916], list of
       works [chronological], list of projected works
       never completed), bibliography, selected dis-
       cography (28 recordings listed).

428.   Orenstein, Arbie. *Ravel: Man and Musician.*
       New York; London: Columbia University
       Press, 1975. xvii, 291 p. ISBN 0-2310-
       3902-6   OCLC 1857936   ML 410 R23 O73

       An effective overview of Ravel's works.

Compositions are considered chronologically.
The author offers a critical examination of
the piano compositions, noting background
data, form, and general characteristics.
There are several photographs of Ravel's
manuscripts. Illustrations, appendixes
(list of works [with data], discography [ex-
tensive; includes Ravel's own recordings]),
bibliography (extensive), name-composition
index.

Anton Grigor'evich Rubinstein
(1829-1894)

429. Norris, Jeremy. "The Piano Concertos of
      Anton Rubinstein." *Music Review* 46
      (November 1985): 241-83.

A critical monograph on the five piano
concerti of Anton Rubinstein. Norris
identifies derivative aspects in the concerti, noting influences of Mendelssohn,
Beethoven, Liszt, and others. The author
systematically compares similar passages
of Rubinstein's scores to concerti of others.
Also, he observes the influence that Rubinstein had on Tchaikovsky's *Concerto in B-
flat Minor* (Op.23). Norris lists structural modifications of existing concerto
forms that Rubinstein employed in his concerti. "Harmonic carelessness" is one of
the many musical weaknesses that Norris ascribes to Rubinstein. A useful study. Musical examples.

Franz Schubert
(1797-1828)

430. Bilson, Malcolm. "Schubert's Piano Music and
      the Pianos of His Time." *Piano Quarterly*
      27 (Winter 1978-79): 56-61.

Performance on period instruments is the
theme of Bilson's article on Schubert and

the piano of his period. He examines the
history of piano actions, with special attention to the Viennese-style instrument (which
Bilson declares to be Schubert's type of instrument). Unfortunately, Bilson does not
examine Schubert's actual instruments, but
rather describes his music in interpretative
terms that conform to the Viennese pianoforte.
There is commentary on performances on re-
stored period instruments.

431. Brodbeck, David. "Dance Music as High Art:
      Schubert's *Twelve Ländler*, op. 171
      (D.790)." In *Schubert: Critical and Ana-
      lytical Studies.* edited by Walter Frisch.
      Lincoln, Neb.: University of Nebraska Press,
      1986. xiv, 256 p. ISBN 0-8032-1971-7
      OCLC 12081518   ML 410 S3 S2985 1986

      The *Twelve Ländler* Op.171 (D.790) are
      formally examined and harmonically and struc-
      turally analyzed. Brodbeck delves into Schu-
      bert's creative process in depth. Documented.
      Musical examples, composers-composition index.

432. Dale, Kathleen. "The Piano Music." in *The
      Music of Schubert.* edited by Gerald
      Abraham. London: Drummond Ltd., 1946.
      298 p. OCLC 13186780 ML 410 S3 A5; Also,
      New York: Norton, 1947. 342 p. OCLC 37-
      6726   ML 410 S3 A56; Reprint. Port Washing-
      ton, N.Y.: Kennikat Press, 1969. OCLC 550-
      969   ML 410 S3 A56 1969; Reprint. Wilming-
      ton, Del.: International Academic Pub.,
      1979. ISBN 0-8976-5473-0   OCLC 4638558
      ML 410 S3 A56 1879

      Critical survey of Schubert's piano mu-
      sic, as to form and harmonic structure.
      Dale often compares Schubert's piano music
      with that of Haydn, Mozart and Beethoven,
      noting influences. A rather dry, analytical
      study. J.A. Westrup covers "The Chamber Mu-
      sic" in a more descriptive style while main-

taining the critical and comparative elements
present in Dale's survey. Musical examples,
chronology, bibliography (extensive), list of
compositions; lacks an index.

433. Feil, Arnold. "Two Analyses." Translated
      by Walter Frisch. In *Schubert: Critical
      and Analytical Studies.* Edited by Walter
      Frisch. Lincoln, Neb.: University of
      Nebraska Press, 1986. xiv, 256 p. ISBN 0-
      8032-1971-7   OCLC 12081518   ML 410 S3
      S2985 1986

      An investigation of rhythm and meter in
      the Schubert *Moment musical* in F Minor,
      Op.94, No.3 (D.780). Musical examples,
      composers-composition index.

434. Hutchings, Arthur. *Schubert.* 3d ed.
      London: Dent, 1956. vi, 233 p. OCLC
      892106   ML 410 S3 H82 1956; Reprint.
      London: Dent; New York: Octagon Books,
      1973. ISBN 0-4600-3118-X   OCLC 7299-
      90   ML 410 S3 H82 1973

      A critical survey of Schubert's piano
      works. Hutchings is frank in expressing
      his personal opinions of the compositions
      e.g., he is not fond of the *Sonata in B-
      Flat Major* (1828) and generally finds
      pianisic deficiencies in the piano works.
      Illustrations, musical examples, appendixes
      (chronology, list of works [by genre], per-
      sonalia, bibliography, poets of Schubert's
      songs), name-composition index.

435. Porter, Ernest Graham. *Schubert's Piano
      Works.* London: Dobson, 1980. viii,
      173 p. ISBN 0-2347-7764-8   OCLC 7603282
      MT 145 S28 P8

      Analysis of Schubert's piano composition
      technique, noting characteristic harmony, mod-

ulation, melody, rhythm and form in his piano
works (including the duets). Analytical descriptions of the compositions are rather
brief, though sections on harmony, modula-
tion, melody, etc. delve into more detail.
Musical examples, appendixes (list of piano
works and a bibliography [seven entries]),
name-composition index.

Robert Schumann
(1810-1856)

436. Chissell, Joan. *Schumann.* rev. ed., Lon-
    don: Dent, 1967. xii, 257 p. OCLC 896056
    ML 410 S4 C4 1967; Reprint. London: Dent,
    1977. ISBN 0-4600-3170-8   OCLC 3743197
    ML 410 S4 C4 1977

    In her concise survey of the piano works
    of Schumann, Chissell notes pianistic style,
    background, and various musical aspects. The
    piano concerto and chamber music are also
    briefly regarded. Illustrations, musical
    examples, chronology, list of works (by
    genre), personalia, bibliography, name-com-
    position index.

437. Dale, Kathleen. "The Piano Music." In
    Schumann; A Symposium, edited by Gerald
    Abraham. London; New York: Oxford Univer-
    sity Press, 1952. vi, 319 p. OCLC 6025-
    48   ML 410 S4 A6317; Reprint. Westport,
    Conn.: Greenwood Press, 1977. ISBN 0-8371-
    9050-9   OCLC 2966761   ML 410 S4 A6317
    1977

    A good historical and stylistic overview
    of Schumann's piano works. Dale offers a
    critical survey of the composer's piano com-
    positions. Maurice Lindsay briefly comments
    on the piano concerto in his chapter, "The
    Works for Solo Instrument and Orchestra,"
    and chamber music is covered by A.E.F. Dick-
    inson in "The Chamber Music." Musical exam-

ples, chronology, bibliography (extensive),
list of compositions.

438.   Schauffler, Robert Haven. *Florestan: The
       Life and Work of Robert Schumann.* New York:
       Henry Holt, 1945. xiv, 574 p.   OCLC 720975
       ML 410 S4 S27; Reprint. New York: Dover,
       1963.   OCLC 603116   ML 410 S4 S27 1963

       Descriptive commentary on the piano works
       of Schumann. Works are not analyzed and the
       coverage is uneven. Illustrations, musical
       examples, appendixes (bibliography, glossary,
       list of works [by opus], discography, geneal-
       ogy), indexes (name-subject, Schumann's in-
       strumental works, vocal works).

439.   Walker, Alan, ed. *Robert Schumann: The Man
       and his Music.* London: Barrie & Jenkins,
       1972. XI, 489 p.   ISBN 0-2146-6805-3
       OCLC 632912   ML 410 S4 W18; Also, New York:
       Barnes and Noble, 1974. OCLC 1029275
       ML 410 S4 W18 1974

       Good coverage of Schumann's piano works.
       The solo piano works are discussed by various
       authors; Yonty Solomon examines the *Sonatas*
       and the *Fantasie*, Bàlint Vàzsonyi regards
       the piano-cycles, John Gardner writes on the
       chamber music, and Alfred Nieman examines the
       concerti. Form, construction, comparison
       with his contemporaries, style, melody, are
       a few of the features observed. There are
       numerous musical examples which help the
       reader understand the specific critical com-
       ments made by the reviewers. All in all,
       the volume offers a great deal of informa-
       tion on the composer and his compositions.
       Illustrations, musical examples, appendix,
       chronology (including Schumann's family tree),
       personalia, bibliography (extensive), list
       of works (by genre, with data), composition
       index, general index.

440. Young, Percy M[arshall]. *Tragic Muse:*
     The Life and Works of Robert Schumann.
     2d ed., enl. London: Dobson Books, 1961.
     256 p. OCLC 6583200   ML 410 S4 Y7 1961

This volume was first published in 1957 and
was written to commemorate the centenary of
Schumann's death (1856). Young devotes
chapters to the piano music and chamber music. He observes analytical aspects such as
form, melodic construction, key relationship, and includes historical background as
well. The *Concerto for Piano and Orchestra*
is examined in the chapter "Music for Orchestra." Illustrations, musical examples, list
of works (by genre), discography (by genre),
bibliography, appendixes (I - the author's article "Schumann and England," which was first
published in German ["*Robert Schumann und die*
englische Musikkultur"] and appeared in *Musik*
und Gesellschaft (July 1960), and II - the
author's BBC script ["Florestan and Eusebius-
The Problem of Robert Schumann"] prepared for
a broadcast of "Music Magazine" which occurred
on 12 July 1960), name-composition index.

Aleksandr Nikolaevich Scriabin
(1872-1915)

441. Steger, Hanns. *Materialstrukturen in den*
     fünf späten Klaviersonaten Alexander
     Skrjabins. [Form in the five late piano
     sonatas of Aleksandr Scriabin] Regensburg:
     Gustav Bosse, 1977. 300 p. ISBN 3-7649-
     2140-4   ML 410 S62 S817

A formal examination of the last five sonatas (Opp. 62, 64, 66, 68, 70) of Scriabin.
Steger analyzes the sonatas in terms of harmonic and linear forms, rhythmic structure,
etc.. Thematic lines are observed in various
forms: transposing, alteration, grouping, etc..
A useful detailed study. Musical examples,
bibliography, editions, no index.

Jan Sibelius
(1865-1957)

442. Blom, Eric. "The Piano Music." in *The
      Music of Sibelius.* edited by Gerald
      Abraham. New York: Norton, 1947. 218 p.
      OCLC 603012   ML 410 S54 A5; Reprint.
      New York: Da Capo Press, 1975. ISBN 0-
      3067-0716-0   OCLC 1682092   ML 410 S54
      A5 1975

      Blom offers a critical summary of Sibelius'
      keyboard writing style as well as a descrip-
      tive survey of the piano compositions. Other
      compositions involving piano are covered by
      Scott Goddard in a chapter on "The Chamber
      Music" with attention to analysis of form.
      Musical examples, chronology, bibliography
      (35 enties), list of compositions; lacks an
      index.

Igor Fydorovich Stravinsky
(1882-1971)

443. Asaf'yev, Boris [Vladimirovich]. *A Book
      About Stravinsky.* Original title: *Kniga
      o Stravinskom.* Translated by Richard F.
      French.   Ann Arbor, Mich.: UMI Research
      Press, 1982.   287 p.   ISBN 0-8357-1320-2
      OCLC 8346426   ML 410 S932 A83 1982

      Kniga o Stravinskom was first published
      in 1929 (Leningrad: Triton) and republished
      in Moscow in 1977. It appears here in trans-
      lation by Richard French. Asaf'yev's criti-
      cal examination and commentary are valuable
      regarding *Piano Rag Music* (1919), *Five Fin-
      gers* (1921), *Concerto for Piano and Winds*
      (1923-24), *Piano Sonata* (1924), *Serenade
      for Piano* (1925), and the Concert Suite from
      Pulcinella for violin and piano (1925).
      Portrait, musical examples, name-composition
      index.

444. Joseph, Charles Mensore. *Stravinsky and the
Piano.* Ann Arbor, Mich.: UMI Research
Press, 1983. xvii, 304 p. ISBN 0-8357-
1426-8   OCLC 9435339   ML 410 S932 J67
1983

An exploration of Stravinsky's association
with the piano. It is Joseph's contention
that the piano works help us to understand
aspects of the composer's broader development as composer and musician. He surveys
Stravinsky's piano works, analyzes many,
notes similar aspects in the non-piano works,
observes influences of other composers in his
piano works, and offers pertinent historical
data. The piano in Stravinsky's life is
traced from the early years. There are many
reflections by Soulima Stravinsky (with whom
the author studied) about his father and his
works. Stravinsky's pieces for player piano
are also examined. A valuable study. Recommended. Illustrations, musical examples, bibliography (extensive), index.

445. Vlad, Roman. *Strawinsky.* Torino: G.
Einaudi, 1958. 253 p. OCLC 10475744
ML 410 S932 V53; Also, Nouva ed. Torino: G.
Einaudi, 1973. ix, 376 p. OCLC 8993533
ML 410 S932 V5 1973; *Stravinsky* 2d ed.
Translated from the Italian by Frederick
Fuller and Ann Fuller. London: Oxford
University Press, 1967. 264 p. OCLC 45-
6117   ML 410 S932 V52; Also, 3rd ed. [Eng-
lish] London; NY: Oxford University Press,
1978, 1985. ISBN 0-1931-5445-5   OCLC 11-
532984   ML 410 S932 V52 1985

The volume is the outcome of a series of
19 broadcasts dedicated to Stravinsky's
works (December 1955-April 1956), for *Radio-
televisione Italiana.* Text material in
this volume is largely the explanatory script
used for the broadcasts. The author has sup-
plemented and enlarged the scope of the material for this volume. Descriptions of the

piano works are scattered throughout the work.
One chapter, "The Piano Works of the Neo-
Classical Period" regards *The Wedding (Les
noces)*, *Five Fingers*, *Concerto for Piano
and Wind Intsruments*, and *Sonata for Piano*.
Illustrations, musical examples, bibliography, general index, composition index.

446.   White, Eric Walter.   *Stravinsky: The Composer
       and His Works*.   Berkeley and Los Angeles:
       University of California Press, 1966.   xv,
       608 p.   OCLC 283025   ML 410 S932 W47; Also,
       London: Faber, 1966.   OCLC 954410   ML 410
       S932 W47 1966

       Descriptions of Stravinsky's compositions.
       The original piano works are viewed, begin-
       ning with the *Sonata in F-Sharp Minor* (1903-
       04) and concluding with *Movements* (piano
       and orchestra; 1958-59).   The descriptions
       are informative and useful.   Illustrations,
       musical examples, appendixes (various writ-
       ings by Stravinsky; selection of letters
       written to Stravinsky [Debussy, Delius, etc.];
       catalogue of manuscripts [1904-52] in Stra-
       vinsky's possession; arrangements for player-
       piano; bibliography [books by Stravinsky,
       books on Stravinsky and his music, other
       publications]), name-place-composition index.

                    Peter Ilich Tchaikovsky
                        (1840-1893)

447.   Blom, Eric.   "Works for Solo Instrument and
       Orchestra."   In *The Music of Tchaikovsky*,
       edited by Gerald Abraham.   New York: Nor-
       ton, 1946.   277 p.   OCLC 385829   ML 410
       C4 A5 1946; Reprint. Port Washington, N.Y.:
       Kennikat Press, 1969.   OCLC 545   ML 410
       C4 A5 1969; Reprint. New York: Norton,
       1974.   ISBN 0-3930-0707-3   OCLC 737083
       ML 410 C4 A5 1974

       A critical examination of Tchaikovsky's

piano concerti. The *Piano Concerto in B-flat Minor Op.23* receives the most attention. Blom examines the concerto as to form, style, etc.. He quotes the critical remarks made by Nicholas Rubinstein regarding the concerto and analyzes the work under categories derived from Rubinstein's critical remarks e.g., the composition was bad as a whole, the music was worthless and trivial, and the piano passages were manufactured and unplayable. A novel approach to examining the concerto. The other concerti are also described. Illustrations, musical examples, bibliography, chronology, list of works; lacks an index.

448.   Dickinson, A.E.F. "The Piano Music." In *The Music of Tchaikovsky,* edited by Gerald Abraham. New York: Norton, 1946. 277 p. OCLC 385829   ML 410 C4 A5 1946; Reprint. Port Washington, N.Y.: Kennikat Press, 1969. OCLC 545   ML 410 C4 A5 1969; Reprint. New York: Norton, 1974. ISBN 0-3930-0707-3   OCLC 737083   ML 410 C4 A5 1974

A critical review of Tchaikovsky's solo piano literature. The author evidently does not admire the piano works of the composer, stating that Tchaikovsky was not inclined towards the piano as Chopin and Liszt were. Descriptions of the compositions are often apologetic in manner. Illustrations, musical examples, chronology, bibliography, list of works; lacks an index.

449.   Warrack, John [Hamilton]. *Tchaikovsky Symphonies and Concertos.* London: British Broadcasting Corporation, 1969. 56 p. ISBN 0-5630-9203-3   OCLC 66453 MT 130 C4 W37; Also, Seattle, Wash.: University of Washington Press, 1971. OCLC 155077   MT 130 C4 W37 1971; Also, 2d ed. London: BBC, 1974. 64 p. ISBN

0-5631-2773-2   OCLC 1460055   MT 130 C4
W37 1974

Warrack regards the *Piano Concerto in B-
Flat Minor*, Op.23; *Piano Concerto in G
Major*, Op.44; *Piano Concerto in E-Flat
Major*, Op.75; and the *Fantaisie de concert
in G Major*, Op.56, largely in terms of background information, with some attention to
form. He includes the controversy between
Nikolai Rubinstein and Tchaikovsky concerning the *Concerto in B-Flat Minor*.   Musical
examples, composition index; lacks a name
index.

ILLUSTRATIONS

Representative Piano Types

Plate 1. PIANO FORTE (1720) by Bartolomeo
Cristofori. Metropolitan Museum of Art, The
Crosby Brown Collection of Musical Instruments,
1889, No. 1219; New York City.
(Courtesy Da Capo Press [New York], agent for
Franz Josef Hirt's *Stringed Keyboard Instruments*,
1981. ISBN 3-8595-1135-1)

Plate 2. PYRAMIDENFLÜGEL [Pyramid Piano] (1745)
by Christian Ernst Friederici. Musée instru-
mental du Conservatoire Royal de Musique, No.
1631; Bruxelles.
(Courtesy Da Capo Press [New York], agent for
Franz Josef Hirt's *Stringed Keyboard Instruments*,
1981. ISBN 3-8595-1135-1)

Plate 3. SQUARE PIANO (1840) by Jean-Henri Pape.
Germanisches Nationalmuseum, Klavierhistorische
Sammlung Neupert, MINe211; Nürnberg.
(Courtesy of Da Capo Press [New York], agent for
Franz Josef Hirt's *Stringed Keyboard Instru-
ments*, 1981. ISBN 3-8595-1135-1)

Plate 4. (top illustration) PIANINO (c.1835) by
A. Flohr. Historisches Museum, No.24773; Bern.
(bottom illustration) PIANINO (early 19th century)
by Andreas Marshall. Norsk Folke Museum, No.88;
Oslo.
(Courtesy of Da Capo Press [New York], agent for
Franz Josef Hirt's *Stringed Keyboard Instruments*,
1981. ISBN 3-8595-1135-1)

Plate 5. PLAYER PIANO (1920s) by Smith & Barnes.
(Courtesy of Vestal Press [Vestal, N.Y.], *Treasures of Mechanical Music* [1981] ISBN 0-9115-
7220-1 by Arthur A. Reblitz and Q. David Bowers)

Plate 6. CONCERT GRAND (contemporary) by Steinway
    & Sons (New York, N.Y.).

Schematics

(Diagrams are from Merle H. Mason's *Piano Parts and
    Their Functions* (1977), courtesy of Piano Tech-
    nicians Guild [Kansas City, Mo.]. Since Mason's
    work deals with nomenclature of piano parts, the
    illustrated parts are given multiple names as used
    by various companies.)

Plates 7-8.   GRAND PIANO ACTION PARTS.

Plates 9-10   VERTICAL PIANO ACTION PARTS.

Plates 11-12   DAMPER PARTS.

Plates 13-14   GRAND PIANO PLATE AND STRINGS.

APPENDIX A

CHRONOLOGY: IMPORTANT EVENTS IN THE
DEVELOPMENT OF THE PIANO

PIANO KEYBOARD - COMPASS

(A-1=lowest A; C-88=highest C on our present keyboard)

c.1700 - (Cristofori)
C-16 to F-69 = 4 Octaves   (54 keys)

c.1700 - c.1790 (Silbermann, Stein, English Pianos)
F-9 to F-69 = 5 Octaves   (61 keys)

c.1800 - (Viennese)
F-9 to F-81 = 6 Octaves   (73 keys)

c.1804 - c.1824
C-4 to F-81 = 6 Octaves and a Fourth
(78 keys)

c.1824 - c.1880
C-4 to C-88 = 7 Octaves   (85 keys)

c.1880 - (Present standard)
A-1 to C-88 = 7 Octaves and a Third (88 keys)

1891 - ([Unique] Bösendorfer Model 275 Concert
Grand)
F below A-1 to C-88 = 7 Octaves and a Fifth
(92 keys)

1904 - ([Unique] Bösendorfer 290 Imperial Concert
Grand)
C below A-1 to C-88 = 8 Octaves (97 keys)

245

ACTION

1716 - Jean Marius' four *clavecins à maillets*
       demonstrate experimentation of several dif-
       ferent forms of actions: primitive (no es-
       capement or damper action), down-strike,
       up-strike, combination of hammers and jacks.
       Drawings patented in France (1716).

1717 - Christoph Gottlieb Schröter devises two
       particular actions: an up-strike and a
       down-strike. The complete construction of
       his prototype hammer instrument never ma-
       terializes. (Germany)

1720 - Cristofori's earliest extant pianoforte con-
       tains an up-strike action that includes a
       spring-loaded escapement jack and dampers.
       (Italy)

1726 - Cristofori demonstrates an improved action
       which is apparent from the extant instru-
       ment of 1726. It has the features of a mod-
       ern action: double lever, escapement, check,
       a synchronized damper system, and an *una corda*
       lever. (Italy)

1770 - Johann Andreas Stein adds an escapement
       to his down-striking action. (Austria)

1777 - Robert Stodart patents the "English" action,
       previously developed by Americus Backers.
       (England)

1786 - John Geib patents the "English Double
       Action." (England)

1807 - William Southwell patents an improved action
       (*sticker action*) for cabinet pianos. (England)

1808 - *Mécanisme à étrier* [repetition action] by
       Sébastien Erard. (France)

1815 - English double action with escapement is
       used in square pianos.

1821 - Sébastien Erard patents his *mécanique à double échappement* [double escapement] action, which forms the working basis of nearly all modern double escapement actions. (France)

1827 - Jean-Henri Pape begins constructing pianos with down-strike actions. (France)

1842 - Robert Wornum patents *tape-check* upright action. (England)

STRINGS

1745 - Christian Ernst Friederici employs oblique stringing for his pyramid piano. (Germany)

1790 - Erard increases stringing resistance by using thicker strings, also utilizes trichord stringing in square pianos. (France)

1790 - Broadwood increases strength with the use of thicker strings. (England)

1802 - Loud utilizes oblique stringing for upright pianos. (England)

1808 - Sébastien Erard invents the *agraffe.* (France)

1820s - High-tensile steel is produced for piano strings.

1821 - Frederick William Collard first uses *aliquot* stringing. (England)

c.1823/25 - Conrad Graf builds a grand piano expressly for Beethoven in which most of the stringing employs four strings per note. A compensation for the composer's deafness. (Austria)

1826 - Pape patents his cross stringing in upright pianos.

1827 - James Stewart invents a process which becomes the basis for modern stringing: instead of using separate strings for unisons, he uses one continuous wire of double length to serve for the two unison strings. (England)

1828 - Pape patents a method of cross stringing (square pianos). (France)

1830 - Babcock patents an iron framing for square pianos with cross stringing. (USA)

1834 - Introduction of cast steel strings, replacing the usual iron or brass strings. (Webster and Horsfall of Birmingham)

1835 - Pierre Fischer uses cross stringing (uprights) in England.

1836 - Wheatley Kirk patents a complete iron frame for an upright piano. (England)

1843 - Henri Hertz patents oblique stringing for grand piano. (France)

1847 - Jacques Vogelsangs of Brussels makes use of cross stringing.

1848 - Claude Montal patents *demi-oblique* stringing for square and upright pianos. (France)

1850 - A double-strung square piano 10,000 kg and a grand piano 13,000 kg. is constructed in Austria.

1859 - Steinway produces first over-strung grand. (USA)

1867 - After the Great Exhibition of Paris, cross stringing becomes the standard practice.

1872 - C.F. Theodore Steinway patents the duplex scale. (USA)

1873 - *Aliquot* system of stringing is patented by Julius Blüthner. (Germany)

1880 - String tension of the average piano corres-
       ponds to a weight of 17,000 to 18,000 kg
       (increased today to 20,000 kg.)

1920 - Pitch of 440 Hz for A-49 is adopted by
       the United States Government.

1939 - Pitch of 440 Hz for A-49 is adopted by
       the International Conference on Pitch in
       London, displacing the 1892 international
       pitch of 435 Hz for A-49.

HAMMERS

1826 - Jean-Henri Pape patents his felt-covered
       hammers of graduated density. (France)

1827 - Edward Dodd invents a hammer in which the
       tightness of the outer layer of leather
       can be adjusted with a screw, varying
       the tone desired. (England)

1845 - Pape invents and patents a hammer with a
       reversible head; when the hammer became
       worn, the head can be turned so as to
       present a fresh surface. (England)

1855 - Felt hammers become universally accepted.

1880 - Alfred Dolge patents an effective machine
       to cover hammers (previously hand covered).

FRAME

1739 - Christoph Gottlieb Schröter's model of a
       tangent action employs the use of an iron
       bar pressing on the strings. (Germany)

1788 - John Broadwood divides the soundboard
       bridge, allowing the bass strings to be
       thicker and more able to sustain higher
       tension. (England)

1799 - Joseph Smith patents the invention of iron
        bracing for pianofortes and square pianos.
        First use of iron reinforcement in frame
        constructions. Normally, reinforcements
        were made of wood. (England)

1800 - Isaak Hawkins patents his portable grand
        pianoforte. The soundboard is framed in
        metal and braced behind with metal rods.
        Wrestplank is also of metal. (USA)

1808 - Erard employs metal bracing. The *agraffe*
        is patented. (France)

1808 - James Shudi Broadwood begins using metal
        framing bars. (England)

1820 - James Thom and William Allen, of the William
        Stodart firm, patent *compensation frame*, a
        system of solid or tubular steel or copper
        supports between hitchpin and wrestplank.
        (England)

1821 - Samuel Hervé, at Broadwood's, invents
        metal hitchpin block and wrestplank.
        (England)

1822 - Erard adopts and patents the *compensation
        frame*. (France)

1825 - Erard abandons the use of the *compensation
        frame*, substituting instead six iron stays
        in framing construction. (France)

1825 - Alpheus Babcock, in Boston, casts a complete
        metal frame with hitch pin block in a sin-
        gle operation and patents his *Cast Iron
        Frame*. (USA)

1825 - Ignaz Pleyel is the first piano builder on
        the continent to make use of the American
        cast iron frame for grand and square pianos.
        (France)

1827 - James Shudi Broadwood patents the *Composite
        Iron Resistance Frame*, connecting the hitch-

pin block (iron) with the wrestplank by
four iron braces. (England)

1831 - In London, William Allen patents his complete cast iron frame (*Cast-Iron grooved
Frame*).

1838 - Erard firm invents a pressure bar (*barre
harmonique*). (France)

1839 - Johannes A. Ibach and sons build first concert grand piano (without metal reinforce-
ment). (Germany)

1840 - Jonas Chickering patents an improved cast
iron frame for square pianos. (USA)

1840 - Erard utilizes cast iron frames. (France)

1843 - Chickering patents a cast iron frame for
grand pianos. (USA)

1866 - Steinway patents a cast iron frame for uprights. (USA)

1867 - Universal acceptance of the cast iron frame,
evident at the Great Paris Exhibition.

1875 - Patent is issued to Steinway & Sons for
the *capo tasto bar* in *cupola* cast iron
plate for grand pianos. (USA)

PEDALS

1774 - Johann Gottlob Wagner builds square pianos
with pedals. (Germany)

1783 - John Broadwood introduces the sustaining
pedal to replace the knee lever. (England)

1860 - Alexandre-François Debain devises a sostenuto pedal mechanism. (France)

1862 - Invention of *pédal de prolongation* [sus-

taining (sostenuto) pedal] by Claude
Montal, Paris.

1874 - Steinway patents improved sostenuto-pedal.
       (USA)

GENERAL

1698 - Bartolomeo Cristofori begins building a key-
       board instrument in which hammers strike the
       strings. (Florence, Italy)

1700 - Cristofori completes building the first
       pianoforte, termed *Gravecembalo col piano,
       e forte* by Scipione Maffei in his detailed
       descriptive article (1711) on Cristofori's
       invention. (Italy)

1711 - Father Wood, an English monk in Rome, builds
       a pianoforte (reproduction of Cristofori's
       instrument). (England)

1711 - Cristofori's invention described by Scipione
       Maffei in *Giornale de' Letterati d'Italia.*
       (Italy)

1716 - Cristofori is put in charge of the Medici
       musical instruments. (Italy)

1716 - Jean Marius submits four models of his
       clavecin à maillets to *l'Académie
       Royale des Sciences.* (France)

1717 - Christoph Gottlieb Schröter of Dresden
       devises two actions, an up-striking and a
       down-striking (models only). The complete
       instrument never materializes. (Germany)

1719 - Scipione Maffei reprints his original re-
       port of 1711 concerning Cristofori's in-
       vention. (Italy)

1720 - Oldest surviving pianoforte by Cristofori.
       (in the Metropolitan Museum of Art, New York)

1722 - Second oldest extant pianoforte by Cristofori. (in the *Museo Strumenti Musicali*, Rome)

1725 - Mattheson publishes, in his paper *Musika-lische Kritik* (Hamburg), a German transla-tion (by Köneg) of Maffei's report. Thus Cristofori's work becomes known in Germany. (Germany)

1726 - The last extant pianoforte built by Cristofori. (in the *Musikinstrumenten-Museum der Karl Marx Universität*, Leipzig)

1726 - Gottfried Silbermann constructs his first models of fortepianos. (Strasbourg)

1731 - Silbermann builds two pianofortes. (Strasbourg)

1732 - *Dodici sonate da Cimbalo di piano e forte, detto volgamente di martelletti.* by Pis-toian composer Lodovico Giustini (published by Don Giovanni de Seixas), in which precise instructions for dynamic expression are given for the first time. Historically acknowledged to be the first compositions written for the pianoforte. (Italy)

1736 - Gottfried Silbermann shows J.S. Bach two of his pianos. (Germany)

1737 - Domenico del Mela (*di Gagliano*) builds his first fortepiano with strings in ver-tical position. (Italy)

1738 - Hammer action slowly gains acceptance.

1739 - Domenico del Mela builds a vertical (*pyramid*) piano. Still extant, housed in the *Conser-vatorio di Musica "Luigi Cherubini"* of Florence. (Italy)

1742 - Square piano built by Johann Söcher in Sonthofen. Oldest surviving square piano. Housed in the *Germanisches Nationalmuseum*, Nürnberg. (Germany)

1745 - Christian Ernst Friederici builds his first
       pyramid pianoforte. (Germany) Housed in
       the *Musee instrumental du Conservatoire Royal
       de Musique*, Brussels.

1747 - J.S. Bach, in Potsdam, plays the improved
       Silbermann pianoforte in the presence of
       Frederick the Great and praises the instru-
       ment.

1752 - Johann Joachim Quantz, in his *Anleitung,
       die Flöte traversière zu spielen* has
       positive comments regarding the pianoforte.
       (Germany)

1753 - C.P.E. Bach publishes his *Versuch über
       die wahre Art, das Klavier zu spielen* which
       includes a supportive statement regarding
       the pianoforte. (Germany)

1755 - William Mason brings back to England a small
       pianoforte purchased in Hamburg. (England)

1757 - *Sonata für Klavicymbel oder Hammerklavier*
       by Johann Christoph Friedrich Bach; first
       German composition for the pianoforte.

1759 - Weltman of Paris exhibits to the French
       Academy of Science his *clavecin à maillet*,
       a "combination instrument" (pianoforte, harp-
       sichord and small organ with bell chimes).

c.1760 - Zumpe and eleven other German piano crafts-
       men (mostly Silbermann pupils) settle in
       London. The square piano begins to be built
       in England.

1760 - Manuel Antunes builds the first pianoforte
       in Portugal.

1766 - *Ten Sonatas* by John Burton are the first
       English works written specifically for the
       piano.

1767 - 16 May; first appearance of the pianoforte
       in a concert hall. London, Covent Garden

Theatre; accompaniments by Charles Dibdin. (England)

1768 - Johann Christian Bach performs on a Zumpe piano in a public recital in London (piece for the piano).

1768 - Piano solos performed at a concert given by Henry Walsh in Dublin, shortly after J.C. Bach's performance in London. (Ireland)

1768 - 8 September; Mlle. Lechantre performs for the first time in Paris on a pianoforte. (France)

1769 - A pianoforte played for the first time in Belgium. (Liège)

1770 - Earliest French square piano in existence, by Johann Kilian Mercken. Housed in the *Conservatoire des Arts et Métiers*, Paris.

1770 - John Broadwood builds his first square piano. (England)

1770 - Introduction of square piano in Sweden.

1771 - Pianoforte manufacturing begins in Russia.

1772 - Americus Backers builds a fortepiano with two pedals. (London)

1775 - John Brent [Johann Behrent] exhibits the first American square piano in Philadelphia. (USA)

1776 - *Sei Concerti per il cembalo o piano e forte* written by J.C. Bach are the first piano concerti.

1777 - Robert Stodart builds his first "combination instrument," a pianoforte and harpsichord. (England)

1777 - Mozart endorses Johann Stein's pianoforte in a letter to his father. (Austria)

1777 - Erard's first square piano. (France)

1779-88 - Importation of London pianos to Boston.
          (USA)

1780 - Josephus Merlin builds a "combination in-
       strument": a grand piano and harpsichord,
       in England. Housed in the *Deutsches Museum*,
       Munich.

1780 - Square piano is popular throughout Europe.

1781 - Mozart and Clementi perform in Vienna for
       Emperor Josef II.

1783 - Broadwood's first Grand Pianoforte. (England)

1784 - Earliest known public two-piano performance,
       given by Clementi and Cramer.

1786 - Pianoforte used in concert for the first
       time in the United States. (Philadelphia)

1786 - First American composition for pianoforte,
       Sonata Piano Forte by Reinagle. (USA)

1788 - John Broadwood builds his first grand pi-
       ano. (England).

1788 - Oldest surviving Swedish square piano, by
       Mathias Petter Kraft of Stockholm.

1789 - Johann Andreas Stein replaces the knee
       levers with foot pedals. (Austria)

1789 - Charles Albrecht builds square pianos in
       Philadelphia. (USA)

1789 - Jean-Jacques Schnell and Tschenky produce
       a *sostenente* piano named *Animo-Corde*,
       in which the strings are caused to vibrate
       by jets of air. (France)

1792 - Johann Matthäus Schmahl builds a trans-
       posing square piano. (Germany) Housed in

the *Schweizerisches Landesmuseum*, in
Zurich.

1794 - William Southwell patents an upright grand
       in the form of a book-case. (England)

1798 - Giraffe upright is built in Vienna.
       (Austria)

1800 - The first upright pianos (strings below the
       keyboard to floor level); John Isaac Hawkins
       in Philadelphia and Mathias Müller in
       Vienna.

1800 - Clementi joins Collard in London to inau-
       gurate their piano firm. (England)

1800 - Isaac Hawkins, father of John Isaac Hawkins,
       patents a *sostenente*-type piano in which
       a device causes the hammers to repeat (there-
       by sustaining the tone) in imitation of
       the *Bebung* effect. (England)

1801 - Edward Ryley obtains the first patent for
       a transposing pianoforte. (England)

1807 - Ignaz Pleyel founds his piano factory in
       Paris.

1811 - Earliest cottage-pianos; William Southwell,
       Frederick William Collard, Robert Wornum.
       (England)

1817 - *Sostinente fortepiano* by Isaac Mott.

1823 - Jonas Chickering establishes himself in
       business with James Stewart under the name
       of Stewart & Chickering; the House of
       Chickering is born. (USA)

1827 - First Pianinos (uprights) in France
       (by Pleyel, Blanchet & Roller).

1828 - Ignaz Bösendorfer receives a permit to
       build pianos in Vienna.

1830 - First Pianinos in Switzerland (c.1835 instrument by Johann Andreas Flohr in the
Historisches Museum, Bern).

1831 - First uprights in Belgium (Herman Lichtenthal's
"dog-kennel" style upright is built about
this time).

1835 - First Pianinos (uprights) in Germany.

1839 - First concert for piano alone, without sup-
porting artists, given by Liszt.

1842 - First roll-operated piano conceived by
Claude-Felix Seytre of Lyons and patented
that year. (France)

1844 - Jonas Chickering becomes the first exporter
of American pianos. (USA)

1849 - Heinrich Engelhard Steinweg (Henry Engelhard
Steinway) and two sons arrive in New York.

1853 - Chickering now producing 2,000 pianos a
year. (USA)

1853 - Carl Bechstein begins building pianos in
Berlin.

1853 - The House of Steinway is founded in New
York City.

1857 - The Kimball Piano Company is founded by
William Wallace Kimball in Chicago.

1860 - North America builds its first uprights.

1862 - Dwight Hamilton Baldwin opens a piano show
room in Cincinnati, Ohio; the beginning
of the Baldwin Piano Company. (Actual piano manufacturing operations don't begin
until 1889.) (USA)

1863 - First pneumatic player-piano (*Pianista*)
patented by Fourneaux. (France)

1867 - Opening of Steinway Hall. (New York City)

1880 - End of the square piano era in America.

1886 - Paul von Jankó publishes *Eine neue Claviatur* [a new keyboard], in which he explains his revolutionary six-tiered keyboard, which he devised in 1882.

c.1887   Nippon Gakki [Yamaha] manufactures the first pianos in Japan.

1889 - Baldwin Piano Company begins manufacturing pianos. (USA)

c.1890 - Seven and one-fourth octave keyboards (88 keys) become standardized.

1891 - Bösendorfer sells its first concert grand (Model 275; 92 keys). (Austria)

1897 - E.S. Votey patents his player-piano system, the basis of Aeolian's *Pianola*. (USA)

1897 - Bailey constructs the first electric piano.

1904 - Welte patents *Mignon* reproducing piano.

1904 - Bösendorfer 290 Imperial Concert Grand with 97 keys (C below A-1). (Austria)

1908 - 364,545 pianos sold in the USA, marking the industry's peak year in this country.

1921 - Emanuel Moór brings out his *duplex coupler* piano in which there are two keyboards tuned an octave apart.

1925-27 - The popularity of the radio has a devastating effect on player piano sales.

1936 - World's largest grand, 11 feet 8 inches long, weighing 1 1/2 tons; longest bass string is 9ft 11in, built by H. Challen & Son of London.

1964 - Robert Moog invents the synthesizer.

1988 - Steinway & Sons celebrate 135 years of
       piano manufacturing by building their
       500,000th instrument. (USA)

APPENDIX B

CATEGORIES OF PIANOS IN FIVE LANGUAGES

ENGLISH NAMES

UPRIGHTS:

Upright Piano
Vertical Piano
Console Piano
  (low upright)
Spinet Piano
  (low upright)
Cabinet Pianoforte
Cottage Piano
Pyramid Piano
Giraffe Piano

GRANDS:

Grand Piano
Baby Grand Piano (under
  five feet)
Boudoir Grand Piano
  (approx. six feet)
Living Room Grand Piano
  (approx. seven feet)
Concert Grand Piano
  (approx. nine feet)

OTHERS:

Square Piano
Pedal Piano

GERMAN NAMES

UPRIGHTS:

Klavier
Pianino
Kleinklavier
Lyraflügel (lyre
  piano)

GRANDS:

Flügel
Stutzflügel (baby
  grand piano)
Salonflügel (medium
  grand piano)

GERMAN NAMES (continued)

Giraffe/Giraffen- flügel (giraffe piano) Pyramidenflügel (pyramid piano)	Konzertflügel/Konzert- piano (concert grand piano)

OTHERS:

Hammerklavier/Hammerflügel (older term for
grand or upright piano)
Querflügel (spinet-shaped square piano)
Tafelklavier (square piano)
Pedalflügel/Pedalklavier (pedal piano)

FRENCH NAMES

UPRIGHTS:	GRANDS:

Piano droit
Piano vertical
Pianino
Piano pyramidal
   (pyramid piano)
Piano giraffe
   (giraffe piano)
	Piano à queue
	Piano à queue mignon
	   (baby grand piano)
	Piano à queue écourtée
	   (baby grand piano)
	Piano à demi-queue
	   (baby grand piano)
	Piano de concert (con-
	cert grand piano)

OTHERS:

Piano à buffet (obsolete term for upright)
Piano à pédalier (pedal piano)
Piano carré (square piano)

ITALIAN NAMES

UPRIGHTS:	GRANDS:
Piano(forte) verticale	Piano(forte) a coda

ITALIAN NAMES (continued)

Piano diritto
Piramidale (pyramid
  piano)

Piano(forte) a mezza
  coda (baby grand
  piano)
Piano(forte) da con-
  certo (concert
  grand piano)

OTHERS:

Pianoforte da tavola (square piano)
Pianoforte organistico (pedal piano)

SPANISH NAMES

UPRIGHTS:

Piano verticale
Jirafa (giraffe
  piano)
Pirámide (pyramid
  piano)

GRANDS:

Piano de cola
Piano cuarto de cola
  (baby grand piano)
Piano de media cola
  (baby grand piano)
Piano de concierto
  (concert grand piano)
Piano de gran cola
  (concert grand piano)

OTHERS:

Piano cuadrado (square piano)
Piano de mesa (square piano)
Piano con teclado de pedales (pedal piano)

AUTHOR-TITLE INDEX

(Citations are Bibliography Entry Numbers)

Burgess, Anthony. "The Well Tempered Revolution; A Consideration of the Piano's Social and Intellectual History," 45

Burk, John Naglee. *The Life and Works of Beethoven*, 364; *Mozart and His Music*, 415

Busoni and the Piano: The Works, the Writings, and the Recordings (Sitsky), 378

Busoni the Composer (Beaumont), 377

Butler, Stanley. *Guide to the Best in Contemporary Piano Music: An Annotated List of Graded Solo Piano Music Published Since 1950*, 336

Butterworth, Neil. *The Music of Aaron Copland*, 386

Calvocoressi, Michael Dimitri. *Mussorgsky*, 421

Campbell, Murray, and Clive Greated. *The Musician's Guide to Acoustics*, 225.

"A Capsule History of the Piano" (Newman), 69

The Carel van Leeuwen Boomkamp Collection of Musical Instruments (Boomkamp; van der Meer), 128

Carmi, Avner, and Hannah Carmi. *The Immortal Piano*, 88

Carter, Susan Blinderman. "The Piano Music of Samuel Barber," 358

Casella, Alfredo. "L'esthétique du piano," 34; *Il pianoforte*, 33

Catalogo, a cura di Natale e Franco Gallini (Gallini, N.; Gallini, F.), 135

Catalogue of Musical Instruments (Victoria and Albert Museum), 141

Catalogue of the Stearns Collection of Musical Instruments (Stanley), 138

César Franck (d'Indy), 394

Challis, John. "New: A 20th Century Piano," 178

"Chamber Piano" (Cooper), 50

Chang, Frederic Ming, and Albert Faurot. *Team Piano Repertoire: A Manual of Music for Multiple Players at One or More Pianos*, 337

Charles Ives and His Music (Cowell, H.; Cowell, S.), 402

Chickering and Sons. *Achievement: An Ascending Scale*, 179

Chissell, Joan. *Schumann*, 436

"[Chopin] Ballades, Fantasy, and Scherzos" (Rawsthorne), 382

The Chopin Companion; Profiles of the Man and the Musician (Walker), 382

Grafing, Keith G. "Alpheus Babcock's Cast-Iron
    Piano Frames," 185
Grame, Theodore. "The Piano in Mozart's Time," 96
Grand Piano (Harrison), 57
"Grand Pianos" (Grossmann), 191
Greated, Clive. See *The Musician's Guide to
    Acoustics*, 225
Greenfield, Jack. "Cristofori Piano Use - Dropped
    in Italy, Continued in Iberian Region," 190;
    "Cristofori's Initial Piano Design," 186; "Cris-
    tofori's Last Work and his Successors," 189;
    Cristofori's Soundboard Design; Cristofori Be-
    comes Curator of Medici Instrument Collection,"
    187; "Home Pianos - Square, Uprights, and Other
    Verticals," 97; "Piano Actions - From Cristofori
    to Erard," 53; "The Piano's Century of Progress:
    1770's - 1870's," 54; "Politics and Music in
    Florence During the Latter Part of Cristofori's
    Career," 188
Gretschel, Heinrich. See *Lehrbuch des Pianoforte-
    baus in seiner Geschichte...*, 153
Grieg: A Symposium (Abraham), 397
"The [Grieg] Chamber Music" (Frank), 397
"The [Grieg] Piano Concerto" (Abraham), 397
"The [Grieg] Piano Music" (Dale), 397
Grossmann, John. "Grand Pianos," 191
Grover, David S. "A History of the Piano from 1709
    to 1980," 170; *The Piano: Its Story from
    Zither to Grand*, 55
"The Growth of National Schools" (Gibb), 297
Grundzüge des modernen Klavierbaues... (Goebel), 158,
    159
Guide to Bartók's Mikrokosmos (Suchoff), 361
*Guide to the Best in Contemporary Piano Music: An
    Annotated List...* (Butler), 336
Guide to the Pianist's Repertoire (Hinson), 343;
    Supplement, 345
A Guide to Tuning Musical Instruments (Meffen), 216
A Guidebook of Automatic Musical Instruments
    (Bowers), 244
Hadley, Benjamin. *Britannica Book of Music*, 1
Hamburger, Paul. "[Chopin] Mazurkas, Waltzes,
    Polonaises," 382
Hamilton, Clarence Grant. *Piano Music, Its Compos-
    ers and Characteristics*, 294
A Handbook to Chopin's Works... (Jonson), 379

Newman, William S. "Beethoven's Pianos Versus His
     Piano Ideals," 239; "A Capsule History of the
     Piano," 69
Nimitz, Daniel. *Keyboard Masters: Study Guide*, 298
*Nineteenth-Century Piano Music: A Handbook for
     Pianists* (Dale), 288
*A Noble Art: Three Lectures on the Evolution and
     Construction of the Piano* (Smith, F.), 169
"Noise in Piano Tone, a Qualitative Element" (Hill),
     227
"Normal Vibration Frequencies of a Stiff Piano
     String" (Fletcher), 229
Norris, Geoffrey. *Rakhmaninov*, 425
Norris, Jeremy. "The Piano Concertos of Anton
     Rubinstein," 429
"Notes on the Grand Romantic Virtuosos and After"
     (Morrison), 50
Notes on the Literature of the Piano (Lockwood),
     349
"Nuova invenzione d'un Gravecembalo col piano, e
     forte; aggiunte alcune considerazioni sopra gli
     strumenti musicali" (Maffei), 196
"Observations on the Vibrations of Piano Strings"
     (Schuck; Young), 229
Ogdon, John. "[Liszt] Solo Piano Works (1861-1886),"
     408; "The Romantic Tradition," 297
*Old English Instruments of Music, Their History and
     Character* (Galpin), 46
Old Pianos (Michel, N.E.), 149
"On Yamaha's Assembly Line" (Stokes), 205
"The Ordeal of Growth..." (Lipman), 45
Ord-Hume, Arthur W.J.G. *Pianola: the History of the
     Self-Playing Piano*, 250; *Player Piano: The
     History of the Mechanical Piano and How to Re-
     pair It*, 248 ; *Restoring Pianolas and Other
     Self-Playing Pianos*, 249
Orenstein, Arbie. *Ravel: Man and Musician*, 428
Oxford Dictionary of Music (Kennedy), 5
Palmieri, Robert. "Artist and Artisan," 70
Parrish, Carl George. "Criticisms of the Piano When
     It Was New," 110; "The Early Piano and Its In-
     fluence on Keyboard Technique and Composi-
     tion in the Eighteenth Century," 109
Parton, James. "The Piano in the United States,"
     263

NAME-SUBJECT INDEX

(Citations are Bibliography Entry Numbers)

Badura-Skoda, Paul, 326, 362, 369, 370
Balantsivadze, Andrei Melitonovich, 310
Baltimore, Md., 263, 267
Balzac, Honoré de, 111
Barber, Samuel, 63, 296, 302, 355, 358, 359; concer-
    to, 358; sonata, 358, 359
Barenboim, Daniel, 369
Bargiel, Woldemar, 325
Bartók, Béla, 127, 297, 360; *Mikrokosmos*, 361
Bax, Arnold, 127, 332
Beach, Amy Cheney (H.H.A.), 304, 317
Beethoven, Johann, 233
Beethoven, Ludwig van
    Influence on instrument, 54, 89, 239
    Music, 2, 26, 28, 62, 73, 99, 126, 238, 287, 289,
        293, 295, 297, 299, 300, 306, 312, 316, 321,
        323, 343, 354, 355, 363, 364, 370, 372-374;
        Bagatelles, 370, 373; *Diabelli Variations*
        (Op.120), 299, 330, 370; *"Für Elise,"* Var-
        iations, Rondos, Waltzes, 373
    Chamber Music, 368; *Sonata in A Major for Vio-
        lin and Piano* (Op.47), 330
    Concerti, 328, 365; (Opp.15, 37, 73), 328
    Compared with C.P.E. Bach, 363; with Clementi,
        385; with Schubert, 432
    Influence of Clementi and Dussek, 372
    Influence on Medtner, 410; on Anton Rubinstein,
        429
    Sonatas, 343, 362, 363, 366, 367, 369-371, 373;
        "Hammerklavier," 363; (Op.31, No.2), 299
    Pedals, Use of, 238, 239, 242
    Performance, 26, 367
    Personal Instruments, 26, 85, 147, 148, 238, 239
        Broadwood Piano, 70, 233, 234, 238, 239, 242
        Erard Piano, 233, 238, 242
        Graf Piano, 70, 209, 233, 238, 242, 370
        Streicher Piano, 70
        Walter Piano, 183, 238
Berg, Alban, 119
Berlioz, Hector, 127
Biancolli, Louis, 412
Bilson, Malcolm, 100
Birkland, Helge, 314
Bizet, George, 315
Blacher, Boris, 119
Blitheman, William, 76

Henselt, Adolph, 325
Hicki-Szabo, H., 129
Hiller, Ferdinand, 325
Hindemith, Paul, 33, 119, 286, 300, 401, *Mathis der Maler*, 401
Hipkins, Alfred James, 46, 134
History of the Piano
  American Pianos: Exhibition, 131, 267
  Austria, 17, 64, 139, 148, 239
  Belgium, 36
  Bibliograpy, 147, 318, 319, 326
  Chronology Lists, 114, 147
  England, 17, 23, 26, 29, 64, 98, 148, 257, 264, 270
  France, 17, 51, 60, 64, 121, 148
  General Survey, 1-7, 9-15, 17, 18, 20, 25-30, 32, 33, 36-38, 40, 41, 44, 47, 52-69, 71-83, 91, 109, 114, 143, 144, 147, 148, 152-154, 169, 171, 223, 225, 228, 230, 291, 294-296, 301, 303, 305, 338
  Germany, 17, 26, 92, 64, 148, 261
  Historical References in Literature, 108, 111
  Italy, 33, 39, 64, 148, 269
  Portugal, 197, 265
  Social, 44, 45, 55, 64, 111, 112, 327
  Spain, 197
  Switzerland, 266
  USA, 17, 19, 50, 64, 121, 148, 253, 258, 267
  USSR, 268
  Vilnius (Lithuania), 84
  White House, 102
History of Piano Music
  Austria, 327, 355
  Bibliography, 318, 319, 326, 348, 351; American composers, 342; black composers, 335
  Chamber Music, 50, 63, 295, 330, 344
  Character Piece, 315
  Classical Period, 49, 50, 62, 65
  Concerto/Works for Piano and Orchestra, 316, 328, 329, 340, 346
  Contemporary Period, 2, 49, 50, 286, 290, 291, 296, 297, 301, 307, 311, 314, 320, 333, 334, 336, 341, 343, 345, 348, 353-355
  Early Music for Piano, 98, 114, 333, 357, 396
  England, 73, 98, 294, 327, 332

318 *Name-Subject Index*

Piano Builders (*continued*)
Babcock, Alpheus, 19, 43, 54, 102, 130, 131, 185
  Dispute with Loud, 185
Backers, Americus, 53, 255
Barrow (with Culliford and Rolfe), 130
Battaglia, Antonio, 135
Beck, Frederick, 59, 78
Blüthner, Julius, 199
Boisselot & Sons, 126
Bösendorfer, Ignaz, 180, 199
Bradbury, William, 102
Brinsmead, John, 32, 104
Broadwood, John & Sons, 15, 18, 38, 54, 65, 81,
    96, 104, 117, 129, 130, 133-135, 137, 138,
    141, 145, 146, 157, 206, 207, 233, 234, 236,
    255, 264
  Comparison with Erard, 125; with Streicher, 182
  Family tree, 206
Broadwood, Thomas, 238
Buntebart, Gabriel (in association with Zumpe),
    130, 146, 264
Bürger, Gaspar Katholnig, 139
Buschmann, Johann David, 106
Canadian, 8
Casteel, Henrique van, 197, 256, 265
Chappell, Samuel, 141
Chickering, Jonas, 19, 54, 102, 104, 130, 131,
    179
Coste, La (of Belgium), 256
Crehore, Benjamin, 131
Cristofori, Bartolomeo, 2-5, 13, 17, 33, 36, 41,
    46-48, 53, 54, 63, 67, 68, 73, 75, 78, 81,
    85, 121, 145, 186-190, 196, 198, 269
  Apprentices
    Ferrini, Giovanni, 189
    Geronimo di Firenza, 189
    Gheraldi di Padua, 189
  Comparison with Stein instrument, 37; with
    Mirabal instrument, 197; with Portuguese
    instruments, 265
  First description (1711) of his invention, 196
  Influence in Portugal, 189, 197, 265; in Spain,
    189, 190, 197
  Inventor, 20, 24, 31, 39, 56, 62, 76, 77, 157,
    187, 196
  List of Extant Instruments, 188